THE HUMOR PRISM IN 20TH-CENTURY AMERICA

THE HUMOR PRISM IN 20TH-CENTURY AMERICA

Edited by Joseph Boskin

Wayne State University Press • *Detroit*

Humor in Life and Letters Series

A complete listing of the books in this series can be found at the back of this volume.

General Editor

Sarah Blacher Cohen
State University of New York, Albany

Advisory Editors

Joseph Boskin
Boston University

Alan Dundes
University of California, Berkeley

William F. Fry, Jr.
Stanford University Medical School

Gerald Gardner
Author and lecturer

Jeffrey H. Goldstein
Temple University and London University

Don L. F. Nilsen
Arizona State University

June Sochen
Northeastern Illinois University

01 00 99 98 97   5 4 3 2 1

Library of Congress Cataloging-in-Publication Data

The humor prism in 20th-century America / edited by Joseph Boskin.
    p. cm. — (Humor in life and letters series)
    Includes bibliographical references.
    ISBN 0–8143–2597–1 (pbk. : alk. paper)
    1. Popular culture—United States—History—20th century. 2. American wit and humor—History and criticism. 3. Ethnic wit and humor—United States—History and criticism. 4. United States—Social conditions—1945–   I. Boskin, Joseph. II. Series: Humor in life and letters.
E169.02.H83   1997
973.91—dc21   97–15521

Every effort was made to secure permission to reprint the essay by Mac E. Barrick titled "Racial Riddles and the Polack Joke," which first appeared in volume 15, number 1 of the Spring 1970 edition of the *Keystone Folklore Quarterly*. The location of the journal is unknown.

Illuminating Camaraderie

Herb Boskin

&

Michael Benari, Ruth Chad, Robert Erwin,

Allen Jay Friedman, Larry Roth

Contents

The
Humor
Prism
in 20th-
Century
America

7

PART III. MULTICULTURAL SPACES

The
Humor
Prism
in 20th-
Century
America

8

PART IV. EVENTS AND SCRIPT

1950s–1960s: Sick and Elephant

1960s: Helen Keller

1950s–1980s: Polish

1970s–1980s: Jewish American Princess (J.A.P.)

1970s–1980s: Light Bulb

1980s–1990s: Disaster

The
Humor
Prism
in 20th-
Century
America

9

Preface

It was late into our final year in college and we had had too many discussions about the draft, the political repression, unfinished term papers, the fading of time, and the foggy future. But it didn't deter him one bit. He pushed away from the small desk, a move I had seen him make many times for over three years, and ran it down: "I don't quite get it. There doesn't seem to be any pattern regarding the professors here. You and I have taken many of the same courses together, listened to a lot of lecturers, and been invited over to their houses for dinner or whatnot. And we've generally been in agreement about them, particularly the ones who stirred in us an idea or idealism, even an anger. Many are progressively left but a number are conservative. They're such a diverse group and differ in so many ways, in personality, speech, even the way they dress, and a couple are even funny-looking. Some are lousy lecturers and haven't written much. But others are real scholars. I can't possibly see anything they have in common! Except that they touched us by their sense of liberation. What *is* it that made us open to what they had to say, and feel genuinely moved by them? What do you think?"

Because I was rarely able to compete with his cascade of observations and questions, I listened with my usual intrigue. With a quizzical shrug along with a few murmured platitudes, I waited for the next moment.

The picture stuck in our heads. We had passed through their courses and presumptuously assumed a familiarity with our professors. Yet as we set out to seek a meaningful pattern, a satisfying connection between us, an awareness of distance loomed. After rummaging around the edges, a befuddlement set in. Nothing seemed to fit all those who had influenced us in one way or another, and concluded that they were, in effect, strangers.

Nonetheless, undaunted as undergraduates, we devised a rough but quantifiable chart, one that would hopefully reveal a theme or focus that bound together the diversified group. On the left side went the list of the names, approximately seven or eight as I now recall, and above a list of characteristics. Included was every salient pertinent quality: knowledge, politics, style, exams, dress, charisma, humor, quirks, sexual aura, and so on. Then we simply filled in the blank boxes with X's.

Diversified was putting it mildly. As the empty spaces disappeared, we started to laugh. A zigzag of crosses, like a bingo card. Then suddenly, the only trait our movers possessed in common was *humor.* "I think I know," exclaimed my roommate, "but what does humor really mean? Some of their humor is uplifting but there's an acerbic quality also."

We got slightly giddy and decided to chuck out all pending assignments. To hell with graduate applications, McCarthyism, and the draft! We divvied up the subject. I became responsible for literature and read the works of James Thurber, Ring Lardner, Jr., Damon Runyon, Robert Benchley, Dorothy Parker, George S. Kaufman, Morrie Ryskind, and countless others. He chose theory and plunged into Sigmund Freud, Henri Bergson, Max Eastman, and wrestled with Aristotle.

Every few days we exchanged information and queried each other. After about four weeks with the subject swirling inside our room—quantities of wine coolers, cigarettes, peanut butter sandwiches, and other sundries buoying our mood—we felt sufficiently confident to embark on the next stage of our campaign.

Our plan called for a visit with each of the professors on our humor hit list. For each encounter we prepared an explanation of our project and particular questions. A mock tryout with some friends in our boardinghouse, some of whom tanked up for the occasion, proved to be hilarious but much less insightful than the ultimate experience.

Much to our gratification, all the professors listened intently, and none threw us out of their office. Overall, the meetings averaged about an hour, and were never short on surprise and further puzzlement. These were mostly males because there were not many women on the faculty in those days. And their ages were as varied as their disciplines.

Regardless of age, religion, or gender, there was general surprise that we had devised, without professorial prodding, a "research" project of our own contrivance. Or was it connivance? This was afterall a small liberal arts college. A touch of paranoia eked out: "Just who among my colleagues put you up to this?"

"What did you say you're majoring in?" "What exactly were you doing in my class?" "Who else have you confronted with this?"

Upon learning that we thought professor so-and-so possessed the quality of humor, more than one vigorously protested: "If so, he's never revealed it to me." In one instance there was a guffaw followed by the comment that "most of my colleagues are assholes." Their eyes widened when we told them of the import of humor in their teaching and, as near as we could guess, in their personal lives as well. Some simply said that they were unaware of its relevance. Was that denial, we thought, or embarrassment? A couple of wiseass kids intruding on their turf?

Why, we asked them, do you often resort to humor in class? There followed a wide variety of answers from the unintentional to the deliberate. More than a few pointed out that student response gratifyingly spurred them on. A number lowered their guard, however, and reached into memory for an intimate experience: a difficult illness, the death of a friend or family member, a harrowing riot. Out of these instances came a conscious attempt to develop a comic spirit: "Well, it was coping or plunging, and fortunately I managed to accomplish the former after initially trying out the latter." Several harkened back to a whimsical parent or relative who saw things through an ironic lens. And one exclaimed that he was a Dadaist and everything in life was so absurd that nothing mattered save laughter.

Yet there was an undercurrent of glee, a kind of collective chortle that came through the conversations. Later, with jazz interspersed with Debussy in the background, we tried to pin down this chortle. If anything, there was surely a sense of bemusement about our probing. In the end, however, we thought that maybe, just maybe, it derived from their having achieved an intellectual, if not personal, liberation, no mean feat at any time.

To our questions about the historical characteristics of humor, there was thoughtful response but not much knowledge. With the exception of the English specialist, none had either researched or read deeply in the subject. Some questioned the viability of humor as an intellectual subject: "Not serious enough." Nevertheless they were intrigued enough to ask us to return and continue the discussion when they had "more time."

None pursued it further, though, even as we later passed them on campus. In the meantime, we squeezed back in our room and crammed for an upcoming examination in physics.

The
Humor
Prism
in 20th-
Century
America

13

I.

Introduction

History and Humor
Joseph Boskin

1.

"History," Robert Heilbroner noted in *The Future of History*, "as it comes into our daily lives, is charged with surprise and shock."[1] It is the opening into the workings of epoch and the comedic.

2.

New prisms through which the past can be viewed are vital to perspective, and a particularly penetrating and refracting slant is humor, especially the relationship between the historic moment and comedic forms.

As a cultural index, a reflector of social change and conflict, humor provides an unusual historical ray into the complex connection between society's concerns and issues. Comedy and change are inextricably entwined, and the related varieties of humor make their points both small and writ large.

Society's laughter poses the issues of community and continuity. Some jokes rankle whereas others are applauded. Some pieces of humor quickly evaporate after the telling while others possess transcendence. What social meaning does humor possess? Why are certain slices of humor rejected while others transmitted to succeeding generations? What, in short, is the relationship between the casting of a joke and story, and its frame of time and setting?

A determining factor clearly centers around societal concern, yet more important, on whether that concern is historically and psychologically relevant to diverse segments of the populace. Forced by shifts surprising or fraught with incongruity, it is not unusual for many people to react in humorous fashion. It happens because, whether oral or written, humor arises from a solidifying participation in a larger unit. Only the group, it has long been noted, can truly comprehend the thrust of a story, the intent of a joke. Thus, if one wishes to know, noted folklorist Alan

Dundes in *Cracking Jokes*, "what is really on a people's collective mind, there is no more direct and accurate way of finding out than by paying attention to precisely what is making the people laugh."[2]

Seminal writings on humor's properties are in considerable agreement regarding this singularity. Sigmund Freud, in his pathbreaking work *Wit and Its Relation to the Unconscious* (1905), posited that humor is wholly a social process wherein the shared actions of the participants allow them to aggress and/or regress together. Similarly, ethologist Konrad Lorenz in his study *On Aggression* (1963) offered that "laughter forms a bond" but simultaneously "draws a line." In this way, laughter produces a "strong fellow feeling among the participants and joint aggressiveness against outsiders."[3]

Supplementing this notion was philosopher Henri Bergson's observation in *Laughter* (1900) that *complicity* is inextricably involved in humor. "Our laughter is always the laughter of a group. You would hardly appreciate the comic if you felt yourself isolated from others. Laughter appears in need of an echo." Bergson offered an illustration: "A man was asked why he did not weep at a sermon when everyone else was shedding tears replied: 'I don't belong to the parish.'"[4]

In his *Essays on the Sociology of Knowledge* (1952), sociologist Karl Mannheim further expounded on how belonging to a specific time and space creates generational cohesion:

> The fact of belonging to the same class, and that of belonging to the same generation or age group, have this in common, that both endow the individuals sharing in them a common location in the social and historical process, and thereby limit them to a specific range of potential experiences, predisposing them for a certain characteristic mode of thought and experience, and a characteristic type of historically relevant action.[5]

Societal laughter, then, mirrors both personal and generational mindsets, transcending time and place and at the same time reflecting time and place. In attempting to capture the sense of an epoch, the historian Carl Becker once proffered a nonquantifiable measure of analysis, which he termed the "climate of opinion."[6] The "climate," in its broadest sense, represents the sum of the various forces impinging on a given culture at a specific time, creating in effect a powerful social tone and an intellectual coherence. Although Becker himself did not offer humor as one of the factors, there is no doubt that a *comic zeitgeist* is an outgrowth of particular social and intellectual forces.

Defined by the group that decides what is and what is not laughable, humor endows a specific cultural hue. Yet not all humor is period bound. There are motifs that transcend cultures, jokes that convey the universality of the human experience. Embracing humor makes a mockery of moment and place, and laughter refracting a common experience that tends to bind us all. "The true balance of life and art, the saving of the human mind as well as the theatre," wrote one of the most notable humorists of the century, James Thurber, "lies in what has long been known as tragicomedy, for humor and pathos, tears and laughter are, in the highest expression of human character and achievement, inseparable."[7]

3.

A study of humor is essentially an exploration of a particular type of cultural language, and to comprehend its dimensions demands an understanding of its characteristics. Like all language, humor organizes and correlates experiences by seeking and creating order and meaning; it strives to clarify the vague through analogue conversion, and as different experiences are absorbed into social awareness, translates them into folk stories and tales. In so doing, humor creates a communal consciousness, binding the generations while at the same time enabling each person a singular connection.

As universal as humor is, it is bounded by a culture code. Devolving from historic patterns and buttressed by basic folk values, the code is the nexus of communal awareness, the elemental factor in the structure of humor. For to be understood and possess meaning, humor must relate to the customs, symbols, and experience of the people. The code creates categories dividing those who are privy to its purpose from those who are outsiders.

In the United States, the code is a complex arrangement, molded by regional, ethnic, race, class, and gender interests and buttressed and enlivened by people's chatter. Emerging from this chatter is a sense of communal awareness writ small and large. Since virtually all joking involves some sort of binding, intimacy is an essential ingredient in humor. Consequently, humor is felt most deeply with others of like mind, and typically within a cozy setting. "How often has the remark been made," concluded Bergson, "that many comic effects are incapable of translation from one language to another, because they refer to the customs and ideas of a particular social group!"[8] Thus do few Californians truly understand the comic contained in the quip New Englanders make about their climate: "If you don't like the weather, wait an hour!"; or a similar jibe made by Minnesotans: "There are two seasons here, July and the rest of the year!" Similarly, African-American jokes are often puzzling to whites, and women's humor is often incomprehensible to men.

As a device of social analysis, therefore, humor illumines the expectations and contradictions of society, its anxieties and confusions, and offers perspective into any historic moment. Freud provided a penetrating insight into the process when he observed that humor is the civilized means by which humans express hidden feelings, the object of the process being to create mirth while the emotions rage. In this sly way, humor confronts reality by wrapping it in a showy package, disguising its contents.

The
Humor
Prism
in 20th-
Century
America

20

4.

Despite humor's import, the scholarly world has largely eschewed the subject as worthy of study. In the early 1970s, Louis Rubin, Jr., rightly complained that "more time and effort has been invested in attempting to study and to understand American tragedy than American comedy, and humorous writing is customarily relegated to a subordinate role. In so doing, we have been guilty of neglecting a valuable insight into the understanding of American society."[9]

It is indeed extraordinary that the historical dimension of American humor has been so short shrifted. More than the sum of its parts, humor mirrors the expanse of American culture, its dreams, anxieties, conflicts, styles, and posture. Since the earliest years of colonization, humor has served as a dynamic, centralizing force in bringing together the disparate elements in society. Humor's role has been vital in ameliorating social conflict, facilitating social change, and forging a national identity.

Humor's import is downplayed because it has been consigned to the nonserious facet of everyday existence. This situation arises from the distinction made in contemporary society between *work* and *play*, the one construed as taking obligations solemnly, the latter as having fun; in effect, evading obligations. As the highly popular phrase "TGIF" suggests, play begins at the moment work ends. This process has been so routinized that the daily 9-to-5 grind is followed by what we term the "Happy Hour." Likewise with the work week in which after many days of toil, a short respite of frolic. The not-so-subtle meaning is evident: (unhappy) work and (happy) play do not mix in the same theatre.

Manufacturers attuned to this dichotomy extol their products accordingly. Hence one of the largest liquor companies in North America in the 1980s featured a billboard advertisement that displayed a prominent bottle lying on its side, the caption announcing, "After the work—the reward."

Consequently, humor in the corporate workplace in the twentieth century has been highly monitored, its practice and content purposely kept at low key. While not exactly banned, organizational policy downright shuns playfulness. "Arnie, what the hell happened to you?" inquires Murray plaintively of his younger brother Arnold, a highly successful businessman, in Herb Gardner's barbed comedy *A Thousand Clowns* (1962). "You got so old. I don't know you any more. When you quit 'Harry the Fur King' . . . you dressed perfectly, homburg, gray suit, cuff links, carrying a briefcase and a rolled umbrella . . . and you came into Harry's office on roller skates. You weren't going to take crap from *any*body."[10]

Constant reminders of humor's distraction from the "business-at-hand" abounds throughout the culture. Colloquial expressions ring out its threat, "This is a serious affair!" / "It's no laughing matter!" And the familiar military admonishment: "Soldier, wipe that smile off your face, throw it on the ground and stamp on it!" Listeners to the highly popular radio show in the 1930s and '40s, *Fibber McGee and Molly*, heard Molly's constant admonishing declaration, "Tain't funny, McGee!"

This approach blunts humor's range. Accordingly, the leader of the Clamshell Alliance at the antinuclear protest in Manchester, New Hampshire in 1978, felt compelled to offer a caveat regarding its whimsical slogan, "Clams Should Be Steamed, But Not Heard": "Our intent is serious, but we don't see any reason why there shouldn't be a lighter side of things, too."[11]

The Humor Prism in 20th-Century America

21

Preindustrial cultures made infrequent distinction between labor and play. Robert W. Malcolmson in his study of popular recreation in eighteenth- and nineteenth-century English-speaking societies observed that "work and recreation were so closely related that they were almost indistinguishable." Mirth coexisted alongside work, storytelling accompanying the labor of spinning and harvesting: "Among some groups of workers one of their members was appointed to read aloud as the others worked."[12]

5.

As inconsequential as humor is perceived to be, its multidimensional forms enliven all facets of American life. In the twentieth century, humor played a crucial role in America's cultural life, from the print and electronic medias to comedy nightclubs and people's jokes. Statistics detailing the latter half-century convey its immersion in all levels of the media. In the print industry diverse publications such as *Dr. Seuss, The Funny Times, The Quayle Quarterly, Freud's Own Cookbook, Oral Sadism and the Vegetarian Personality, The Whole Mirth Catalogue,* as well as pseudo-collections of "tasteless" jokes, cartoons, short stories and other edited books, filled the bookstores. Columnists Art Buchwald, Erma Bombeck, and Russell Baker were nationally syndicated throughout the mid-1900s, joined later by Dave Barry, P. J. O'Rourke, and Molly Ivins. The *New York Times Book Review* best-seller list in January 1992 contained four humor books among the top fifteen, several of which had been long-standing, including Dr. Seuss's *Oh, The Places You'll Go!,* P. J. O'Rourke's *Parliament of Whores,* and Bill Cosby's *Childhood.*

Newspapers continually expanded their comic strips and cartoon section, so that by the early 1990s such papers as the *Boston Globe, Tampa Tribune, Sarasota Herald-Tribune,* and *Los Angeles Times* offered between twenty-four and twenty-seven strips. Socially relevant and generational comic strips made their appearance, including Garry Trudeau's *Doonesbury,* Gary Larson's *The Far Side,* and Nicole Hollander's *Sylvia.*

Figures for the ten top prime-time programs on television in the 1980s exhibited the nation's craving for humor. Although *60 Minutes* headed the list, it was immediately followed by two of the decade's most popular sitcoms, *Cheers* and the long-running *Bill Cosby Show,* as well as the short-lived *America's Funniest Home*

Videos and *America's Funniest People.*[13] And in continuous opera-
tion from the mid-1970s was *Saturday Night Live,* which offered
socially conscious and politically satirical sketches.

Other comedy revues and satiric sitcoms from the 1950s to
the 1990s amplified the comedic atmosphere: *I Love Lucy, All in
the Family, The Honeymooners, The Jeffersons, The Mary Tyler Moore
Show, You Bet Your Life!, Sanford and Son, the Jack Benny Show, The
George Burns and Gracie Allen Show, Laugh-In, That Was the Week
That Was, MASH, Roseanne, Frasier,* and many others.

Supplementing the electronic scene were stand-up performances and concerts: Lenny Bruce demolished the boundaries
surrounding public comedy; Dick Gregory pried open the racial
boundary; Hal Holbrook presented the life of Mark Twain; Lily
Tomlin offered the manifold levels of women's existence; Bill
Cosby tendered the multiracial issues of middle-class urban life;
Garrison Keillor peered into Lake Wobegon's mythical midwestern lives; Richard Pryor flaunted society's mores; George Carlin
undercut religious and linguistic taboos; Robin Williams mani-
cally dissected every subject imaginable. On hundreds of comedy
stages and cable television stations were a multitude of stand-up
comics who offered a range of multicultural issues.

Comic inducements appealed to people's consumerist impulses. Jesting signs in a small pizza and submarine shop, "Seven
days without pizza makes one week"; on a Howard Johnson's
menu, "Having an Affair? Our Experienced Catering Staff Will
Be Happy to Assist You"; on a trolley car, "I Know I'm Having a
Good Time When the Conversation Gets as Deep as the Pizza";
on Pizza Hut paper plates, "How to Give a Pizza Six-appeal"; on a
landscaper's truck, "A House without Shrubs Isn't Fit for a Dog";
on a party announcement for young Jewish professionals, "The
Matzo Ball"; on subway station ads showing a smiling black
youth, "You Don't Have to be Jewish to Like Levi's Rye Bread."
Whimsical products became fads—the pet rock, mood ring, silly
putty, hula hoop, Slinky.

Humor's grip on the culture extended in other ways, such
as in the film industry: in 1986 seven of the highest grossing films
were comedies or comedy-adventures.[14] No longer able to deny
the impact of humor, scholarly interest initiated a series of international conferences beginning in the late 1960s, and incorporated into university curriculums topics ranging from the comedies of Aristophanes and Shakespeare to films such as Charlie

The
Humor
Prism
in 20th-
Century
America

23

Chaplin's *Modern Times*, Stanley Kubrick's *Dr. Strangelove*, Mel Brooks's *Blazing Saddles*, and Woody Allen's *Annie Hall.*

The potential accorded humor carried over to individual quests, for example, to Stanley Myron Handelman's identification as a "religious comedian" and his efforts to separate humor from the secular. Handelman had made his mark as a highly respectable stand-up comic in the 1950s and '60s but had redirected his career with a firm belief in "the religion of comedy," since "like other religions, it is based on love and trust. . . . It is something that inspires comradery and reveals our universal nature." Convinced that the government was subverting humor's spiritual goal, Handelman refused to pay his taxes and petitioned the Internal Revenue Service to recognize the new religion. He lost.[15]

6.

The
Humor
Prism
in 20th-
Century
America

24

Undergirding and supplementing the vast stage of public comedy was an equally vigorous underground river of people's humor. Different forms—jokes, graffiti, quips, anecdotes, cycles—speedily traversed the country, the consequence of an elaborate electronic system that, in effect, created a national ear. Due to the telephone, internet, fax machine, and e-mail, the comedic came to possess almost geographical simultaneity.

Parenthetically, people's jokes have always moved rapidly along the cultural grapevine. A folklorist researching early American nineteenth-century tales that ridiculed bad roads and miserable traveller accommodations noted that such "stories passed back and forth between the oral tradition and print as they travelled from north to south and east to west."[16]

In the latter half of the century, the flow of people's humor accelerated exponentially. Reacting to rapidly changing social mores and institutions, ethnic/racial/gender conflicts, technological disasters, and other national events, people deluged the electronic airwaves with a raillery rarely seen in American history. So, too, did many a local occurrence pique humor, as indicated by this two-town predicament in the 1980s:

> In 1981, a two-mile, newly constructed high-arched bridge over the upper Mississippi River, the most direct link between Prairie du Chien, Wisconsin and Marquette, Iowa, was suddenly and indefinitely closed when an inspection dis-

closed that it might collapse at any moment. Planned, extravagant celebrations at its opening—the new bridge had replaced an aged, rickety suspension structure—were cancelled and both towns feared severe economic repercussions. Because neither the ancient bridge nor its replacement had actually collapsed, the towns could not apply for federal disaster funds.

This catch-22 situation instantly produced acerbic joking among the residents of the towns. One of the mayors, decidedly portly in girth, suggested that he and the governor, equal in size, jump up and down on the bridge together. A retailer volunteered to drive his truck over the bridge every fifteen minutes until it fell. Residents tied red ribbons around trees signifying that the bridge was being held hostage by federal regulations; and a newspaper displayed a drawing of the new bridge on its masthead over a caption: "Closed. Prairie Held Hostage, Day 18." The mayor of Prairie suggested that the town secede from the Union, declare war, blow up the bridge and surrender—all in one day. Then the government "would be down here right away to help rebuild."[17]

7.

Exploring the dynamics and disguised messages behind humor, especially people's humor, is the overall thrust of this volume. Of all humor's characteristics the correlation between an event and its comedic expression is surely one of the most intriguing. Presented here are diverse essays that analyze the social and intellectual function of humor framed by the question: to what extent and in what ways does humor reflect moments small and circumstances large? These pieces also explore the character and major influences on American humor in the present century, tracing the relationship between social change and conflict as they were reflected and transformed in the national humor.

The volume comprises four distinct sections. Complementing the opening essay is an article on humor's primary relationship to the culture code. The following section analyzes the contours of American humor, its social and intellectual roots from which it draws its energies, idiosyncratic patterns and peculiarities, and a special class of stand-up comics. A third part explores the tenor of humor devolving from the requirements and dynamics of the metropolis, the predominant minorities, and other

The Humor Prism in 20th-Century America

25

alienated groups. The final section presents the major joke cycles from the post–World War II period to the 1990s, and discusses how each responded to profound social change and perceived contradiction.

The stage on which all this has played out exists in the minds of people who, when confronted with unanticipated social twists and change, threatening challenges to accepted values and institutions, and redefining identities, employed humor as a means of grappling with events and generating new meaning. By so doing, they also ameliorated anxieties, solidified resolve, and obtained critical perspective.

8.

"For God's sake, shall we laugh?" asks a figure in Christopher Fry's drama, *The Lady's Not for Burning.* "For what reason?" he is challenged.

> For the reason of laughter, since laughter is surely
> The surest touch of genius in creation,
> Would *you* ever have thought of it, I ask you,
> If you had been making man, stuffing him full
> Of such hopping greeds and passions that he has
> To blow himself to pieces as often as he
> Conveniently can manage it—would it also
> Have occurred to you to make him burst himself
> With such a phenomenon as cachinnation?
> That same laughter, madam, is an irrelevancy
> Which almost amounts to revelation.[18]

The
Humor
Prism
in 20th-
Century
America

26

Notes

1. Robert Heilbroner, *The Future as History* (Grove Press, 1959), 13.

2. Alan Dundes, *Cracking Jokes: Studies of Sick Humor Cycles and Stereotypes* (Ten Speed Press, 1987), 168.

3. Sigmund Freud, *Wit and Its Relation to the Unconscious* (Routledge and Kegan Paul, 1922); Konrad Lorenz, *On Aggression* (Bantam Books, 1963), 284.

4. Henri Bergson, Laughter, in *Comedy*, ed. Wylie Sypher (Doubleday & Co., 1956), 64.

5. Karl Mannheim, *On the Sociology of Knowledge* (Routledge & Paul, 1952), 291.

6. Carl Becker, *Freedom and Responsibility in the American Way of Life* (Vintage Press, 1945), xv.

7. James Thurber, *Lanterns and Lances* (Harper & Bros., 1955), 143.

8. Bergson, *Laughter*, 64–65.

9. Louis D. Rubin, Jr., "The Great American Joke," *The South Atlantic Quarterly* 72 (Winter 1973): 83.

10. Herb Gardner, *A Thousand Clowns* (Random House, 1961), 101–102.

11. Michael Kenney, "Pronuclear leader: It's for the children," *Boston Globe*, June 23, 1978, 26.

12. Robert W. Malcolmson, *Popular Recreations in English Society, 1700–1850* (Cambridge University Press, 1973), 15–16.

13. *New York Times*, January 19, 1992; *Wall Street Journal*, January 9, 1992.

14. Bob Thomas, "Comedy Is King at the Movies," *Boston Globe*, July 15, 1986, 86; Aljean Harmetz, "Drama Inches Up on Comedy at the Movies," *New York Times*, January 17, 1989, C15, 20; Stephen Holden, "New Kind of Arts Festival, With Laughs," *New York Times*, June 4, 1993, C3; "Going for Broke on the Laugh Track," *Newsweek* 106 (August 19, 1985), 58–60.

15. Stanley Myron Handelman, letter to author, circa early 1980s; "From the Sublime to the Ridiculous," in *The Handbook of Humor Research*, ed. paul E. McGee and Jeffrey Goldstein (Springer-Verlag, 1983), 24–31.

16. John Q. Anderson, "Some Migratory Anecdotes in American Folk Humor," *Mississippi Quarterly* 25 (Fall 1972): 447.

17. Barry Siegal, "Bridge Cracks and Town's Economy Sags," *Los Angeles Times* (15 February 1981): 1, 7–8.

18. Christopher Fry, *The Lady's Not for Burning* (Oxford University Press, 1950), 49.

The
Humor
Prism
in 20th-
Century
America

27

What Makes People Laugh?: Cracking the Cultural Code

Arthur Asa Berger

The
Humor
Prism
in 20th-
Century
America

28

Humor is directly tied to the "cultural code" of a given country—to the assumptions people make about time and space, to the values they hold, to their historic experience, etc.— though in certain cases humor can transcend particular codes and have a universal appeal. In such cases people from different countries may not understand the full significance of what makes them laugh, but there is enough to tickle their fancy. I can't imagine that the English (or French) can relate to the gags in a Marx brothers film the way Americans can, but there is still enough zaniness and anarchism for non-American audiences to find them hilarious.

Even foreign students of the film, who study the Marx brothers and are aware, *intellectually* speaking, of their humor, cannot relate to it the way Americans do. As Pierre Bourdieu has written in "Systems of Education and Systems of Thought":

> Culture is not merely a common code or even a common catalogue of answers to recurring problems; it is a common set of previously assimilated master patterns from which, by an "art of invention" similar to that involved in the writing of music, an infinite number of individual patterns directly applicable to specific situations are generated. The *topoi* are not only commonplaces but also patterns of invention and supports for improvisation.

Bourdieu argues that the educational institutions of a country play a pivotal role in the transmittal and modification of culture and "its express function is to transform the collective heritage

Reprinted from *ETC: A Review of General Semantics*, vol. 32, no. 4, with permission of the International Society for General Semantics, Concord, California.

into an individual and common unconscious." What is important for our purpose is that we acknowledge the existence of this "cultural unconscious" and recognize that humor is tied to it.

When a comedian makes an allusion to some event which is politically embarrassing to the government, or to some individual, the allusion has power only because it is connected to historical experience and because Americans (and many other people) find embarrassment humorous. I once showed a copy of *The New Yorker* to a Japanese Fulbright student taking a course on humor. He looked at the cartoons with curiosity, but didn't crack a smile at any of them. This was because the cartoons were, for the most part, intimately connected with American culture—and American upper middle class culture, at that—and the allusions and revelations in the cartoons meant nothing to him.

It may be that I am somewhat like that Japanese student when it comes to English humor in that my ideas about what humor should be like are tied to my social class, my profession, and my expectations as an American. On the other hand, I do think that there are certain standards which can be used to judge humor (and perhaps all kinds of cultural performances) regardless of where one is or what the audience is like. It is argued that *person*'s taste is intimately related to his education, social class, and culture. But it strikes me as quite foolish to suggest that all things are necessarily equal in all respects, and that the question of individual preference is not a factor to be considered.

A person has a right to his tastes, for that is an individual decision, but this does not mean that one person's taste is as good as the next person's, for when we enter into the realm of social phenomena there are canons that can be used to judge artistic performances. Thus I believe it is possible to evaluate humor even when it is somewhat foreign to the kind of humor to which we are normally accustomed.

Actually the evaluation process is of secondary importance to me. I am interested in the cultural codes behind the humor and believe that humor can be "used" to gain valuable insights into the ethos and worldview of other cultures.

The
Humor
Prism
in 20th-
Century
America

29

II.

The Contours of
American Laughter

The Great American Joke

Louis D. Rubin, Jr.

The American literary imagination has from its earliest days been at least as much comic in nature as tragic. Perhaps this is only what might be expected; for while the national experience has involved sadness, disappointment, failure, and even despair, it has also involved much joy, hopefulness, accomplishment. The tragic mode, therefore, could not of itself comprehend the experience of the American people. All in all, and with some notable exceptions, the story of America has been pretty much a success story. The type of society that has evolved in the northern portion of the Western Hemisphere bears no notable resemblance either to Eden or to Utopia, of course, since from the start it has been inhabited by human beings who have remained very human and therefore most fallible. Even so, if one views American history as a whole, it would be very difficult to pronounce it a tragedy or to suggest that the society of man would have been better off if it had never taken place.

Yet for all that, it is remarkable how comparatively little attention has been paid to American humor and to the comic imagination in general by those who have chronicled and interpreted American literature. Thalia, the muse of comedy, has always been something of a wallflower in critical circles, and the attention has gone principally to Melpomene and her celebrants of tragedy. In large part, of course, this is because in the hierarchy of letters, comedy has always occupied a position below and inferior to tragedy. We have tended to equate gravity with importance. The highest accolade we give to a humorist is when we say that even so he is a serious writer—which is to say that although he makes us laugh, his ultimate obective is to say something more about the human condition than merely that it is amusing. This implies that comedy is un-serious. We thus play a

The
Humor
Prism
in 20th-
Century
America

33

This essay was first published in the *South Atlantic Quarterly* vol. 72, no. 1 (Winter 1973). Copyright 1973, Duke University Press. Reprinted with permission.

verbal trick, for we use "serious" to mean both "important" and "without humor," when the truth is that there is no reason at all why something cannot be at once very important and very comic.

In any event, a geat deal more time and effort have been invested in attempting to study and to understand American tragedy than American comedy, and humorous writing is customarily relegated to a subordinate role. In rating it, we have been guilty of neglecting a valuable insight into the understanding of American society. For not only have so many American writers been comic writers, but the very nature of comedy would seem to make it particularly useful in studying life in the United States. The essence of comedy is incongruity, the perception of the ridiculous. The seventeenth-century English critic Dennis's remark, that "the design of Comedy is to amend the follies of Mankind, by exposing them," points to the value of humor in searching out the shortcomings and the liabilities of society. In a democracy, the capacity for self-criticism would seem to be an essential function of the body politic, and surely this has been one of the chief tasks of the American writer. From Colonial times onward, Americans have spent a great deal of time and effort criticizing themselves, pointing out their shortcomings, exploring the incongruities and the contradictions within American society. As Robert Penn Warren has put it,

The
Humor
Prism
in 20th-
Century
America

34

> America was based on a big promise—a great big one: the Declaration of Independence. When you have to live with that in the house, that's quite a problem—particularly when you've got to make money and get ahead, open world markets, do all the things you have to, raise your children, and so forth. America is stuck with its self-definition put on paper in 1776, and that was just like putting a burr under the metaphysical saddle of America—you see, that saddle's going to jump now and then and it pricks.

Literature has been one of the important ways whereby the American people have registered their discomfort at those pricks, and repeatedly the discomfort has been expressed in the form of humor—often enough through just such a homely metaphor as Warren used. For if we look at Warren's remark, what we will notice is that it makes use of a central motif of American humor: the contrast, the incongruity between the ideal and the real, in which a common, vernacular metaphor is used to put a somewhat abstract statement involving values—self-definition, metaphysical—into a homely context. The statement, in other words, makes its point through working an incongruity between two modes of language—the formal, literary language of traditional culture and learning, and the informal, vernacular language of everyday life.

This incongruity lies at the heart of American experience. It is emblematic of the nature and the problem of democracy. On the one hand there are the ideals of freedom, equality, and self-government, the conviction that ordinary people can evince the wisdom to vote wisely and demonstrate the capacity for understanding and cherishing the highest human values through embodying them in their political and social institutions. On the other hand there is the reality of the fact that the individual citizens of a democracy are indeed ordinary people, who speak, think, and act in ordinary terms, with a suspicion of the abstract ideas and values. The problem of democracy and culture is one of how, in short, a democracy can reach down to include all its citizens in its decision making, without at the same time cheapening and vulgarizing its highest social, cultural, and ethical ideals. Who, that is, will commission the Esterhazy quartets? Confronting this problem, Thomas Jefferson called for the *aristoi*, an aristocracy of intellect. He believed that through public education the civilized values of truth, knowledge, and culture that he cherished could be embodied and safeguarded in the democratic process so that leadership could be produced which would not be demagogic and debasing. His good friend John Adams was skeptical of this ever coming to pass, and Adams's great-grandson, Henry Adams, lived to chronicle and deplore a time when the workings of political and economic democracy made heroes of the vulgar and the greedy and had no place in the spectrum of power, he thought, for an Adams who by virtue of inbred inheritance still believed in the disinterested morality, as he saw it, of the Founding Fathers. What Henry Adams could not fathom was why the public could nominate for the presidency of the United States a Ulysses Grant, a James A. Garfield, a James G. Blaine, and then vote for him. He could only conclude that the "the moral law had expired—like the Constitution." "The progress of evolution from President Washington to President Grant," he concluded, "was alone evidence enough to upset Darwin."

The problem has been part of American experience from the start, and it is at least as crucial today as in the past. Though

The
Humor
Prism
in 20th-
Century
America

35

it is by no means purely or uniquely American, it is nevertheless distinctively so, and if we look at American literary history, we will quickly recognize that the writers have been dealing with it all along the way. Herman Melville's famous invocation to the muses in *Moby Dick* faces it squarely:

> If, then, to meanest mariners, and renegades and cast-aways, I shall hereafter ascribe high qualities, though dark; weave round them tragic graces; if even the most mournful, perchance the most abased, among them all, shall at times lift himself to exalted mounts; if I shall touch that work-man's arm with some ethereal light; if I shall spread a rain-bow over his disastrous set of sun; then against all mortal spirits bear me out in it, thou just Spirit of Equality, which hast spread one royal mantle of humanity over all my kind! Bear me out in it, thou great democratic God! . . .

Melville wanted to create a tragedy along metaphysical lines, and yet he wanted to write about the Nantucket whaling fleet; his problem was how to render the everyday experience of life aboard a whaling vessel while creating a tragic protagonist, one who, in Aristotle's classic formula, could arouse pity and terror through his fall from eminence. Obviously such a protoganist, Aristotle declared, "must be one who is highly renowned and prosperous—a personage like Oedipus, Thyestes, or other illus-trious men of such families." How to give a whaling captain such heroic stature? Melville's solution was partly one of language. He separated the two elements. He used a literary, highly poetic, Shakespearean diction to chronicle Ahab, and a much more ver-nacular, colloquial diction to report on the activities of the crew. He made the language distance between tragic captain and mot-ley crew serve his ultimate meaning.

In so doing, however, Melville was forced to distort the ex-perience of a whaling captain. He could not make (nor did he wish to make) Captain Ahab into a "typical" Nantucket whaling skipper. He had to leave out a great deal of what an ordinary whaling captain does and says and thinks. To achieve the magni-ficent tragedy of Captain Ahab against the universe, he was forced to sacrifice most of what a whaling captain was *as a whal-ing captain*. The "realism" of *Moby Dick* does not extend to the captain of the *Pequod*. No one would lament the loss; *Moby Dick* is worth whatever it cost to make it possible. But all the same, the problem remains. How does the writer evoke the civilized values

—of language, religion, philosophy, culture in general—that have traditionally been used to give order and delineate meaning in society, while at the same time remaining faithful to the everyday texture of "low life" experience? How may a whaling captain grapple with the eternal verities and yet be shown doing it in the terms in which such things would confront a whaling captain, and in a mode of language that can reproduce his experience *as* a whaling captain? How to make a whaling captain into a tragic hero, in other words, without making him into the literary image of Shakespearean king and investing him with the language conventions of Shakespearean tragedy? This has been the dilemma of the American writer from colonial times onward.

Henry James, in a famous passage about Nathaniel Hawthorne, expressed the cultural problem quite (I will not say succinctly, for that is no word for the style of even the early Henry James) appropriately. Taking his cue from something that Hawthorne himself wrote, James declared that

> one might enumerate the forms of high civilization, as it exists in other countries, which are absent from the texture of American life, until it should be a wonder to know what was left. No State, in the European sense of the word, and indeed barely a specific national name. No sovereign, no court, no personal loyalty, no aristocracy, no church, no clergy, no army, no diplomatic service, no country gentlemen, no palaces, no castles, nor manors, nor old century-houses, nor parsonages, not thatched cottages nor ivied ruins; no cathedrals, nor abbeys, nor little Norman churches; no great Universities nor public schools—no Oxford, nor Eton, nor Harrow; no literature, no novels, no museums, no pictures, no political society, no sporting class—no Epsom nor Ascot! Some such list as that might be drawn up of the absent things in American life—especially in the American life of forty years ago, the effect of which, upon an English or a French imagination, would probably as a general thing be appalling.

But James does not stop there.

> The American knows that a good deal remains; what it is that remains—that is his secret, his joke, as one may say. It would be cruel, in this terrible denudation, to deny him the consolation of his national gift, that "American humor" of which of late years we have heard so much.

The
Humor
Prism
in 20th-
Century
America

38

James's words are appropriately chosen, for so much of American literature has focused upon just that national "joke"—by which I take him to mean the fact that in a popular democracy the customary and characteristic institutions that have traditionally embodied cultural, social, and ethical values are missing from the scene, and yet the values themselves, and the attitudes that derive from and serve to maintain them, remain very much part of the national experience. This is what Robert Penn Warren meant by the "burr under the metaphysical saddle of America," which pricks whenever the saddle jumps. Out of the incongruity between mundane circumstance and heroic ideal, material fact and spiritual hunger, democratic, middle-class society and desire for cultural definition, theory of equality and fact of social and economic inequality, the Declaration of Independence and the Prohibition Act, the Gettysburg Address and the Gross National Product, the Battle Hymn of the Republic and Dollar Diplomacy, the Horatio Alger ideal and the New York Social Register—between what men would be and must be, as acted out in American experience, have come a great deal of pathos, no small bit of tragedy, and also a great deal of humor. Both the pathos and the humor have been present from the start, and the writers have been busy pointing them out. This, then, is what has been called "the great American joke," which comedy has explored and imaged.

One of the more amusing sketches in Joseph Glover Baldwin's *The Flush Times of Alabama and Mississippi* (1853) is that entitled "Simon Suggs, Jr., Esq: A Legal Biography." Baldwin took his character's name from that given to the old scoundrel in Johnson Jones Hooper's Simon Suggs stories. Like his father, Suggs, Jr., was a semiliterate and a complete rogue. The sketch opens with some correspondence between Suggs, Jr., and the promoters of a New York biographical magazine, who write to inform him that he has been honored by having been chosen to have his biographical sketch apear in public print, and asking him to furnish biographical details and a suitable daguerrotype. The letter to Suggs, Jr., is couched in the most formal and flowery of terms, but its message is in effect a suggestion that by having his biography appear in the magazine suitably worded, Suggs, Jr., will perhaps be chosen to be a judge some day. To this elaborately worded invitation—"We know from experience, that the characteristic diffidence of the profession, in many instances, shrinks from the seeming, though falsely seeming, indelicacy of an egotistical parade of one's own talents and accomplishments . . ."—Suggs, Jr., responds with misspelled alacrity: "I'm obleeged to you for your perlite say so, and so forth. I got a friend to rite it —my own ritin being mostly perfeshunal. He done it—but he rites such a cussed bad hand I cant rede it: I reckon its all ker-rect tho'." He doesn't have a daguerrotype available, but the engraving of his famous father appearing in Hooper's *Some Adventures of Simon Suggs* will do for him if retouched to make him look a bit younger. He then receives another letter from the publisher, thanking him for his sketch, "the description of a lawyer distinguished in the out-door labors of the profession, and directing great energies to the preparation of proof." In a postscript, however, the editor informs Suggs, Jr., that "our delicacy caused us to omit . . . mention what we suppose was generally understood, viz., the fact that the cost to us of preparing engravings &c. &c., for the sketches or memoirs, is one hundred and fifty dollars, which sum it is expected, of course, the gentleman who is perpetuated in our work, will forward to us before the insertion of his biography."

Suggs, Jr., now realizes what is going on, and he writes, *"Dear Mr. Editor*—In your p.s. which seems to be the creem of your correspondents you say I can't get in your book without paying one hundred and fifty dollars—pretty tall entrants fee!" He tells them "I believe I will pass. I'll enter a nolly prossy q. O-n-e-h-u-n-d-r-e-d-dollars and fifty better! Je-whellikens." He has begun "to see the pint of many things which was very vague and ondefinit before." And so on.

Following this exchange of correspondence, we then get the text of the biographical sketch which was prepared by Simon Suggs, Jr.'s, friend for inclusion in the magazine. It is cast in the elegiac, flowery tone of such self-adulatory biographical sketches, and it makes the most of a very checkered career, putting the kindest construction possible on the events of that career. What is described is the story of various slick dealings by a consummate rogue and trickster, involving much swindling, knavery, and dishonesty, and it is couched throughout in the most formal and literary of tones. The humor consists of the self-important pomposity of the literary method of narration as it contrasts with the very undignified vernacular antics being described. To wit:

Col. Suggs also extricated a client and his sureties from a forfeited recognizance, by having the defaulting defendant's obituary notice somewhat prematurely inserted in the newspapers; the solicitor, seeing which, discontinued proceedings; for which service, the deceased, immediately after the adjournment of court, returned to the officer his particular acknowledgements.

The sketch concludes with Simon Suggs, Jr., in Washington attempting to settle claims on behalf of the Choctaw Indians, and with the suggestion that "may the Indians live to get their dividends of the arrears paid to their agent."

Now the humor of this sketch, like that of most of the writings of the humorists of the old nineteenth-century Southern frontier, comes out of the clash of language modes. Baldwin is perhaps the most extreme of all of them in this respect. A well-educated and highly literate man, he adopts the persona of a cultivated gentleman to describe the wild, untutored, catch-as-catch-can doings of the old frontier regions. The tone is that of condescension, and the humor arises out of the inappropriateness of the way in which vernacular and usually crass activities are described in quite ornate and pompous language. But although the author's spokesman is a man of culture and refinement who is amused by and somewhat contemptuous of the uninhibited, semicivilized crudeness of the frontier folk, there is also an element of respect for the way that the low-life characters can get right to the point and deal directly with experience. Suggs, Jr.'s, shrewdness in spotting what the invitation to submit a sketch for the magazine really involves, his failure to be taken in by the flowery language and erudite circumlocutions of the thing, are, in the context, quite admirable. Suggs, Jr., is a rogue, to be sure, as his biographical sketch admirably demonstrates, but he does not pretend to be anything other than that. The New York entrepreneur, by contrast, is every bit as dishonest. Though his magazine is supposedly designed to supply "a desideratum American literature, namely, the commemoration and perpetuation of the names, characters, and personal and professional traits and histories of American lawyers and jurists," and though he says that Simon, Jr., has been selected for inclusion by "many of the most prominent gentlemen in public and private life, who have the honor of your acquaintance," what he is really doing is selling self-advertisements in the guise of biographical

The
Humor
Prism
in 20th-
Century
America

40

sketches. Unlike Simon, Jr., however, he pretends to be doing so "from motives purely patriotic and disinterested," in order that "through our labors, the reputation of distinguished men of the country, constituting its moral treasure, may be preserved for the admiration and direction of mankind, not for a day, but for all time." Suggs, Jr., in brief, is a barbaric but honest rogue, and the editor of the magazine is a civilized but hypocritical confidence man.

Here, indeed, is the elementary, basic American humorous situation—the "great American joke," and in one very obvious form. The humor arises out of the gap between the cultural ideal and the everyday fact, with the ideal shown to be somewhat hollow and hypocritical, and the fact crude and disgusting.

The so-called frontier humor was admirably constituted to image the problems of meaning and existence in a society that is very much caught up in the process of formation. In the Old Southwest—Georgia, West Florida, Alabama, Mississippi—of the 1820s, 1830s, and 1840s, virgin wilderness was almost overnight being converted into farmland, and towns and cities coming into being where the forest trails crossed. New wealth was being created, and old fortunes either vastly augmented or lost overnight. Rich and poor flocked into the new lands, and the social distinctions brought from the older society of the Eastern seaboard were very much disordered and distorted by the new circumstance. Society, in other words, was being reordered, and former distinctions of class and caste rearranged in accordance with the realities of wealth and power in a changed community. Since language, education, and culture are always ultimately grounded in social position, the social confusion of an open frontier society is reflected in a confusion of language and cultural modes and attitudes. It will take several generations for the descendants of a Simon Suggs, Jr., to acquire the social polish and cultural sophistication that educational advantages made possible by new wealth can ultimately afford them; and the effort to chronicle the checkered career of an opportunistic rascal in the sophisticated language appropriate to a biographical sketch in an Eastern magazine provides the rich incongruity that Baldwin could draw on for purposes of humor.

The clash between the ideal and the real, between value and fact, is of course not an exclusively American institution. Cervantes rang the changes on it in *Don Quixote*, and Aristophanes before him. But a society based theoretically upon the equality of all men, yet made up of human beings very unequal in individual endowment and containing within it many striking social, economic, and racial differences, is more than ordinarily blessed with such problems in human and social definition, and the incongruities are likely to be especially observable. The very conditions of a frontier society, with its absence of settled patterns and with its opportunities for freedom and individuality, are ideally suited for this kind of humor. One finds it already in flower long before the Declaration of Independence. Consider a work such as William Byrd II's *History of the Dividing Line.* An English-educated planter trained for the law in the Middle Temple, member of the Royal Society, one accustomed to command and to receiving the deference due a wealthy planter, goes off with a surveying party to determine the boundary line between the Virginia and the North Carolina colonies. There in the Dismal Swamp he encounters rustics who are without culture, refinement, ambition, or wealth, and who moreover do not seem to feel the lack of such commodities very much. Here he observes North Carolinians:

The
Humor
Prism
in 20th-
Century
America

42

> The Men, for their Parts, just like the Indians, impose all their Work upon the poor Women. They make their Wives rise out of their beds early in the Morning, at the same time that they lye and Snore, till the Sun has run one third of his course, and disperst all the unwholesome Damps. Then, after Stretching and Yawning for half an Hour, they light their Pipes, and, under the Protection of a cloud of Smoak, venture out into the open Air; tho', if it happens to be never so little cold, they quickly return Shivering into the Chimney corner. When the weather is mild, they stand leaning with both their arms upon the corn-field fence, and gravely consider whether they had best go and take a Small Heat at the Hough: but generally find reasons to put it off till another time.
>
> Thus they loiter away their Lives, like Solomon's Sluggard, with their Arms across, and at the Winding up of the Year Scarcely have Bread to Eat.
>
> To speak the Truth, tis a thorough Aversion to Labor that makes people file off to N. Carolina, where Plenty and a Warm Sun confirm them in their Disposition to Laziness for their whole Lives.

William Byrd, the aristocrat, the man of culture, confronts the spectacle of low-life settlers whose crudeness and laziness strike him as an affront to civilized dignity. His response is to poke fun at them, to use ridicule to rebuke the failure of the vulgar fact to approximate the cultural and social ideal. So he adopts a mode of language that through its inappropriateness to the triviality of the occasion makes the settlers appear ludicrous: they "stand leaning with both their arms upon the corn-field fence, and *gravely consider* whether they had best go and take a Small Heat at the Hough . . ." [italics mine]. Here again is the same clash of modes that Baldwin and the Southwestern Humorists would use to chronicle the New Men in the New Territory. In both instances the fact—the ordinary man, as he is, unregenerate and uncaring—is satirized by being described in a language mode customarily reserved for more elevated subject matter. But where in Byrd the satire is all directed at the low-life objects, in Baldwin it is not so one-sided. For though Baldwin is a Virginian and a Whig and a man of education and culture, he is enough of a democratic American to admire the independence and the practicality of his low-life characters just a little, and so he does not confine his ridicule to them. He turns the language mode, the elevated diction, back on itself. He is consciously overelegant, overgenteel in his choice of phraseology, so that the formal diction, the language of Culture, is also being mocked. The Great American Joke thus works both ways, and the incongruity illuminates the shortcomings of both modes.

Neither Byrd's *History of the Dividing Line* nor Baldwin's *Flush Times in Alabama and Mississippi* is, strictly speaking, literature, so much as subliterature. The one is narrative history, the other humorous journalism. Neither was designed purely or primarily as full-fledged art. But the same kind of incongruity they offer, the clash of genteel and vulgar modes, has been incorporated into the comic art of many of America's best and most respected writers. A single example will suffice to illustrate. William Faulkner has not only written certain novels that are possibly the only genuine literary tragedy produced by an American author in this century but is also one of the finest comic writers in American literature. In his comic masterpiece, *The Hamlet*, Flem Snopes and a Texan bring a herd of wild Texas horses to Mississippi and offer them for sale at very low prices. They are snapped up by the inhabitants, who are men invited to claim the horses

The
Humor
Prism
in 20th-
Century
America

43

they have purchased. Before very long wild horses are being pursued all over the landscape; they jump fences, leap over people, run into houses, overturn wagons, until as nighttime comes they are scattered over miles of countryside. One hapless purchaser, felled by the stampeding Texas herd, is carried unconscious into a house by some of his friends. Afterward they go outside:

> They went out; they didn't look back. They tiptoed up the hall and crossed the veranda and descended into the moonlight. Now that they could pay attention to it, the silver air seemed to be filled with faint and sourceless sounds—shouts, thin and distant, again a brief thunder of hooves on a wooden bridge, more shouts faint and thin and earnest and clear as bells; once they even distinguished the words: "Whooey. Head him."

Once again, both language modes are at work: the heightened literary diction, drawing on the full resources of cadenced prose and metaphor, and the vivid colloquial counterthrust. The haunting, beautiful description of the pursuit over the pastoral landscape is undercut by the broad vulgar comedy of the actual fact itself—the hoodwinked farmers vainly attempting to corral their untamable purchases. But Faulkner is not satirizing his characters; the human dignity he has given them as they go about the activities that are the plot of *The Hamlet* is such that, though they are "low-life," they are not thereby debased. Thus when, with the escape of the wild horses and their pursuit, he moves into the mode of formal literary diction and metaphor to describe what happens, the effect of incongruity does not produce satire and ridicule so much as delightful counterpoint of modes that plays them back and forth, against and around and along with each other. The shouting *is* "faint and thin and earnest and clear as bells," even as they *do* call out "Whooey. Head him." The contrast of literary language and poetic description with vernacular fact and colloquial speech is developed into as marvelously comic a scene as any in American literature. Both elements are at work, and in their juxtaposition each delineates the other. It is a masterful intensification of the same brand of humor as that of Byrd's *Dividing Line,* Baldwin's *Flush Times,* Irving's *Knickerbocker History,* Longstreet's *Georgia Scenes,* Clemens' *Connecticut Yankee,* Hemingway's *Torrents of Spring,* Barth's *Sot-Weed Factor,* and many another work of American comedy. It is the interplay of the ornamental and the elemental, the language of culture and the language of toil, the democratic ideal and the recalcitrance of fallen human nature—the Great American Joke.

The
Humor
Prism
in 20th-
Century
America

Our Native Humor

Sculley Bradley

A painstaking scholar recently classified 30,000 jokes in pigeonholes, finding that there were only thirty original jokes (which was more than one would suspect). Afterward, he discovered another, and he had to rearrange the entire lot in thirty-one categories. This was probably a useful enterprise, but simple folk, who prefer their laughter undiluted, are inclined to seek another pigeonhole for the critic.

Yet humor, of all human qualities, lies closest to the heart. Other animals share with man the ability to think, but not that highest perception of the intellect which flowers into laughter. The true nature of an individual is revealed by what makes him laugh. If Lucrezia Borgia ever smiled, no one has remembered it, but the laughter of the wise and good, of the Buddhas and the Shakespeares, is immortalized in bronze or in their own words.

As with individuals, so with nations—the collective laughter of a race will reveal its most secret qualities. It is not simply accident that has given each nation a distinctive humor. Above the bedrock of universal humor, the common heritage of mankind and understood everywhere, lies the topsoil formed by the erosion of national life. Humor is deeper and more fertile in the United States than in some less fortunate places. Critics are just beginning to see it as an important key to our national character. To understand its spiritual sources is to comprehend more fully the American attitudes revealed in the sober pursuit of our daily lives, and in our language, literature, and art.

The common origins of the English and the earlier American cultures have produced certain similarities in humorous points of view. Since the Anglo-Saxon is always a moralist, the laughter both of England and America is prevailingly corrective. Yet there is an important difference: the corrective laughter of

This essay was originally published in the *North American Review*, vol. 224, no. 2 (Winter 1936–1937). Reprinted with permission of the University of Northern Iowa.

England is satiric; that of America is ironic. The British laugh at a thing for being so ridiculously what it is; Americans are more prone to be laughing because the thing is not what it should be, or what they expected it would be. This American attitude was demonstrated, years ago, by the wide currency of stories about the Ford car. And after that remarkable machine had achieved a perfection beyond humor, our typical jokes fastened themselves upon certain blond or platinum personalities in Hollywood, and then, more recently, found a perfect subject in the depression. British life offers little parallel for this sort of humor, a blend of admiration or awe with irony.

English humor rejoices in the simple humor of a situation. For instance, when Sheridan learned that the theater which afforded him his livelihood was burning, he repaired with a friend to an alehouse across the street where he watched the destruction over a comforting glass. As their spirits revived, a formal little gentleman at an adjoining table, not recognizing the writer, admonished them sternly for their gaiety, "while poor Mr. Sheridan's theatre was burning down."

"Well," said Sheridan, "things are at a pretty pass when a man dare not be merry at his own fireside."

This, of course, is a variation of a universal comic situation, the "downfall of dignity." In its simple form it generally suffices for British humor. When Americans employ it, however, they are tempted to treat it with embellishment or exaggeration which would seem in bad taste to our English cousins. An old American story, for example, deals with the corpulent and dignified Senator who sprawled on the icy steps of the Capitol and slid to the bottom. Part way down he encountered a stout lady, who crumpled up helplessly on his chest and rode to the sidewalk below. There the Senator lay panting, "Madam, you will have to get off now; this is the end of my route." Thus a simple and universal comic situation is made American.

Characteristic English humor is defensive, while American humor prefers to strike first. The English enjoy the sudden, defensive brilliance of wit under fire. They do not understand why Americans like to play jokes on the unwary. It does not occur to an Englishman to give his friend a cigar that will explode. The British tell another story of Sheridan which is one of the best examples of defensive wit. As dramatic critic for a periodical, he had praised a play which some spectators had thought to be im-

The
Humor
Prism
in 20th-
Century
America

47

moral. An irate lady of sturdy principles wrote a letter to the editor, remarking that for the opinions of such a man she "would not give three skips of a louse." Sheridan published the letter with the comment that, although the language was violent, a woman must always be forgiven for mentioning whatever was going through her head at the moment.

Americans employ such defensiveness, of course, but even more they seem to enjoy the unexpected and unprovoked attack. They tell of the explorer in the jungle who was informed by his wife that a tiger was pursuing his mother-in-law: "What do I care what happens to a tiger!" replied the explorer. Judged by British standards, this story is in bad taste; in America, it is simply funny. Far-reaching differences in social history are responsible for these divergent attitudes.

The national characteristics of American humor are plainly rooted in the conditions of American life. A people chiefly occupied with the conquest of a wild and unfriendly continent will develop unique attitudes which their humor must represent. The frontier spirit has been the strongest element in our national consciousness for three hundred years. In 1607 the frontier, for Captain John Smith, was Pocahontas in Virginia; in 1900 it was the great Northwest. But as the margin of conquest moved westward it left behind an increasing area of frontier consciousness which survives today even in eastern cities. Frontiersmen must live their lives with the mother of invention. They must be quick and cunning and strong. They must not be taken in by the appearance of things. They will come to value simple integrity of character and homely philosophy. As these attitudes grew in American thought they were reflected in American humor, and they still persist.

A principal trait of American humor is its anti-romanticism. We love to puncture an illusion, to burst an iridescent bubble of hot air. Pretensions of grandeur, false family pride, snobbishness, or conceit annoy us, and we enjoy destroying them with the sharp weapon of irreverence. As a necessary corollary to our anti-romanticism, we have chosen as our most comic figure the "sucker." He is the "goat," the victim of our practical jokes, the romancer who is fooled by the mere surface of things. At different periods he was the tenderfoot who walked blithely into an Indian ambush, the fool who thought he could go up in a balloon, the loon who believed a carriage would run without a horse, the apprentice who runs to fetch a left-handed monkey wrench or a bucket of steam, the sucker who "bites" on the leading question, or the simple soul who is taken in by those odd novelties, decent and otherwise, in which American merchants do a thriving business just before the first of April. The more easily the American "sucker" may be "taken," the funnier he is.

Reflect upon the origins of all this in pioneer life. From the time of Columbus onward, European publicity men and real-estate brokers painted alluring pictures of America in the effort to induce colonization and stimulate trade. The land flowed with milk and honey, gold lay in lumps on the ground, and wild game obligingly came into the settlements to be shot. As late as 1880, according to the story, an Irish immigrant, leaving the immigrant station in New York, saw a blind beggar standing outside, with a ten dollar gold-piece glittering at his feet. Stooping down, Pat tossed the coin into the beggar's cup with the remark that "the poor divil couldn't see thim fer himself."

Whether in New York in 1880 or in Virginia in 1607, the expectations of the immigrant were to receive a rude shock. The Indians were not noticeably friendly, the game was unaccountably shy, the trees were tough and the gold turned out to be chiefly iron pyrites. A family of settlers would pole a raft laboriously up the mammoth tides of the Mississippi or Missouri, past the forlorn settlements, looking for a place less muddy and unfriendly. At last, finding it all to be the same, they would choose a spot and build a log house. In three weeks of perspiring toil they would achieve a romantic dream of abode. Then one night, just as the new mansion was nearly completed, the floods would descend, the river would capriciously change its course, and the house would become an island, if indeed it did not float off toward the gulf.

Experiences of this nature were the common lot of our forefathers. If you could not laugh at this or at yourself in the role of the sucker, you were doomed. And the laughter grew. It became a national trait. Such anti-romanticism is a fundamental quality of our typical humorists, writers like Mark Twain, for instance, whose *Petrified Man* is as characteristic a story as we have. It deals with a party of silver miners in Nevada. They have labored across the continent and up the steep hills. They have sweated fruitlessly through many veins of pure quartz, with no trace of silver. At last they strike something different. They do

The Humor Prism in 20th-Century America

not understand it, but hope springs high. For days they labor to uncover the curious object. At last it is revealed, a gigantic petrified man. There he had been sitting hundreds of years, facing eastward toward the oncoming pioneers, his nose and thumb cooperating "in the immemorial gesture of derision."

This story is almost a perfect pattern for the anti-romantic American story. It was a fertile field for Davy Crockett, Petroleum Nasby, Artemus Ward, John Phoenix, and almost every other early American humorist. It is a principal characteristic in our humorous fiction. It is a fundamental American stamp on the work of such contemporary writers as Dorothy Parker, Ogden Nash, Robert Benchley, or Clarence Day. In John Phoenix, for example, the anti-romantic climax emerges exuberantly in the case of the ingenious surveyor who invented a pedometer for measuring distances in road building. The instrument had a neat dial which was hung on the "seat of the pants," and a long rod attached to the knee. Unfortunately the surveyor stopped at a tavern for some frontier whiskey, and in the next ten miles achieved a speedometer reading which suggested a transcontinental journey. When a bottle of Phoenix' hair tonic was accidentally broken on a marble step, a doormat grew up at once. In our modern humorists there is only a change of setting; the principle of anticlimax is retained. A typical heroine of Dorothy Parker has looked forward to a certain dance as a big moment of her life. She is carefully dressed for the advent of Prince Charming. Suddenly her garter snaps and her stocking begins to slither down. To her horror she finds that she is on the side of the room remote from the haven of feminine repair. She spends the evening as a gloomy wallflower, holding her knee, waiting for the guests to leave, with thoughts of such brilliant ineptitude as only Mrs. Parker can master. Clarence Day's *Father* was a master of the anti-romantic conclusion. Stephen Leacock thrives upon it, as for instance in *My Financial Career*, in which a "simple soul" goes crazy opening his first bank account. Anti-romantic expectation is so deeply rooted in our national consciousness that even today, in any part of the country, the current slang of "So what?" or "Oh, yeah?" are conclusive if impolite remedies for inflated illusions.

Contemporary writers still employ frontier irreverence. Ogden Nash's *Quartet for Prosperous Love-Children* ("the banker, the broker, the Washington joker," and the Forgotten Man), coming pat

The
Humor
Prism
in 20th-
Century
America

50

upon the inevitable moment in national politics, was convincing proof that the appeal of irreverence is as strong now as it was when Major Jack Downing poked fun at President Jackson, or when Abe Lincoln kept thirty important political leaders waiting while he read to Sumner the satiric remarks on politicians from the pen of Petroleum V. Nasby, or when Will Rogers, in *Letters of a Self-Made Diplomat*, addressed President Coolidge by cable as Calcool, or called the United States Senate "just a cheap club that ninety-six men belong to, and pay no dues." This sort of thing will naturally give pain to British critics, one of whom recently reviewed Ogden Nash as a poet who might produce important work if he could learn the use of rhyme.

Another element noted in our humor by the critical is its endless capacity for exaggeration. To this the English have impolitely referred as the habit "of telling a lie and laughing at the person who believes it." This disparagement may indicate a natural resentment on the part of the British. Again and again, stories from American newspapers and magazines, which no American was intended to believe and which passed as good hoaxes at home, have been reprinted in England as the solemn truth. There was the story, out of a frontier newspaper in Nevada, of the invention of "solar armor," a refrigerating device intended for use in crossing the great southern deserts; and how its inventor, neglecting to turn off the refrigerator at the proper time, had been found frozen to death. English papers reprinted this, with grave comments on the usefulness of such an invention for the British army in the tropics. This sort of episode has continually embarrassed our foreign diplomacy.

Actually, the exaggeration in our humor has the same cultural sources as our anti-romanticism. Probably the first settlers who ever wroter letters home began the practice. Many of them had come over against the earnest advice of family and friends and they all were anxious, above all else, to make good. Children who have left home against their parents' wishes are notoriously unreliable in reporting their adventures; and young wives who have made questionable marriages are given to the public praise of their husbands. Just so, we may imagine, the new settlers tried to enhance the attractiveness of their new situation. The letters home passed into literature as books about the new country. Captain John Smith, as early as 1608, began his remarkable series of publications about Virginia, and today their charm as literature rests chiefly on the quaint exaggerations which render them wholly unreliable as history. As late as 1778 the same attitude was still prevalent among writers on the new country. In that

The Humor Prism in 20th-Century America

year one Samuel Peters, a clergyman, published a *History of Connecticut*, which reads as though some portions of it had been written by Sir John Mandeville's ghost. The rapids of the Connecticut River, for instance, were said to be so swift that an iron crowbar would float there.

Another powerful impulse to exaggeration was the worship of strength and size, which were principal requisites for survival in forest and frontier life. The traditional exploits of the frontiersman are unblushingly exaggerated for humorous effect. He could run down a deer. He had killed a bear so big that he could not carry the pelt. Davy Crockett told of shooting an eye through the head of a weathercock across the Ohio River. At the same distance he punctured a pail of milk which a girl was carrying on her head. Bill Merriweather lost his brother in an extraordinary manner. During a drenching rain his new deerskin breeches shrank so rapidly that he was shot high into the air and never was seen again. Paul Bunyan, at the age of two, built Niagara Falls for a cold shower.

Fishermen and huntsmen even today preserve the frontier tradition, and an allusion to "the one that got away" will always provoke a knowing wink. Sporting magazines unblushingly conduct a Liar's Club while the amalgamated reformers are undisturbed by this menace to the public virtue.

Indeed, the "tall story" was highly regarded in early American life. Such yarns were repeated until they constituted a native folklore; they were reprinted in the newspapers as a regular branch of journalism from the Jacksonian era until long after the Civil War. They inspired a school of fiction which flourished for a half-century. The adventures of Simon Suggs, Major Jones, or Sut Lovingood are unfamiliar now, and such authors as Longstreet, Baldwin, Thorpe, and W. T. Thompson have passed from memory, but they were the popular literature of the generation of Mark Twain. It is natural, therefore, that exaggeration should leaven every anecdote in *Roughing It* or *Tom Sawyer*; or that *A Connecticut Yankee* should be a tall tale of Arthurian times.

The tall story survives exuberantly today in our daily conversation, in our jokes, in the anecdotes which we so shamelessly tell about our friends. Our speech is full of absurd "gags" which we continuously employ. The one about the man so tall that he had to climb a ladder to shave himself is very old, but one recently heard of the professor so absent-minded that he put his trousers to bed and hung himself over a chair-back where he froze to death. Any reader can add a score of such current oddities. And recently one of the most popular features on the American radio was Baron Munchausen who fascinated millions of auditors every week by the monstrous audacity of his lies. It seems unlikely that this could have occurred in any other country.

Two principal elements of American humor have been indicated. It is interesting to see exaggeration and anti-romantic irreverence joining forces to give the typical American quality to Mark Twain's work. A certain heroine, he said, was "virtuous to the verge of eccentricity." "In this chapel," wrote the Innocent, "were the ashes of St. John. We had seen St. John's ashes before, in another church. We could not bring ourselves to think St. John had two sets of ashes." Romantic Italy proved to be a place where you couldn't get a bath. "Each of us had an Italian farm on his back. We could have felt affluent if we had been officially surveyed and fenced in." The coyote of the Western plains proved to be not a noble wolf, but "a living, breathing allegory of want, . . . and even the fleas would desert him for a velocipede." Mark Twain's enduring popularity rests in large measure upon his ability to make immortal use of the qualities which differentiate our native character.

Today these are still the principal traits of our humorists. I have before me one of those omnibus volumes of contemporary mischief containing nearly a hundred widely varied pieces from pens of such writers as Lardner, Benchley, Leacock, Sullivan, Nash, Thurber, Stewart, and Mrs. Parker. Almost every one of these sketches achieves its quality and strength through the same combination. "I was a poor little girl born in a tenement and my mother and father used to be drunk all the time and beat me so I grew up to be sweet and pure and beautiful." . . . "Only an expert can tell a live Penguin from a stuffed one. It is probable that most Penguins are stuffed." . . . "Children are embarrassed to have their parents along when they are attending certain movies or plays. A child never knows at what point in a play his uninformed old father will start to giggle." . . . "I knew if I came to this dinner, I'd draw something like this baby on my left. I should have stayed at home. I could have had something on a tray. The head of John the Baptist, or something." These quotations fall at random from various parts of the volume, and they all bear the same stamp. It is not so much the tradition of Mark Twain as it is the democracy of frontier laughter amid the sophistication of New York City today.

Finally, our humor is distinguished by homeliness. This, again, is the result of our homespun past. It has a blunt directness, learned along gunsights. It preserves the laconic reflectiveness of wide and lonely vistas. It is the philosophy of the countless crossroads stores that dotted the countryside a few years ago. The bustling towns sprung up around the old Corners have not forgotten the circle of chairs about the woodstove at night, the box of sawdust with its brown stains, and the slow wisdom. It is as though the shrewd commonsense of *Poor Richard* had been sharpened to laughter by adversity. Our most typical humor still preserves the vernacular and seldom employs the balanced brilliance of wit. Across the pages of our social history moves an array of characters with linsey-woolsey names— Jack Downing, Hosea Biglow, Petroleum Nasby, Bill 'Arp, Artemus Ward, Josh Billings, Mr. Dooley, and many others. They have made our humor as characteristically American as the California redwoods or a baseball game.

Courage and necessity were the original sources of our especial variety of humor. It lined the faces of men and women who were crossing prairies, and conquering forests, and building cities. It may be that with all its strength it is a bit boisterous. Perhaps it lacks refinement or finish according to British standards. But if we were free to choose, we should probably prefer the American variety. As Mr. Dooley said, "a man can be r-right an' be the President, but he can't be both at the same time."

The
Humor
Prism
in 20th-
Century
America

54

Entropy and Transformation: Two Types of American Humor

Arlen J. Hansen

In the twentieth century, American humor found new expression in two contrasting kinds of media—silent movies (picture without sound) and radio (sound without picture). That American humor could adapt itself readily and brilliantly to both media bespeaks its dual nature. A glance at nineteenth-century literature confirms the presence of two general tendencies in American humor, one to show someone doing some funny thing, and a second to show someone saying something funny. Almost as if in anticipation of film and radio, the literature of the last century encouraged its reader to visualize funny action and to "hear" funny talk. In the nineteenth century, these two modes were seldom separated; Petroleum V. Nasby (David Ross Locke) in the lecture hall and Huckleberry Finn in print both *did* and *said* funny things. For that matter, only if one looks back from the perspective afforded by subsequent developments can the two tendencies be recognized as distinct modes of humor. When the technology of the twentieth century developed silent movies and radio, the two modes became more discrete and exploitable. The funny talkers gravitated toward radio; the actors, to film. And the American audience was equally fascinated with both. The same person who saw Laurel and Hardy on Friday night listened to Amos and Andy on Saturday.

The distinct characteristics of oral and visual humor in America reveal a fundamental difference in vision and attitude between the two kinds of humorists. This is not, for example, the same kind of difference proposed and explored by Constance Rourke in her seminal study, *American Humor*. Rourke discerns

The
Humor
Prism
in 20th-
Century
America

55

Reprinted from *The American Scholar*, vol. 43, no. 3 (Summer 1994). Copyright © 1974 by the Phi Beta Kappa Society.

two lines of humor, one originating in the Yankee's understatement and the other in the backwoodsman's exaggeration. Eiron and Alazon, however, can be recognized by either their actions or their talk. That is, American visual humor can easily accommodate both the Yankee and the backwoodsman (or their descendants), and so can oral humor. The assumptions and values of the oral humorist, whether he understates or exaggerates, tend to differ as a rule from those of the visual humorist.

In general the active, visual humor appeals to the American's fondness for breaking up systems. It is a humor of entropy. Perhaps an extension of the spirit of democracy, this humor presupposes an innate attraction to anarchy, iconoclasm and—to an extent—chaos. It feeds the hunger for chase and activity, and its usual effect is the breaking down of an established, "normal" system, causing both the matter and the structure of that system to deteriorate. Seen from Bergson's position, this humor dramatizes the collapse of mechanical and habitual behavior when such behavior is confronted with new, unexpected and vitalizing challenges. In contrast, oral humor exploits properties of language rather than the dynamics of physical activity. Although Americans may share the English fondness for witty retorts and clever sayings, American oral humor typically is of another sort. It is founded upon the transforming and creative power of language. Unlike entropy, which describes a system in disintegration, transformation describes the process of synthesis, the creation of a new and other totality. The humor of transformation is achieved usually by an imaginative persona who generates and sustains fantasies through his powers of language. He is a storymaker. Growing out of the American's fondness for dreams and fantasy, the humor of transformation involves creative, unmalicious fabrication—the magnificent lie.

The
Humor
Prism
in 20th-
Century
America

56

Imagine a large estate, such a one as might be found in a 1920 Hollywood two-reeler. Isolated by acres of neatly manicured lawn, the hilltop mansion is accessible only by means of a sidewalk and steps. Two figures, their backs to us, are working their way up the path. The house itself is virtually a closed, self-contained system. Inside are chandeliers, thick carpets, a piano, highly polished banisters, swinging doors that lead off to the kitchen. A dinner party is about to begin. The petite French maid hangs up shawls and coats; men in starched collars and boiled shirts escort buxom and bejeweled *grandes dames* into the sparkling dining room. Everything suggests control and order; the system is functioning nearly perfectly. Only the two waiters have yet to arrive—waiters who had to be hired at the last minute from the Acme Employment Agency. In fact, it is the two waiters, one fat and one skinny, who have just now made their way up the walk. With the best of intentions in mind and reflecting happily on the prospect of associating with the upper class, Stan Laurel and Oliver Hardy reach the door of the manor. Stanley raises his hand to knock, but Ollie stops him. *I* will knock, Ollie's gestures suggest; he gives the act the flourish proper for such a promising occasion. The butler comes, and they are hastily pulled inside—the heavy door closing behind them. They have entered the system. The camera's eye need no longer follow them; it may simply fix on the exterior of the house, for everyone can readily imagine what is happening inside. The system is breaking down. Matter is converting to energy, energy to heat; heat is virtually radiating from the vibrating walls. Twenty minutes later only the outer shell remains; inside, all has been leveled. The chesty matrons have been dematronized; collars have been torn; mirrors, pianos and conventions all reduced to rubble. When the door opens, Ollie and Stanley emerge, disheveled but undaunted. Quickly dusting off their gloves and brushing a fleck or two from their jackets, they adjust their bowlers and walk merrily off—this time across the lawn. The system has deteriorated. Sterile, artificial and solemn order has given way to the fun of chaos. And not a word need have been spoken; it is visual humor, for entropy of this sort is a visible phenomenon. Language could have been included: Ollie's remarks to Stanley when they knock on the door, or Stanley's remark to a society lady inside, might well contribute to the fun of the picture; but at base, this humor is a result of physical, visible activity.

The Marx brothers frequently build their material out of entropic situations, Groucho's wit notwithstanding. In *A Night at the Opera* Groucho attempts to smuggle three stowaways (Alan Jones, Chico and Harpo) into the United States disguised as foreign pilots. Complete with baggy pants and long beards, the obviously phony pilots are led to a speakers' platform for an elaborate welcoming ceremony. The imposters dutifully stand in front of the large crowd listening to themselves being celebrated as courageous and exemplary men. Then, following the testaments to their bravery, the frauds are invited to address the crowd. In his transparent Italian accent, Chico speaks first. "The first time-a we start-a to fly to the U.S. we get-a half-a way across when we run out of gasoline and we gotta go back. . . ." Chico's jokes are funny to be sure, but the mute Harpo comes next and with him (surely!) a culminating hysteria. The game is up, one suspects— it's time to cut and run. But there they stand, content to watch Harpo drink what seems to be gallons of water in an attempt to stall. Groucho quips, "We're all right as long as the water supply holds out." Anyone else, it seems, would have run long before. Eventually the breaking point is reached; the system collapses. Harpo's beard falls, people begin shouting and shoving, and the imposters are exposed. Among the noise and chaos, Groucho gets in one last wisecrack: "You realize, of course, that this means war!" And the chase is on. The dynamics are virtually consistent with the law of the conservation of energy: as the situation becomes unstable and begins to disintegrate, tempers and temperatures rise, and the dissolution accelerates in a geometric progression. Chico's and Groucho's jokes only add to the basically visual humor of the scene in disintegration.

As these illustrations suggest, the humor of entropy is, or pretends to be, spontaneous. The Marx brothers have no master plan for accomplishing their ends. Indeed, they have only a vague notion, if any notion at all, of what their goals are. They improvise their way through the dilemmas of their collective life. While Harpo drinks glass after glass of water, the others simply wait to see what will happen. As they wait, the tensions build. Groucho's tiny stateroom becomes packed with plumbers, janitors, manicurists, waiters, brothers, *ad absurdum*, precisely because Groucho chooses not to anticipate the future. He keeps hauling them into his quarters until the equilibrium of the system breaks. The only plan, if it can be called a plan, is to extemporize once the system can tolerate no more and begins to disintegrate. In their hotel, the brothers let a policeman pursue them around and around their rooms—even though they seem to have several chances to escape—until they all are on the verge of collapse from fatigue. Similarly, on the night of the opera, they do not leave, no matter what opportunities are afforded, until the potentials of the entire system are virtually exhausted. Groucho's dissemblances, puns and witticisms contribute either to his attempts to ride out the situation until it breaks, or to the accelerating dissolution of the situation after the equilibrium has broken. But Groucho's language augments, rather than sustains, the picture. Years later, a context for exploiting Groucho's witty oral humor was created in the format of a quiz show, "You Bet Your Life." The medium, of course, was radio.

A word should be said about Charlie Chaplin, whose prominence and importance make him impossible to ignore. One could argue, perhaps, that Chaplin's work fits well into the category of entropic humor, for the Chaplin character seems frequently to be breaking down established systems and formalized postures. On the other hand, Chaplin's own description of his humor points to its transformational aspects. Emphasizing his persona's determination to maintain his illusions of himself, Chaplin wrote in *American Magazine* (1918):

> All my pictures are built around the idea of getting me into trouble and so giving me the chance to be desperately serious in my attempt to appear as a normal little gentleman. That is why, no matter how desperate the predicament is, I am always very much in earnest about clutching my cane, straightening my derby hat, and fixing my tie, even though I have just landed on my head.

It may be that Chaplin's especially rich humor comes from a fruitful synthesis of both transformational and entropic tendencies. I suggest, however, that Chaplin's humor partakes *only slightly* of any antecedent American tradition. Trained in the British music halls, Chaplin developed a humor that was substantially English. Given his skills at pantomime and ballet, his humor seems to be indebted also to continental tradition. At any rate, he did not learn his humorous techniques only in America or only from Americans. In the book *Comedy Films,* John Montgomery argues persuasively that when Essanay began to produce such Chaplin films as "His New Job," "The Champion" and "The Tramp"—which are "all titles Fred Karno might have given to his famous [British] music-hall sketches, . . . English humor had conquered the American screen." Chaplain is not, strictly speaking, representative of *American* humor.

The sources of American entropic humor can be found in the sketches of the nineteenth-century backwoodsman and riverboatman. A common beginning for these sketches depicts a

The
Humor
Prism
in 20th-
Century
America

59

"gamecock of the wilderness" insulting or threatening a "dandy," and thereby precipitating a fight or a verbal exchange, which disrupts the composure of the scene. As one such ring-tailed roarer claims in a sketch popular in the 1830s:

> I was ridin along the Mississippi in my wagon, when I came acrost a feller floating down stream, settin in the starn of his boat fast asleep. Well, I hadn't had a fight for ten days; felt as tho' I should have to kiver myself up in a salt barrel, to keep so wolfy about the shoulders. So says I, hallo stranger, if you don't mind your boat will run off and leave you. . . .

Even though what ensues is an extended boast, which calls forth a vivid and imaginative use of language and thereby appeals to the other, the transformational, mode of humor, this first act—the confrontation—appeals to a sense of humorous entropy. Perhaps what Americans enjoy about roughhouse brawls is the prospect of well-composed systems being challenged, whether it is the squatter confronting the dandy or Groucho accepting the test that Margaret Dumont and her wealth pose. Entropy is a natural and humorous result of that challenge as it comes to fruition.

One figure in particular out of the nineteenth century represents this line of humor at its most compelling: G. W. Harris's Rabelaisian character, Sut Lovingood. As with the Marx brothers or Laurel and Hardy, Sut's presence and conduct is usually the catalytic agent that begins the funny entropic process. Consistently finding himself excluded from the systems around him, Sut attempts innocently to remedy or puckishly to revenge his alienation. Like Groucho's, his is not a grand plan, but rather a series of extemporaneous gestures. On his way to Bill Carr's farm one day, Sut recounts in "Sicily Burns's Wedding," he sees a crowd gathered at the Burns place. Sicily Burns and Clapshaw, the circuit rider, are to be married that day. Perhaps partially motivated by a desire for revenge for Sicily's soda trick on him (as related in an earlier story), Sut is also motivated by a thinly disguised erotic fascination for Sicily. She is, after all, the woman whose "pint am tu drive men folks plum crazy" and whose "buzzim [is like] two snow balls wif a strawberry stuck but-ainded into bof on em." Sut also feels slighted by the family: "I wur slunging round the outside ove the house, fur they hedn't had the manners to axe me in, when they sot down tu dinner." While momentarily considering his revenge (shaving the tails off the horses in the barn), Sut sees that ol' Sock, Burns's bull, "wer a-nosing 'round, an' cum up ontu a big baskit what hilt a littil shattered co'n; he dipp'd in his head tu git hit, an' I slipp'd up an' jerked the handil over his ho'ns." This impromptu and relatively innocent act proves to be far-reaching and devastating. Pulling the bucket over Sock's head is merely the first in a seemingly irrevocable series of chain reactions that generate a chaos of chases, bellows, bee stings, shattered glass and broken walls. Significantly, Sut's act is one of convenience rather than contrivance, and it is the first and only act in the chain of events over which a human has any control. In a story following up the wedding, Sut comments:

> Well, the vardick ove the neighborhood wer, that I wer the cause ove all the hole thing. Greater injestice wer never dun; fur all that I did in the worild, wer jist tu help ole Sock git a few grains ove shatter'd co'n, by liftin the baskit over his ho'ns; an' when I did hit, the fuss warn't begun at all. Arter'ards, I did nuffin but stan clear ove danger, an' watch things happen.

It is almost as if the system that Sut encounters is in such a delicate balance that the slightest jostling initiates an inexorable process of disintegration. The suggestion seems to be that in Sut's world, at least, the ultimate consequence of any initial act is unknowable—chaos lies so near the surface. Who would think, for example, that Sut's impulsive act would culminate in keeping Sicily and her new husband from sleeping together "fur ni ontu a week"? Even in his wildest dreams Sut could not have designed a plan more commensurate with his secret wishes than this.

Since Harris's stories are recounted in dialect, the reader is clearly aware of their oral qualities. Nevertheless, the humor lies principally in the *activity* of the stories. Sut's descriptions are vivid, to be sure, but they are not transforming descriptions. His language attempts to indicate, not remake, what has happened; his use of metaphor and analogy serve him the better to describe the action. In a detailed study of Harris's imagery, Milton Rickels has observed that "the first effect of [the] imagery is speed and intensity. The reader is whirled into the illusion of sheer delight in motion and wild action." Sut's stories—like the antics of the Marx brothers or Laurel and Hardy—must be visualized to be funny for they present the activity of a system in disintegration.

The
Humor
Prism
in 20th-
Century
America

62

The humor of entropy had its counterpart on radio in the 1930s and 1940s. Although the success of Fanny Brice's "Baby Snooks" and Red Skelton's "mean little kid" indicates that entropic humor was not precluded by the medium of radio, most of the radio humor was different. There was the clever wit of Fred Allen, the folksy talk of Lum and Abner, and the funny sounds and mispronounciations of Baron Munchausen. But, above and beyond these, there was another kind of humor, one that was built upon an American tradition perhaps even older and more highly developed than the tradition behind entropic humor. Whereas Sut's and Groucho's humor is visual and basically active, this humor relies primarily on language. It speaks to the American characteristic of transforming reality through creative and inventive talk. Richard Poirier and Tony Tanner, in their studies of American literature, have addressed the serious writers' efforts along this line—efforts, that is, to create by means of language "worlds elsewhere." The transformational humorist usually develops a speaking persona who attempts to disguise his (the persona's) nature or to fantasize away his actual lot in life. The humor arises naturally from the discrepancy between his actual condition and his transformed version of it—between, that is, the persona as the audience sees him and as he represents himself in language. Jack Benny's radio persona, for example, transparently tried to hide his stinginess; he spoke of himself as a brilliant violinist, and yet he played atrociously; and he maintained firmly that he was thirty-nine years old—year after year. Through an exaggerated recounting of some past event, Fibber McGee frequently attempted to make himself out to be a person of consequence, of some effect, in his "Wistful Vista" neighborhood. Trying to make himself appear clever and witty, McGee was often merely corny, as Molly's "t'ain't funny, McGee" warmly reminded him. Significantly, Benny and McGee attempted to break down no systems; indeed, they manufactured their own. They constructed fantasies through talk which their very talk betrayed. Radio was therefore well suited to these transforming personae, including Benny and McGee, as well as the Great Gildersleeve, George Burns, Gracie Allen, Andy and the Kingfish, Jane Sherwood and Charlie McCarthy.

It should not be supposed that the medium of radio prevented the transformational humorist from encouraging his audience to visualize his dilemma. Just as entropic humor could be augmented by clever language, transformational humor could be augmented by the audience's visualizing imagination. When Jack Benny was accosted by a thief who demanded, "Your money or your life," Benny's subsequent pause invited the radio audience to picture the stingy Benny's predicament. When he finally capped the silence with "I'm thinking! I'm thinking!" Benny's voice most likely confirmed the listener's speculation. A visual imagination, however, was not so essential for responding to Benny's humor as it was for, say, Baby Snooks's humor, wherein one needed to imagine specific scenes of breaking vases, chases around sofas and other entropic activities. The subordinate relationship of picture to talk in the humor of transformation is well illustrated by the achievement of perhaps the outstanding transforming persona of the twentieth century—W. C. Fields. The hat and gloves he wears in a poker game in a western saloon in *My Little Chickadee* give a visual correlative of his more fundamental verbal behavior. By substituting the mellifluous "Godfrey Daniel" for "godammit," Fields reveals his penchant for prettifying his world, the same characteristic that dictates his wearing gloves, top hat and braces in the saloon. The picture strengthens and extends to a visual level the transformation that Fields usually accomplishes through language. Fields was eminently successful in both film and radio, but his humor virtually required sound. It was in the "talkies," not the silent movies, that Fields scored his greatest successes.

As Sheriff Cuthbert J. Twillie, in *My Little Chickadee*, Fields at one point faces a hostile mob ready to lynch him. In accordance with filmic tradition, Twillie is asked if he has any final requests. "Yes," the sheriff pronounces, oblivious to his predicament, "I'd like to see Paris before I die." Then, as the snarls of the mob increase and the noose is set around his neck, the sheriff raises his hand and says, "Vote for Cuthbert J. Twillie!" Cuthbert J. Twillie, in a world all his own, is politician to the very end. He does not hang, of course; but neither does the system collapse. He is saved, innocence and fantasy intact, by a masked bandit, *deus ex machina*. Blind to the nature of his actual situation because of his grand fantasy, Twillie occupies another, a larger and more grandiose, world. "My little chickadee"—that's what he calls the brazen and libidinous Mae West, who neither his, little, nor by any stretch of the ordinary imagination a chickadee. Condemned to walk the earth with names like Cuthbert Twillie or Larson E.

Whipsnade (mispronounced as "Larceny Whipsnake"), it is perhaps hardly surprising that the Fields persona is eager to remake, if only in his own mind, the conditions of his life. It's a better world the Fields persona lives in, a world made by language—and he loves language. With his gift for transforming, who can blame him? He is a rhapsodic storyteller. While lining up a three-cushion bank shot, addressing a golf ball, or drying a whiskey glass, the Fields persona drifts off into story. If he seems to pause to rechalk his cue, to reexamine the golf ball, or to buff a spot off the glass, very likely he is actually pausing so as not to hurry through the verbal construct he is bringing into being. He savors his fantasies. "Did I ever tell you of the time me and Shorty here was tending bar in the Bowery?" One can still hear the nasal drawl, the strung-out and slowly paced words as Fields catches up pieces of fancy and fact and weaves them into a new reality. Language is his natural medium.

The humor of transformation was exceptionally popular and richly developed in the nineteenth century. It appeared in its most primitive form perhaps as the splendid boast of the boatman or backwoodsman and as the tall tale recounted at campfire. The humor of these forms usually stemmed from the inventiveness and vividness of the hyperboles employed. One such exaggerator is T. B. Thorpe's Jim Doggett. Asked to tell his fellow riverboat passengers about bear hunting, Doggett—the self-proclaimed "big bar of Arkansas"—admits that "it is told in two sentences—a bar is started, and he is killed. The thing is somewhat monotonous now. . . ." When pressed for a "description of a particular hunt," Doggett responds by saying, "Yes, I have it! I will give you *an idea* of a hunt. . . ." Doggett's ensuing narrative therefore has basically an expressive function. He tries to articulate a sense, an "idea," of life in the lush backcountry of Arkansas. To describe the natural opulence and solitary existence, which must have been alternately monotonous and exhilarating, may well defy ordinary descriptive language. In order to suggest truthfully some of the qualities of fear, pride and loneliness that lay near to the surface of his existence, Doggett needs to transform the routine of his life by means of vivid and hyperbolic language.

Transformational humor was not restricted to backwoods bravado; indeed, this humor was artistically cultivated by such writers as A. B. Longstreet, Joseph Baldwin and Mark Twain.

"The Dance" illustrates the relatively innocent humor that Longstreet elicits from a transforming persona. This story is described as "a personal experience of the author," even though the narrating persona is called "Abram Baldwin," and not Augustus Baldwin Longstreet. While attending a country dance, the middle-aged Abram Baldwin is moved to recollect his adolescence, specifically his first romance with Polly Jackson. As the dance progresses he begins to see in the young dancers before him various characteristics of his own friends from his youth: "Jim Johnson kept up the double shuffle from the beginning to the end of the reel: and here was Jim over again in Sammy Tant." The more the narrator sees of Polly Gibson, the more certain he is that she is the Polly Jackson of his youth. And so he discovers her to be. Before he confronts her with the happy news of his own identity, he reminisces: "I thought of the sad history of many of her companions and mine. . . . I compared my after life with the cloudless days of my attachment to Polly." Abram Baldwin recalls further that he had abandoned this state of youthful bliss "in pursuit of those imaginary joys which seemed to encircle the seat of fame." His joy warmed by memory, he approaches Polly and asks her to dance, hinting broadly that she "surely will dance with an old friend and sweetheart." Her puzzled response provokes his affectionate jest, "Have you forgot your old sweetheart, Abram Baldwin?" She has indeed. What is worse, she *does* remember others from their mutual past—Jim Johnson, Bill Martin, Becky Lewis. The story ends with the narrator having returned to his city life. There he receives a note from Polly's husband, who writes somewhat apologetically, "Since you left here, Polly has been thinking about old times, and she says, to save her life, she can't recollect you." Faced with Polly's version of their mutual past, which her memory has apparently severely edited, the narrator is forced to recognize that he has also transformed the past, endowing it with a special texture and preciousness. Another author might have employed a narrator bitter with disillusionrnent, but not Longstreet. The warm tone throughout the story precludes any sense of bitterness. The narrator, for example, does not assign to Polly any blame for forgetting him; moreover, the methodical construction of his story suggests that the narrator is well aware that he is retelling a joke on himself. In effect, the narrator has suffered a poignant embarrassment, and he willingly shares it with the reader. Although he remains in the end somewhat bewildered, uncertain as to what his true relation-ship with Polly Jackson had been those many years ago, he has forgiven himself for distorting the past and for thereby making himself vulnerable to embarrassment. He has recognized and ac-cepted his innocent transformation with humor.

Longstreet's narrator is in a situation similar to the narrator in Washington Irving's story "The Stout Gentleman." Destined to spend some time in a gloomy and uninteresting country inn, Irv-ing's narrator unwittingly generates an intriguing story to occupy himself. Overhearing several references to a "stout gentleman" who occupies an upstairs room in the inn, the narrator begins to imagine what the stout gentleman must be like. Circumstances encourage the narrator to envision him as unyieldingly aristo-cratic and openly lascivious (both characteristics may well be projections of the narrator's own latent nature). In the end, as the stout gentleman boards a carriage, the narrator gets only a glimpse of the man's expansive posterior. In essence the story in-volves the narrator's abilities to turn the tedium of the inn into a mildly exciting and speculative adventure. Like Longstreet's nar-rating persona, Irving's is given naturally to transforming aspects of his experience into events and relationships that are consider-ably more enjoyable and stimulating. Longstreet's narrator, how-ever, is forced to face and acknowledge his alteration of the past, whereas the broad breeches of the stout gentleman do not neces-sarily compel Irving's narrator to abandon or repudiate his ima-ginary construct. Both authors suggest with fundamental compas-sion that such acts of transformation are innately and spontaneously natural to man.

This type of humor reached a new stage of development in the work of Joseph Baldwin, a well-known lawyer-politician in Mississippi and Alabama during and after the "flush times" of the late 1830s. It became the humor of the magnificent liar. Bald-win's Ovid Bolus, Esq., was a "natural liar," who did not lie from commercial interest, from a personal vanity, from ignorance, or from temptation. Far above such mundane concerns, Ovid Bolus apparently lied for the same inexplicable reason artists create their art. He "lied with a relish: he lied from the delight of inven-tion and the charm of fictitious narrative." That is to say, Bolus lied consciously and with care: "The truth was too small for him." To be sure, Bolus used his natural skills on occasion to earn a liv-ing and to nurture his own ego, as might anyone, poet or plumber. But his affection for transformation had its selfless side as well: "There was something sublime in the idea—this elevating the spirit of man to its true and primeval dominion over things of sense and grosser matter." By enveloping the things of matter in language, particularly in *his* language, Bolus achieved a control over them; he restored man to his rightful role as controller of the materiality of the world. His use of language, like that of W. C. Fields, altered the very nature of his existence. But in the end Bolus's language could not save him from the wrath of his fellow men whom he had duped. If Fields's Twillie is rescued by a masked bandit at the last minute, Baldwin's Bolus is not; he is driven into exile—run out of town, to state it in its untransformed form. His genius, however, is not the less for his exile.

As the careers of Ovid Bolus and Cuthbert Twillie illustrate, they can dream and transform all they want, it seems, when it comes to inanimate nature. They can regard themselves as refined gentlemen with souls as spotless and genteel as the white gloves they wear. But when a fellowman points out "realistically" that the gloves are frayed and ludicrously out of place, the liar's transformation is directly challenged. Either his dream or he himself must go—if, that is, the "realist's" view is to obtain. The liar can fool some of the people some of the time, perhaps, but when enough of them object and carry him off to the gallows or demand their money back, well, it is time for facing reality. The humor of the situation often lies in the confrontation of the dreamer and his lie with the nondreamer and his facts. But tragedy also lies nearby, ever threatening to injure, if not destroy, the magnificent liar. Huck Finn, whose detestation of the King and the Duke borders at times on downright contempt, is moved to sorrow when he sees the two exemplary liars tarred and feathered by an outraged mob. It would seem that the safest transformation—the one most purely humorous and least potentially tragic—is achieved by the hermit, in private and away from the exposure and ridicule of his fellowman. When Bolus is run out of town, he does not flee to another society: "With a hermit's disgust at the degradation of the world, . . . he pitched his tabernacle amidst the smiling prairies that sleep in vernal beauty. . . . There let his mighty genius rest. It has earned repose. We leave Themistocles to his voluntary exile." Bolus, safely away, can dream on.

The
Humor
Prism
in 20th-
Century
America

67

Mark Twain's imaginative liars are loners, if not hermits. As solitary figures they are allowed to keep their lies, and as lonely men they are perhaps moved further to cultivate and refine them. Jim Baker, for example, is "a middle-aged, simple-hearted miner who had lived in a lonely corner of California . . . and had studied the ways of his only neighbors, the beasts and the birds. . . ." As Baker drifts into his narrative of the blue jay, he reveals that "seven year ago the last man in this region but me, moved away." When Baker says—in regard to the jay's chatter and appearance of befuddlement as it flits about the hole in the roof— that he "never [saw] a bird take on so about a little thing," the reader may well be tempted to make the same observation with regard to Baker himself. Jim Baker seems as intrigued and mystified by the fascinating jay as the jay is by the apparently bottomless hole in the roof. They both are moved to expressive and vivid interpolation by the enigmas with which they are faced. In effect, both Baker and the jay are filling an emptiness—with language and acorns respectively. But the futility of the jay's efforts becomes clear when a fellow bluejay investigates and "the whole absurdity of the contract that that first jay had tackled hit him home and he fell over backward suffocating with laughter. . . ." Baker, fortunately, has no one to point out the futility of his attempt to render his existence less empty and solitary. Baker succeeds in creating meaning, fellowship and delight where little, if any, had existed; and his language embodies, makes manifest, this new life. Meanwhile, over in Calaveras County, in another of Twain's tales, Simon Wheeler sits alone by a "bar-room stove of [a] dilapidated tavern in [a] decayed mining camp." Like Jim Baker, Wheeler transforms the nature of his existence through his imaginative and creative use of language. And, his linguistic re-creation rivals the most splendid things of the corporeal world. The celebrated jumping frog must surely have been a sight to behold. A most remarkable frog it was which, in response to Smiley's call of "Flies, Dan'l, flies!" would "spring straight up and snake a fly off'n the counter there, and flop down on the floor ag'in as solid as a gob of mud, and fall to scratching the side of his head with his hind foot as indifferent as if he hadn't no idea he'd been doin' any more'n any frog might do." As remarkable as the frog's feats of skill, it might be said that Simon Wheeler's achievements outshine them. Wheeler's language, in this and virtually every other sentence, is little short of amazing. "*Snake* a fly off'n the counter," "solid as a *gob of mud*," and the picture of the indifferent frog scratching his head —all show Wheeler's ability to treat experience, real or imagined, with a genius's touch. I, for one, would rather *hear* Simon Wheeler describe a frog "whirling through the air like a doughnut," than *see* the frog do it, impressive though the sight would be. Language does wonders for these men's experiences. So much does language improve even the most celebrated of events that it is hardly surprising that they are reluctant to ever stop talking. In fact, Twain's yarn spinners seldom stop of their own choosing. Just as Fields's Cuthbert J. Twillie is about to make a final speech as his noose tightens, Twain's Simon Wheeler is about to launch into a story about a "yaller one-eyed cow" with "jest a short stump like a bannanner" for a tail, when the narrator takes his leave.

Unlike the visual humor of entropy, transformational humor does not necessarily involve physical activity. When compared with Groucho, who can swing Tarzan-like from opera curtains or whisk shapely ladies across dance floors, W. C. Fields seems virtually inert. One gets the impression that excessive physical motion is repugnant to Fields, who never walks when he can ride—even if it means being dragged behind an Indian pony. Similarly, Jim Baker and Simon Wheeler, two other talkers, seem never to leave their rocking chairs. But not Sut and Groucho. Participating in the general entropy of things, they expend energy, disrupt equilibrium, and bring about the deterioration of nearly all proximate systems. In distinct contrast to the sense of frenzy and chaos generated by the Lovingoods and the Marxes, Fields and Clemens, in the guises of their respective transforming personae, seem to lean back and weave new and fantastic wholes with the colorful yarn of narrative.

American humor depicts dreamers and levelers, both of which the culture seems to cherish. The transformers have an overarching vision, and all things and events are made to conform to or reinforce that vision. Bolus, Wheeler and Twillie are quasi artists, whose creative imaginations add dignity and coherence to their worlds and make their lives less vulgar and less lonely. It is a personal matter. The dream is made manifest, kept intact, and perpetuated by an individual's language; it is also exposed by the very language that gives it existence. To recognize and enjoy the creations of the fantasizing transformer requires a

The
Humor
Prism
in 20th-
Century
America

69

high level of sympathetic tolerance and an appreciation of linguistic feats of skill. To enjoy the humor generated by the levelers, those who set established systems into irreversible entropy, requires a different disposition, one which is unsympathetic to artificial or mechanical order. Entropic humor concerns social matters. The subject and object are distinct: it is Groucho Marx who exposes Margaret Dumont (as opposed to Cuthbert Twillie who exposes Cuthbert Twillie). Two forces are pictured in energetic contention, and the audience welcomes the contest, for it is given that the established, artificial system will decompose. Groucho and Sut are the American democratic warriors, fighting the "good" fight against established systems that undemocratically exclude them (and "us"). The entropist, that is, has action to perform, something to do—something for the audience to see; he has little to tell, other than, perhaps, to recount his battles. In contrast, the transformer has his dream, his magnificent lie, to make and relate in language. The one relies on being seen; the other, on being heard.

The
Humor
Prism
in 20th-
Century
America

70

American Political Humor: Touchables and Taboos

Joseph Boskin

> Here in America we have an immensely humorous
> people in a land of milk and honey and wit, who
> cherish the ideal or the 'sense' of humor and at the
> same time are highly suspicious of anything that is
> nonserious.
> —White and White, 1941

Consensus and Black Holes

Contemporary views about political humor in America are usually expressed in crisp and certain terms. It is explicitly declared that its historical dimension is boundless, its character egalitarian, its breadth all-encompassing, and its expression open and innovative. An oft-stated remark is that political irreverence is, and persistently remains, a distinctive American trait that subjects every form of power to humorous scrutiny and/or comedic skepticism. Intriguingly, these statements command an extraordinary consensus among the public and social scientists alike. A poll on the subject would undoubtedly demonstrate that the majority of people believe their national humor is as democratic as their politics.

Yet these various declarations have rarely been carefully scrutinized. Taken at face value because of their self-serving quality, the claim of an unfettered national humor has been buttressed by the complementary belief that no level of the political process escapes humorous attention. Understandably, these claims are founded on certain a priori assumptions. Is not the open expression of humor a crucial index of democratic culture,

The
Humor
Prism
in 20th-
Century
America

71

This essay was originally published in the *International Political Science Review*, vol. 11, no. 4 (October 1990), Butterworth Heinemann Journals, Oxford, England. Reprinted with permission.

a distinctive feature separating one form of government from another? One society permits, indeed welcomes, critical humor; another restricts, indeed represses, particular forms of comedy. Such thinking naturally has led to the conclusion that the United States is one of those rare societies in which the eloquence and experience of humor is an axiomatic byproduct of its devotion to freedom, nurturing as well as exacting.

Although these propositions have a degree of validity, at the same time their unquestioned acceptance poses serious problems. Just as the practice of democracy is often at variance with its principles, so too is its humorous idiom. An examination of American political humor—that is, humor that speaks not only to its joking and joshing elements but more importantly to its relation to the power structure and to the decision-making processes—reveals specific limitations and unspoken taboos. Restraints on political humor lie deeply hidden within society's psyche. In other words, there appear to exist substantial black holes in political humor's space. Pinpointing them, however, has not been of primary interest to scholars or others involved in humor studies.

A Tepid Cup of Political Tea

So far as its historical antecedents are concerned, a variety of humor forms operated within Colonial and Revolutionary settlements. The language of politics was infused with humorous references, and, reinforced by repeated experiences, was employed as a means of furthering political ideas and institutions. William F. Fry has convincingly observed that "the historical era during which this country was born was a period of ferment and ebullience for political humor. As the monarchy cult waned in dominance, common citizens found greater and greater freedom in pointing out the foibles of their 'betters.' The citizenry also discovered satirical and ironical humor to be effective instruments in communicating their viewpoints and wishes, and in influencing the decisions of government at all levels" (Fry, 1977).

Disclaimers to several of these characteristics, however, were already advanced by some foreign visitors in the decades before the Civil War, not a few of whom also wrote glowingly of the great experiment in Western society. Alexis de Tocqueville, in *Democracy in America*, in the 1830s wrote admiringly that "having little knowledge of the dead languages, democratic nations are apt to borrow words from living tongues" and thereby "make an innovation in language" upon which humor must devolve (de Tocqueville, 1945: II, 70). Yet, the German-born American citizen Francis J. Grund, in *The Americans in their Moral, Social, and Political Relations*, observed in the same decade that despite the powerful wit in the country, "Americans do not laugh at honest bluntness, or good-natured simplicity." Rather, they are "very fond of laughing at the expense of their neighbors," namely, Western European nations. Grund had observed that since Americans had come to regard their birthplace as decadent, it was perforce within the bounds of haughty spoofing.

No doubt Grund was peeved at this chauvinist attitude. He himself had adopted the United States as his domicile because he believed that American ideals and practices ought to be those of all civilized people. But his comments about the structure of American humor cannot be easily dismissed because they highlighted a characteristic of American behavior, one that persists to the present. Wrote Grund critically:

> I know no object more deserving of pity, than a comic actor on an American stage. He is always expected to say something witty; yet he is to give no offence to any part of his audience. His doings and sayings are to be pointed; yet, in whatever direction he turns, he is sure to give offence, and to have his transgressions *visited on his head.* He is to be a politician, and yet offend no party; he is to ridicule the whims and follies of women, but not offend any of the ladies present; he is obliged to please the taste of the rich, who are best capable of rewarding his merits; but he must take care lest, by offending the poor, he may be hissed off the stage, and when too late be made to repent of his folly (Grund, 1968: 78–80).

Not all of Grund's observations have validity in current terms. One aspect of his assessment, though, fingered a particular American yearning for a centrist position. Just as politics has become the art of ameliorating controversy and arriving at consensus—the eschewing of ideology—so too has the character of political humor itself. Over the decades, the reverence that enveloped the two-party system and the inherited divisions or government further affected the forms of humor. A particular consequence is that humor of, by, and for the political scene rarely challenges the basic system. If on occasion a small ray of funny light pierces the foundation's darkness, the exaggerated importance attached to it gives away the false impression of openness.

Serious scrutiny, then, has been muted, and censorious observations not allowed to flow beyond specific boundaries. Levity has been permitted only to the extent that it does not undermine the essential political structure or undercut its symbolic representation. American political humor is more frequently than not a tepid cup of tea.

Modes of Operation

How, though, does the culture accomplish this task of seemingly subjecting the system to humorous scrutiny while at the same time exempting it from any radical examination? The modus operandi has been to separate the *structure* from its *leaders*, the *process* from its *decision-makers*, and to obscure the existence of *power* as such. Everything political is presented as if it were a natural process, functioning automatically for the good of the entire community.

These curious dichotomies have not been lost on certain clever politicans. Even though he had been a two-term governor of California, for example, Ronald Reagan constantly portrayed himself as the political outsider in his quest for the presidency. By smartly fabricating a distance between himself and "politics," Reagan was able to give the appearance of political "purity."

Even in its formative years, as Arthur P. Dudden has pointedly noted, rarely did American political humor "overreach its own bounds to decry democracy's ideals or to dispute the people's faith in their capacity to govern themselves" (Dudden, 1987: 51). The result of these juxtapositions has been, on the one hand, a body of humor that is highly innovative in language and form; and, on the other hand, a humor tightly bound in scope and direction.

To be sure, these are not always immutable patterns. Occasionally, the system is flayed and its principles satirized. On the whole, though, the culture focuses its laughter elsewhere. All this is by way of saying that democracy, the branches of government, and, to a lesser extent, the two parties have led charmed existences. They are largely immune from humor's inquiry. The amount of political humor directed at the Supreme Court and the judiciary system, for example, would fill a thimble. It might be argued that the Court, the most sacrosanct of all American institutions, prevents criticism. But this reverence encompasses virtually the entire political edifice. Few take potshots at the presidency, and even Congress is let off lightly. It is even rarer to hear humor directed toward city or state legislatures.

A Hero but Mostly the Villain

If democratic theory and establishment are largely off limits to humor's thrust, where then is political humor directed? The one constant variable, the figure most often kept in the sights is the linchpin of the American value system itself—the political individual: a unique entity only coincidentally or indeterminately connected to institutions, social class, or concepts of governance. "Politics and poker, politics and poker," chorused the seedy group trying to select a candidate for Congress in the musical *Fiorello!* (1960), one of the few theatrical dramas involving politics: "If politics seem more / Predictable that's because usually you can stack the deck!" (Weidman and Abbott, 1960: 22–29).

Essential to the system but at the same time its clearest threat as well, the career politician has become the mainstay of humor's repertoire. This would explain Ambrose Bierce's caustic definition of an American politician as "an eel in the fundamental mud upon which the superstructure or organized society is reared. When he wriggles he mistakes the agitation of his tail for the trembling of the edifice. As compared with the stateman, he suffers the disadvantage or being alive" (Bierce, 1960: 328). A typical joke, related in the early 1960s, illustrates the public's apprehension regarding the politician's ways:

The Humor Prism in 20th-Century America

75

> It seems that President John Kennedy, Attorney General Robert Kennedy, and Chicago Mayor Richard Daley were in a row boat. Suddenly it sprang a leak and it became clear that two of them aboard would have to jump overboard if the boat were to remain afloat. The President stood up and said, "As President I represent the free world. If I go under, the free world will perish." He sat down. The Attorney General stood up and said, "As Attorney General I represent law and order. If I go under, law and order will perish." He sat down. The Mayor stood up and said, "As Mayor, I represent the diversity and vitality of all cities. If I go under, all cities

will perish." He sat down. They decided to put the matter to
a vote. Daley won, 5–2 (Author's notes, 1962).

Anecdotal and fictional accounts have consistently limned
the corrupt politician as the primary threat to the democratic system. On *Hollywood Squares*, a highly popular television show of
the 1970s and 1980s, the host asked humorist George Gobel:
"According to a University of Rochester study, do most criminals
return to the scene of a crime?" "No," replied Gobel dryly to in-
stantaneous applause and considerable laughter, "they have to
get re-elected first."

Because they possess the power to render the system inef-
fective—to undermine and ravage it—the defective character of
the politician has furnished an endless supply of aggresive retort,
as if laughter can lighten such anxiety or perhaps force the politician to rearrange his priorities. An illustrative story, the counterpart to tales of the urban boss, has its locale in rural Connecticut. A farmer named Boyd decided to run for county office:

The
Humor
Prism
in 20th-
Century
America

76

> A leader of his political party in the county seat thought
> he'd make a few inquiries and one day spotted another
> farmer, a neighbor of Boyd, buying some nails at the hard-
> ware store. He approached this old man and asked him
> what he thought of Boyd as a candidate for office. The
> farmer ran his hand through his beard and looked wise and
> said nothing.
>   "Would you say he's an honest man," the questioner
> persisted; "or would you rate him as a liar?"
>   The old farmer considered for a few moments and
> then answered slowly: "I wouldn't go so fur as to call him a
> liar, but I've heered tell that when he wants his pigs to come
> in for their feedin', he has to git somebody else to call em"
> (Smith, 1968: 67).

Another, more serious menace to the system, however, derives from the politicians' refusal to directly confront problems
and decisions. Wrote Keith Preston in *Epitaph*, a biting ode to
those individuals who assiduously avoid dealing with the issues:
"Here lies beneath this mossy stone / A politician who /
Touched a live issue without gloves / And never did come to"
(Preston, 1955: 631).

The politicians' shortcomings in this respect has led to a
chorus of satirical responses. Comedian Will Rogers' remark in

the 1930s, "Politics ain't worrying this country one-tenth as much as where to find a parking space," was a gentle but illustrative jibe. Essayist Art Buchwald's satirical piece on the political poll as the supposed authentic voice of the people reflects a more biting probe. "What would have happened," Buchwald mused, "if there had been political pollsters in the early days of this country?" Buchwald then posed a series of questions relevant to the period: "Were the British doing a good job?" "Did the dumping of tea in Boston harbor by the militants hurt or help the taxation laws?" "What do you think our image is in England after the Minute Men attacked the British at Lexington?" and so on. On the basis of the responses to the polls, Buchwald noted that the militant Colonials decided "they did not have enough popular support to foment a revolution and gave up the idea of creating a United States of America" (Buchwald, 1962).

The politician with feet of clay has thus been the target of political humor for several centuries. His entrance onto the American scene occurred long before the founding of the nation, as Robert K. Dodge observed in his collection, *Early American Almanac Humor* (1987). A considerable portion of the comic stories that abounded in the Colonial period involved authority figures, particularly lawyers and other court officers. Politicians and magistrates were judged to be as long-winded and boring as the clergy and guilty of cupidity and lying as well. Indeed, there were times when they were accused of contracting with the Devil himself.

Vilifying the politician has never ceased and the figure remains the focus of much humor in the contemporary period: lampooned in newspaper and magazine cartoons on a daily basis; satirized as hopelessly sleazy in such films as *The Senator Was Indiscreet* (1947) and *Born Yesterday* (1950); portrayed as the windbag Senator Claghorn so dubbed by comedian Fred Allen on his radio program in the 1930s and 1940s; skewered as pompous, silly, and fraudulent on such television programs as *That Was the Week That Was* (1960s), *Laugh-In* (1970s), and *Saturday Night Live* (1970s–1980s); rendered foolishly inept by such literary humorists as Mark Twain, Finley Peter Dunne, H. L. Mencken, Art Buchwald, and Russell Baker; flattened intellectually by storytellers such as Will Rogers and Mort Sahl; and ridiculed for their antics almost nightly by talk show host Johnny Carson.

As expected, the politician around whom the mass of political humor revolves is the president. All incumbents have been the object of humorous attention that more often than not involves dichotomous feelings. That is, the dual expression of adulation and rejection appears to undergird the laughter directed toward the head of the American state. In part this is due to the symbolic nature of the office itself. Finley Peter Dunne, the popular dialect humorist at the turn of the century, captured the nub of it when he quipped, ". . . a man can be r-right an' be the President, but he can't be both at the same time" (Bradley, 1984: 69).

The sharpness of humor directed at President Ronald Reagan, mainly in his second term, serves as an illustration of this dictum. Commercial greeting cards in stationery stores and full-sized plywood cutouts on city streets for a "Picture with the President" colorfully displayed his boyish smile, slicked pompadour, and tailored dark serge suit in a way that allowed for personal affection *and* comical connection. A series of jokes, relayed by comics in public and people in private, mocked his personal style, film background, and slipping memory. Virtually no aspect or his ebbing energy went unmentioned, no slip unnoticed. Thus the quip that appeared in the final year in office was fondly caustic: "Did you hear that IBM has come out with a new typewriter called the President? It has no memory or colon" (Author's notes, 1987).

Unlike most of his predecessors, however, Reagan pointedly embraced and utilized humorous repartee. He was often able to deflect the criticisms directed toward his style and philosophy. At the convention of the American Association of Editorial Cartoonists in 1987, for example, Reagan was confronted with an editorial page caricature in which he displayed a lofty finger and an equally lofty hair set as he declaimed: "Let me clarify the last clarification of the previous clarification on the earlier clarification on the '85 tax issue. I've tried every way I can to make my hair stand up that way, but it just won't take" (*Boston Globe*, 1987: 10).

That the President's status does not prohibit his being spoofed, even ridiculed, was pointedly observed by one of the premier satirists in the twentieth century. In a speech at a naturalized citizens' ceremony in 1986, Art Buchwald observed that the country "honors those who make fun of their leaders—and not only cheers them on but invites them to appear on television talk shows to be witty and clever." He then delivered several public anti-Reagan jokes that had been spawned by the Iran-Contra controversy in 1987: "When did the President know what was going on—and when did he forget it?"; "Have you heard that President Reagan has lost many sleepless days over the Middle East?" (*New York Times*, 1986: 43). This episode clearly exhibits humor's powerful access but specific locus within the political culture.

The Invisible Establishment

Amid all the jokes and skits, though, one seldom bears any reference to the system itself that continually produces corrupt individuals, generation after generation. Few humorists spoof the public's practice of re-electing pompous, small-minded, and venal politicians after constantly excoriating them in jokes. Although politicians individually and as a type serve as the butt of humor, this is not the case with other powerful individuals. A careful perusal of American laughter suggests that within the broad reach of American culture there are definite taboos involving humor's involvement and intent. Certain classes and issues are outside humor's purview, so much so that merely to mention or delineate this situation is to rouse immediate pique and certain challenge.

Specifically, there is a gaping absence of humor involving the corporate world, its leaders, structure, and practices. Who would ever know from an analysis of American humor in the twentieth century, the epoch in which the industrial and financial sectors have come to dominate American culture, that this society is guided by the ethos of the corporation? One searches in vain for humor directed at the business establishment. It is only in a rare book, *The Peter Principle* (1969) by Laurence J. Peter or *Up the Organization* (1970) by Robert Townsend, or an occasional film, *The Great McGinty* (1940) by Preston Sturges and *Fun With Dick and Jane* (1974), or an uncommon play, *Of Thee I Sing* (1932) by George S. Kaufman and Morrie Ryskind, George and Ira Gershwin, and *You Can't Take It With You* (1937) by George S. Kaufman and Moss Hart that one can locate humorous themes about America's corporations. Otherwise, where are the literary treatises, the public jokes, and the visual caricatures involving the leading 500 corporate institutions? Where are the guffaws about General Motors, ITT, AT&T, E. F. Hutton, Chase Manhattan Bank, U.S. Steel, Du Pont, *Time* magazine, and so on? Who jokes about the way allied institutions, the universities and churches, genuflect to wealth? The foibles and foolishness, contradictions and conflicts, or the corporate leaders and their satellites have been assiduously avoided by America's humorists, the sit-down writers and stand-up comics. Does unquestionable immense power prevent such humorous intrusion into personal experiences and decisions? To what extent does the taboo arise from the elemental connection of business to all aspects of American life? As President Calvin Coolidge laconically put it, "The business of America is business." Would subjecting the corporation to humorous analysis render it less effective and efficient? Would mocking it subvert the national mission? Of all the weapons in the human repertoire, it is certain that the force of humor is the most potent in unsettling the pysche, whether personal or national.

It must be immediately noted that these institutions are not barren of internal humor. In their enclosed confines can be heard much furtive laughter that arises from spontaneous circumstances or arranged amusements. Within the workplace, raillery is frequently employed to define social place and status as well as to ameliorate conflict and intense pressures. Moreover, there can be little doubt that humor by executives in corporate society is employed in ways similar to that of other organizations. The difference is that the humor and the concerns which give rise to it in private corporations are rarely revealed or integrated into the public's consciousness. Laughter in the corporation is effectively confined to its boundaries.

Consider, in addition, the public's image of corporate and industrial figures. Stereotypes about certain stock powerful types, including the politician, lawyer, and clergyman, have always abounded in American humor, stereotypes that provide a familiar face in the theater, films, and novels in good times and bad. Yet, their counterparts in the corporate world—the executive, manager, financier, and advertiser—only occasionally make their appearance. Corporate leaders, to put it baldly, are faceless.

To the extent that corporations and their executives ever become the specific objects of national humor, a severe reversal

The
Humor
Prism
in 20th-
Century
America

80

in the economy is usually the cause, not a shift of values. This was precisely the situation in the 1890s and again in the 1930s when the financial system unraveled and the country was plunged into vast depressions; and once again in the 1970s when a spiraling inflation and recession wreaked havoc with the economy. In plays, films, and cartoons in the 1930s, for example, bankers and businessmen were mercilessly fingered as culprits. Derogatory portraits became commonplace. A *New Yorker* cartoon of the period pictured a portly man in a prison suit tacking up a sign announcing a baseball game on prison grounds pitting the Trusties vs. Wall Street. On movie screens, executives were often shown as men of rotund physique and bumbling mentality, while their wives and children were highlighted for their pretentious airs and childish cares.

Similarly, hostile humor was directed at the managerial class in the mid- and late 1970s. In this decade, they were singled out in a mini-joke cycle. Lumped together under the stinging acronym WASP—White, Anglo-Saxon, Protestant—the upper classes were again reviled. The spirit of this joke cycle was traceable to a 19th-century anonymous couplet that scorned their haughty demeanor:

> You can always tell the Irish,
>> You can always tell the Dutch;
> You can always tell a Yankee,
>> But you cannot tell him much

The
Humor
Prism
in 20th-
Century
America

81

The WASP broadside of the contemporary period took aim at the lifestyle of the old rich by mocking their values and financial activities. On their vaunted individualism: *How can you tell the WASPs at a Chinese dinner? / They're the ones who won't share the food.* On their hedonistic practices: *What is a WASP's idea of an orgy? / Price-fixing.* On their sexual energies: *What do you call a WASP woman who makes love more than once a month? / A nymphomaniac.* On their sense of importance in the universe: *Why do WASPs smile at lightning? / Because they think they're having their pictures taken* (Author's notes, 1975).

There is another exception to the protective covering of executives, one related to the bureaucratic character of the corporation. Since the 1950s, a kind of graphic sniping at managerial pieties has become widespread. Appearing on standard stationery, circulated in business and corporate offices across the country, thousands of anonymous drawings, statements, anecdotes, and stories express contempt for organizational practices and executive values and behavior. Written from the white collar worker's vantage point, they portray the workplace as uncaring, rigidly hierarchical, and often cruel. A brief but not untypical graffito, for example, points up the impossibility of accomplishing company goals:

> The objective of all dedicated Company employees should be to thoroughly analyze all situations, anticipate all problems prior to their occurrence, have answers for those problems when called upon;
>
> HOWEVER
>
> When you are up to your ass in alligators, it is difficult to remind yourself that your initial objective was to drain the swamp.

The extensive use of this alienated humor throughout the marketplace has been made technically possible by duplicating machines. But the underlying motivation of this behavior was insightfully explained by the political observer Dwight MacDonald, who likened it to guerrilla warfare. Success depends on traveling light, striking unexpectedly, and getting away unobserved, he noted. It is highly significant that the majority of these underground productions name no companies or executives. To cite one illustration, an "Organization Chart" that symbolizes the nature of all corporations was circulated in many offices. Roughly drawn was a string of office workers, all of whom are on their knees kissing everyone before them, the line eventually concluding at the feet of a single, erect, beaming CEO, a halo hovering over his head.

With the exception of an occasional play or film, a novel or television special, then, the short-lived WASP joke cycle and the anonymous graphic office leaflets represent the only substantial humorous challenge to the American power elite and its infrastructure in the twentieth century.

Contradiction and the Comedic Fix

Ultimately, then, humor about public affairs in the United States has been shaped by the contradiction between a democratic justification and a docile belief in formalities and authorized procedures. To put it bluntly, the theory of an open society has been thwarted by a political system so sanctified that humor cannot be brought to bear on its various components.

Similarly wrapped in a cocoon are the corporations and their executive officers. Whether the protection given to the financial sector results from a conscious but subtle campaign by the corporation itself to suppress humorous scrutiny or from a subconscious queasiness on the part of the populace stemming from a fear of harming capitalism is not at all certain. To repeat, what has been overlooked is that America's financial organizations are virtually outside humor's bounds.

There have been occasional challenges to this situation and they are, of course, cited as representing the health of democratic humor in the country. Corruption in government, specifically, the Harding administration of the 1920s and the Watergate and Iran-Contra scandals of the 1970s and 1980s, were uncovered by the media and satirically skewered by humorists. Sudden economic disasters have brought out the barbs and quips. As expected, though, even at the time it was forcibly argued that these were but temporary blemishes on the body politic, the fault of flawed individuals.

Consequently, no continuous body of political humor directly impinges on the system. To repeat, this situation has gone largely unnoticed because to define the national humor in terms of its limitations and taboos wreaks havoc with democracy's self-image. There would appear to be an ironic undertone to a remark by the writer E. B. White, one of the most influential literary humorists of the century, who noted that "Whatever else an American believes or disbelieves about himself, he is absolutely sure he has a sense of humor" (White and White, 1941: xx). And, extending White's observation; it should be duly noted that practically everyone further subscribes to that complementary notion of a national sense of humor as well.

The outcome of this dubious belief has been a body of folk-humor of impressive latitude that reaches its best expression mainly when directed at selected aspects of particular politicians. Given America's infatuation with the uniqueness of the individual, perhaps this was to be the expected outcome. As sociologist Robert Ross cleverly exclaimed, America's national anthem is not the "Star-Spangled Banner" but Frank Sinatra's song, "My Way."

In this context, the political humor that does exist possesses an imaginative play combined with a simple directness. It emphasizes the shortcomings and quirkiness of specific individuals. The following is a story that circulated during the presidential primary campaign in 1988:

> Jimmy Carter, Richard Nixon, Gary Hart, Joe Biden, Michael Dukakis, and Ronald Reagan were on a ship that began to sink. Carter yelled, "Women and children first." Nixon said, "Screw them." Hart asked, "Is there time?" Biden said, "Is there time?" Dukakis responded, "Did you hear what Biden said?" Reagan exclaimed, "Is there something going on I don't know about?"

Thus, American political humor shuns the real centers of economic and political power that have developed over the centuries. Laughter has yet to be extended to certain decision-making institutions or their representatives in the political firmament. Rather, it concentrates upon the most visible and vulnerable unit in the structure: the political official. In contrast with those powerful sectors that remain hidden to humor's scrutiny, the person on the stump has had nowhere to hide. It is precisely at this place on the stage, on the spotlighted self, that America's humor illuminates its political democracy.

The
Humor
Prism
in 20th-
Century
America

84

References

Bierce, A. (1960). *The Collected Works of Ambrose Bierce.* Secaucus, N.J.: Citadel Press.

Bradley, S. (1984). "Our Native Humor," in *Critical Essays on American Humor* (W. B. Clark and W. C. Turner, eds.), p. 69. Boston: G. K. Hall.

Buchwald, A. (1962). "Reading the Tea Leaves in Boston Harbor." IV: 1 (3rd May). *Boston Globe.*

de Tocqueville, A. (1945). *Democracy in America,* II: 70. New York: Vintage Books.

Dodge, R. K. (1987). *Early American Almanac Humor,* pp. 131–155. Bowling Green: Bowling Green State University Popular Press.

Dudden, A. P. (1987). "The Record of Political Humor." In *American Humor* (A. P. Dudden, ed.), p. 51. New York: Oxford University Press.

Fry, W. F., Jr. (1977). "Popular Humor in American Politics." Unpublished paper.

Grund, F. J. (1968). *The Americans in Their Moral, Social, and Political Relations.* I and II: 78–80. New York: Johnson Reprint Corporation.

Preston, K. (1955). "Epitath." in *The American Treasury, 1455–1955* (Clifton Fadiman, ed.), p. 631. New York: Harper & Row, Publishers.

Smith, H. A. (1968). *Buskin with H. Allen Smith,* p. 67. Los Angeles: Trident Press.

Weidman, H. and G. Abbott (1960). *Fiorello!* pp. 22–29. New York: Random House.

White, E. B. and K. S. White, eds. (1941). *A Subtreasury of American Humor,* p. xx. New York: Coward-McCann, Publishers.

The
Humor
Prism
in 20th-
Century
America

85

The Standup Comedian as Anthropologist: Intentional Culture Critic

Stephanie Koziski

> People laugh and tell jokes, and if you can learn
> the humor of a people and really control it, you
> know that you are also in control of nearly every-
> thing else.[1]

The
Humor
Prism
in 20th-
Century
America

86

Anthropologist Edward Hall maintained that an understanding of a people's sense of humor is one key to the structure
of that society. By control, he means that a person who can en-
gender good feelings by verbal facility and charisma holds social
authority over his or her fellows. This social authority is not
based on legality or even tradition, but by the extraordinary impact of some personalities to catalyze and negotiate interaction
among others, manipulating role performances.[2] The importance of affirming the existence of tacit knowledge in society is
another tenet of Hall's scholarship. He noted that "culture hides
much more than it reveals, and strangely enough, what it hides,
it hides most effectively from its own participants. Years of study
have convinced me that the real job is not to understand foreign
culture, but to understand our own."[3] Documenting areas of tacit
knowledge and bringing them to the conscious awareness of
their particular audiences are important functions performed by
the anthropologist and the standup comedian in their respective
roles. The social and cultural function of popular culture materials along with the anthropologist's and standup comedian's perspectives as social critics fused for me, as I considered the role of

This essay was originally published in the *Journal of Popular Culture*, vol. 18, no. 2 (Fall
1984). Reprinted with permission.

the standup comedian in American culture through an examination and analysis of selected recorded comedy routines.

An examination of the material used in the routines of standup comedians—Bill Cosby, George Carlin, Dick Gregory, Hal Holbrook, Steve Martin, Bob Newhart, Richard Pryor, Flip Wilson and Lily Tomlin, to name but a few—shows them to be sensitive culture critics. They pattern their comic material close to everyday reality, making obvious behavioral patterns, explicit and tacit operating knowledge and other insights about American society objects of conscious reflection. Contrasting a familiar society with an alien one, anthropologists' observations may evoke in their scholarly audiences a new perception by incongruity, as something of the pan-humanity of man is glimpsed through their explanations of culture. Many standup comedians jar their audience's sensibilities by making individuals experience a shock of recognition. This occurs as deeply held popular beliefs about themselves—even the hidden underpinnings of their culture— are brought to an audience's level of conscious awareness. The standup comedian can elevate his audience to a new cultural focus.

Content analysis of standup comedians' routines, especially projections of covert culture through figurative modes of expression—repetitive metaphors and imagery used to describe similar phenomena—can be analyzed for the artist's response, conscious and unconscious, to covert traits of culture.[4] The comedian may associate a particular regionalism with a type of cultural inferiority or superiority, prescribe for the ideal community of men or offer explanations of change as innovative, destructive, cathartic, threatening or inevitable. As an example, Lenny Bruce perceived economics as the base upon which society turned. Dick Gregory's picture of the universe focuses on class conflict and institutional power structures that obstruct equality for all citizens. Female comedians may be acutely aware of a male-dominated society and the social handicaps that society places upon women and other minorities. Such analysis can provide insights into the unstated ideas of a society—ideas that may not otherwise be visible. Standup comedians often talk about conventions that are "simply too basic, too much an assumed constant of life to be rendered fully visible and self-conscious."[5]

Some standup comedians specifically look at the array of seemingly unrelated customs, behaviors and artifacts in their so-

The
Humor
Prism
in 20th-
Century
America

87

ciety, as does the anthropologist, and see novel interconnections. They break down social life into its basic elements—searching for categories, isolating domains and identifying rules. They may talk about social behavior in terms of analytic concepts used by the anthropologist—that is, language, social structure, kinship rules, economics, technology and the effects of these on every-man in the audience. These comedians may describe the net-work of customs that are immediately linked to a particular cul-tural practice.

For example, in Bob Newhart's routine "Introducing To-bacco to Civilization" he tries to imagine what the world would be like without tobacco and coffee. Newhart envisions a tele-phone conversation from America to England during the seven-teenth century between Sir Walter Raleigh and the head of the West Indies Company. The Company head opens the conversa-tion as Raleigh tries to explain the uses of tobacco and coffee to someone who has never experienced them:

> What is it this time, Walt? You got another winner for us, do you? Tobacco. What's tobacco, Walt? It's a kind of leaf? And you bought eighty tons of it! . . . This may come as kind of a surprise to you, Walt, but come fall in England now, Walt, we're kind of up to our, uh . . . (laughs). It isn't that kind of leaf? What is it, a special food of some kind is it, Walt? Huh? Not exactly. It has a lot of different uses? Are you saying "snuff," Walt? What's snuff? Ya take a pinch of tobacco (laughs) and you shove it up your nose. And it makes you sneeze, huh? I imagine it would, Walt, yeah. Gee, goldenrod seems to do it pretty well over here."[6]

The
Humor
Prism
in 20th-
Century
America

88

Bob Newhart skillfully communicates to the audience through his incredulous reactions to Raleigh's descriptions of the new cultural practices, the Company head's estimation of Raleigh as something of a nincompoop:

> It has some other uses, though? You can chew it or put it in a pipe or you can shred it up and put it in a piece of paper and roll it up, ha ha. Don't tell me, Walt, don't tell me. You stick it in your ear, right, Walt? No, between your lips, then what do you do to it, Walt? (laughs). You set fire to it, Walt? Then what do you do? You inhale the smoke? You know, Walt, it seems offhand like you could stand in front of your fireplace and get the same thing! . . . I think you're going to

have a tough time convincing people to stick burning leaves in their mouths. It's going very well over there, you say?[7]

We can envision ourselves responding as the Company executive to Raleigh's explanations as ludicrous ones if we did not intimately know and accept the cultural practices surrounding the use of tobacco and coffee.

> What's the matter, Walt? You what? You spilled your c-o-f-f-e-e (pronounces very slowly). What's coffee, Walt? That's a drink you make out of beans? That's going over big there too, is it? A lot of people have their coffee after their first cigarette in the morning? Is that what you call the burning leaves there, Walt, cigarettes? Why don't you send us a boatload of those beans too? If you can talk people into putting those burning leaves in their mouths, they gotta go for those beans, Walt.[8]

The way we as people characteristically look out on the universe may be held up for our gaze by the standup comedian. He or she may call attention to general features of our cultural landscape by naming the themes that run through the context of American culture like the major ideas of a novel.

The comedic response as a vehicle for making visible to an audience tacit areas of unacknowledged human attitudes and behaviors, residing in private, unofficial realms, is worthy of study. As cultural anthropologist John Caughey notes, "Americanists are well aware that trying to understand one's own society poses problems as interesting and challenging as those encountered in studying another culture and that—as in studying an alien society—much of the complex work involves rendering tacit culture explicit."[9]

As an example of private, tacit behavior, comedian George Carlin describes things people may have done but haven't told to another person:

> Anything that we all do and we never talk about? It's funny, man. Here's something I discovered that was more universal than I'd ever suspected. I found out by asking people, "When you take a piss, do you do this? Ooooooh!" What is that, man? It has no name. I call it the piss shiver. It's nature's way of shaking off.[10]

Some tacit knowledge involves negotiating ordinary activities. Bill Cosby, for example, examines the logic of a game of golf:

> I got to tell you first of all that there are two sports that I think happen to be very dumb. And the first one is golf. Golf is dumb because you take the ball out of your pocket, you put it down and you hit it—WHACK!, and then you walk after it. Now think about that. You hit the ball—let's take it step by step. (LOUDER VOICE). You had the ball. It was in your hand. You were home free, and then you put it down and then you beat it away. You didn't want it . . . but then you went after it again.[11]

Other tacit realms are profound and extremely sensitive. Covert behavior is not merely hidden because informally learned, but includes a component of ignored, repressed behavior patterns and commonly learned attitudes running counter to the culture's articulated ideals.[12] These disparate threads render covert culture difficult to detect and examine. Speaking of covert culture, Bernard Bowron, Leo Marx and Arnold Rose believe hidden areas of our culture "may be of the greatest importance in certain emotionally charged areas of behavior, such as racial or sexual relations or religion."[13] Known for her outspoken acceptance of sexuality in her Las Vegas nightclub routines, stand-up comedian Rusty Warren said of sexual areas of human behavior, "if we can open them up and make laughs with them, or see them in picture form, people are bound to loosen up. I'd like to think I help them become less a part of that inner tightness because, when you are tight inside, you can't function as a man or a woman."[14]

The comedian may investigate with an audience tacit areas of behavior not easily discussed, especially this realm of sexual behavior. As an example, George Carlin discusses masturbation in one of his comedy routines. He imagines a discussion with a friend in a bar setting:

> Did you ever do Betty Ryan? I said, "Yeah." He said, "How was she, man?" Well, I believe in masturbation. I think if God intended us not to masturbate, he would have made our arms shorter. One thing I never did was to accept money from myself. One time, I caught myself with another hand. Never let your left hand know. . . .[15]

The
Humor
Prism
in 20th-
Century
America

90

Taken-for-granted behavior patterns may have been present in a group for some time, attracting little attention, until the introduction of a new catalyst—such as a new cultural focus prompting social change. In one of Dick Gregory's routines, he ridicules himself to make a point about the pervasive atmosphere of racism in America from his perspective. Exaggerating the requisite operating knowledge necessary for a minority to fit into America's white social structure, Dick Gregory describes the behaviors expected from a Black who moves into an all-white Chicago neighborhood:

> . . . the other day, I'm out raking my snow . . . And I don't want to rake no snow but any time you the first Negro to move into an all white neighborhood in this town, the N.A.A.C.P. send you dat little booklet because you there and you got to impress 'em. . . . Page two says you *will* (emphasis) wear an Ivy League suit and a tee shirt and no coat 'cause we want to make 'em think we healthy. . . . No stocking cap. . . .[16]

Because most informally learned behavior tends to be invisible, such behavior needs to be carefully re-defined to be fully understood in its implications to society. What many standup comedians and anthropologists do is, as anthropologist Victor Turner describes, "cut out a piece of society for the inspection of his audience [and] set up a frame within which image and symbols of what has been sectioned off can be scrutinized, assessed, and perhaps remodeled."[17]

The anthropologist operates as a participant observer in an alien group from a stance of cultural distance, and writes back to his own people about an unknown culture. His methodology involves collecting, analyzing and comparing how various groups structure their reality. Anthropologists, like standup comedians, are sensitive to the common pattern of things. From the fieldwork situation, the ethnographer publicly witnesses socially enacted behavior which he or she describes and reports literally, accurately and with scientific objectivity in a written document, a lecture, a museum display or a film.[18] He communicates basically to a scholarly audience. The isolates he has selected to scrutinize are fitted into a theoretical model of the studied society. He creates a scholarly artifice from a social reality. The anthropologist's audience responds to him or her as one who is reporting observations and replying to others' theories. The delivery of the an-thropologist's message in a lecture situation is not unlike the so-cial environment in which a standup comedian shares his views of reality with an audience. The audience can choose to accept the new knowledge or discount the anthropologist's findings in light of their own theories. But these theories are not meant to be entertaining. The comedian's basic thrust as he or she stands before an audience, however, is to be entertaining rather than to elucidate culture theory.

The standup comedian is charged with a different commu-nication function than the anthropologist is. Both study living cultures (unless the anthropologist is studying an extinct culture) in order to reveal something of the habits and thoughts of that culture and the functions of that culture's institutions. Both make a commentary on the human condition from the perspec-tive of people who profoundly understand human nature. The comedian publicly witnesses or reads about socially enacted be-havior. However, he exaggerates or distorts his observations as a participant observer talking to people in his own society about the familiar cultural rules and behavior patterns in *their* and *his* own society. The audience may hear their own behavior de-scribed as if it is an alien culture in the sense that they knew that information all along but no one ever said it like that to them before. However, even though the comedian and his audience share culture, part of the cultural knowledge with which they operate is tacit (that is, hitherto unspoken).

The typical cultural scene in which anthropologists operate is the researcher acting with scientific objectivity in an alien soci-ety. Anthropologist Laura Bohannan's understanding of tacit areas of African culture and the dramatic cultural performance she enacted to mediate its effects as it impacted on her daily real-ity came closest to approximating the characteristic scene of the standup comedian. In her novel *Return to Laughter* she recounted her detection, understanding and dealing with tacit areas of cul-tural knowledge during fieldwork among the Tiv in northern Ni-geria. Soon after her arrival in their village, she sensed a deep belief in witchcraft. Knowing that Europeans disbelieved in and disapproved of witchcraft, the Tiv were evasive in response to her questions about the actual existence and hidden nature of magic and witchcraft. One villager assured her she asked about things that did not exist. This private realm of belief was brought to dramatic cultural visibility when one of her informants was accused of causing a woman's death through witchcraft. Bohannan was caught in the resulting factional struggle between the chief of the tribe and rival witch, Yabo. By association with the accused, Bohannan was negatively branded a witch by the villagers' system of knowledge—their cultural categories for organizing reality. This underlying web of belief which defied explanation in terms of her own system of knowledge brought her into contact with the tacit area of belief imbedded deep in Tiv tribal consciousness. She said of the villagers' responses that defied her logic, "I never found out just what happened that day, before my very eyes."[19] By using her craft of cultural insight, however, she was able to restore the situation to harmony by glimpsing the tacit web of meanings underlying their witchcraft belief and using that knowledge to her advantage. She enacted a cultural drama in the style of the dramatic performer in terms the Tiv culture would understand. She intended no humor in her performance however; her dramatic enactment was intended as magic. Only in retrospect was the ceremony humorous to Bohannan and to an American audience.

She enacted a ceremony composed of associating a fear of metal with witches and neutralizing witch owl infestations in the village with preventive ritual magic. She used the deep sepulchral tone the Tiv utter for magical incantations over bird-scarers made from tin cans, modeled from the ones her mother used in her vegetable garden back home in America. Her utterances involved a rendition of the paternoster in Latin, fragments from the Book of Psalms, Song of Solomon and one of Catullus' more impassioned love lyrics in a completely new context. The sudden incongruity between means and ends, she recalled, and a flashback to the quiet schoolroom where she learned the lyrics became superimposed mentally on the scene in which she found herself, bringing Bohannan's performance to an abrupt halt. Her dramatic enactment was accepted by the villagers as a successful prevention against further visits from the witch owls. She cleared her identity from the stigma of witch and silently congratulated herself, thinking, "Poe just didn't know how to handle that raven."[20]

This scene from an anthropologist's field experience differs markedly from the comedian's enactment before an audience for purposes of sheer entertainment. Bohannan did not utilize humor as an analytic expression. In retrospect, her performance was humorous to her but not intended in the instant of the act to be received humorously by her African audience. Recounting these emotional experiences by constructing an inner portrait with some humorous conventions in a novel to an American audience, she approaches the way the standup comedian transforms experience into an artistic construction—the comedy performance.

In a similar vein, anthropologist Clifford Geertz and his wife broke the silent treatment accorded them in the initial stages of fieldwork in a Balinese village when they fled with Balinese onlookers from an illegal cockfight. At the approach of law enforcement agents, villagers bounded over hedges and down dusty roads. The Geertzes ran into the courtyard of a Balinese home on the heels of its owner, seating themselves at an outdoor table as if on cue. They acted as if they had been taking tea for some time while the illegal gambling occurred in the marketplace. As the police came on the scene and questioned Geertz's Balinese host (until this moment but another stranger amid the aloof villagers), to Geertz's surprise the man described in minute detail Geertz's identity and purpose in his village. Geertz's identification with the fleeing villagers rather than choosing to invoke his immunity from Balinese law provided by his exalted status as a foreign anthropologist, won his acceptance into the Balinese community. He identified with the community in an instant of mutual danger. He had not intended his actions to be funny, yet, as he relates this incident to an audience of scholars in his essay "Deep Play: Notes on the Balinese Cockfight" his cultural observations are laced with humor as were Bohannan's descriptions of incidents that confronted her among the Nigerians. Using humor to recount their lives in a foreign culture to an American audience through an emotional, inner portrait and with humorous conventions, these particular anthropologists approach the way certain standup comedians transform the stuff of their experiences into an artistic construction—the comedy performance. The intent is to channel a direct and immediate humor response in a particular audience. One step removed from the dangerous or embarrassing situation described by the anthropologist or the standup comedian, their respective audiences can find amusement in those situations. However, humor as used by anthropologists is an occasional convention

The
Humor
Prism
in 20th-
Century
America

94

used to enhance the explanation process rather than a characteristic analytic tool.

These inner transforming experiences are sometimes described to us as standup comedians talk about their perceptions of what they do for an audience through the vehicle of comedy. Standup comedian Rusty Warren remarked in an interview, "I talk the truth with comedy—the audiences know it, they understand. You could say I hold up a mirror for people to see themselves as they are."[21]

The comedian's and anthropologist's explanations of reality are built from many observations over time. Both have the ability through training or natural inclination to survey behavior, discover the knowledge upon which particular behaviors are founded and to construct an explanation form to answer questions about human experience. Journalist Phil Berger, who interviewed many standup comedians for his book *The Last Laugh: The World of Standup Comics,* said of them: "Part of the game was memory. All the great comics drew on their experience."[22] The comedian finds, frames and edits reality into an artistic construction—the comedy routine. Robert Klein is described by Berger as one comedian who "took his experiences and distilled them to comic quick. . . . In this, he was aided by a remarkable memory, one able to retrieve an inordinate amount of data. . . . It was that knack for details of a '50s past that lent his comic fragments of it their liveliness."[23]

Both the anthropologist and the standup comedian highlight aspects of human life and bring these phenomena into a public area for examination, discussion, analysis and clarification. This analytic ability involves a penetrating and challenging habit of mind that allows deeper insight into the essence of humanity and the structure of society. Penetrations into the components of society and the revelations that both the anthropologist and the standup comedian isolate for their respective audiences illuminate the tacit and explicit cultural knowledge that undergirds the outlook of particular population segments. However, while the anthropologist reports literally and with scientific objectivity the closer structural observations of a society, the comedian's observations of his culture are broadly refracted and highly distilled, although recognizable, images from his own culture.

There may be some truth to attributing a "marginal man" label to some anthropologists and standup comedians. Their sensitivity to and insight into the dynamics of culture might be viewed as a mediating strategy to compensate for their own feelings of isolation from mainstream society and to bring them into closer fellowship with American core culture.

The anthropoligist is—by training—*a sympathetic outsider,* while the comedian is, in most cases—by temperament—*a cynical insider.* A survey of the writings of anthropologists like Ruth Benedict, Margaret Mead, John Adair, Clifford Geertz, James Spradley and David McCurdy indicates optimism about human potential. Most hold hope for the possibilities available to human society, in contrast to standup comedians who are informed by anger and despair as the inherent weak, stupid and evil tendencies in human nature. The comedian's pessimism goads him or her into looking for society's flaws and broadcasting those revelations through a special kind of enacted social drama to a select public.

This cynicism about the human race is conveyed brilliantly by Hal Holbrook in bringing the character and writings of Mark Twain alive on the stage. Experiencing the impressions of a nineteenth-century artist-spokesman from twentieth-century viewpoints, today's audience can experience new cultural meanings through incongruity, as past interfaces with present. Holbrook relates, "You probably noticed that the human race is a curiosity. Originally, man started out a little lower than the angels and he has been getting lower ever since. . . ."[24]

Mark Twain pinpoints the hypocrisy of the human race, especially in man's profession of religion:

> Oh, man is a marvel, he is. He's invented himself a heaven and emptied into it all the nations of the earth, all in one common jumble, and all of them on an equality absolute. They have to be brothers. They have to mix together and pray together and harp together and hosanna together. Whites, Negroes, Jews—everybody. There is no distinctions and yet, down here on earth, all the nations hate each other and fight each other, and every one of them persecutes the Jews.[25]

Mark Twain exposes the pretense of brotherly love in the human creature and ends his soliloquy on a humorous note—"yet every pious person adores that heaven and wants to get into it, he really does, now isn't that marvelous? And when he is in a heavenly rapture, he thinks that if he can only get up there, he would take that whole populace to his heart and hug and hug and hug."[26]

Holbrook postpones the delivery of his punch line with a long and purposeful pause. He relieves the serious reception of his message about equality by equating man's creation with another forebearer in the evolutionary chain, stating, "I wonder if God invented man because he was disappointed in the monkey?"[27]

Holbrook as Mark Twain reports his imagined success in training a variety of animals to live peacefully together in a cage, but relates that in a similar experiment with an Irish Catholic, Presbyterian, Turk, Methodist, Buddhist and a Salvation Army Colonel, these human creatures killed one another over theological details. Mark Twain's skepticism about the value of religion and man's hypocrisy are enumerated forcefully:

> Man is the only animal that deals in the atrocity of war. He is the only one that for assorted wages, goes forth to exterminate his own kind. He has a motto for this, "Our country, right or wrong." Any man who fails to shout it is a traitor. . . . Man is the only patriot.[28]

Mark Twain links war-making and land acquisition behavior to the grand scheme of the human species:

> He sets himself apart in his own country under his own flag; sneers at the other nations; keeps uninformed assassins at heavy expense to grab slices of other people's countries and keep them from grabbing slices of his, with the result that there's not an acre of ground on the globe that's in the rightful possession of its rightful owner and in the intervals between campaigns, he washes the blood from his hands and works for the brotherhood of man, with his mouth. . . .[29]

George Carlin's comparison of athletic games to the larger world picture of territorial acquisition among nations makes the same points as Holbrook's routine:

> Football is weird anyway, man. Football is. . . . What is football? Our national pastime game now. And what is it really except eleven guys line up and beat the shit out of the other guys and take their land. It's a land acquisition game. Except we take it 10 yards at a time. That's what we did to the Indi-

ans—work them a little at a time. First in Pennsylvania; Midwest is next to go. . . .[30]

As an artistic construction composed of truth and distortion, the standup comedian's routine in and of itself will not yield up to students of culture its corroborative insights about America *verbatim*. It is not an exact mirror image of American culture, for the standup comedian does not relate his experiences and observations with literal accuracy. Relevant cultural evidence from factual information and transmuted impressions are interwoven skillfully into the comic's humorous conventions. The comedian's texts can be examined for what is expressive and revealing about the content of minds. Sociological forces at work in the material, glimpsed through character portrayal, mode of expression and attitudes imbedded in dialogue, can be analyzed for preoccupations individually held by the comedian or those entertained by a broader segment of Americans. Distinct character types brought to artistic life by American humorists can be examined as potential embodiments of their place in American society as participants or alienated beings. Character types may also express the comedian's general awareness of social class as it operates in American society.[31]

Stances of moral judgment in characters may chart the boundaries of what the comedian or segments of his culture perceive to be the normative outlines of good or bad human behavior. Those stances may bracket the value system endorsed by the comedian or the segment of society for whom he or she speaks. For example, regarding his boyhood in Hannibal, Missouri, Samuel Clemens peppered his literary works with characters reminiscent of his beloved hometown. Remembering his observations of the different experiences of Blacks and whites in Hannibal, he came to regard Blacks with compassion and rejected the hypocrisy of orthodox religion with contempt. His work experiences on Mississippi River steamboats brought him into contact with a collage of American types from all strata of society. He married into a prominent New York family which regarded him as a maverick shaped by less than a genteel tradition. He was accorded by his in-laws less than full acceptance. His maverick status followed the Southwestern humorist into established Eastern literary circles where he was a member. All of these conditioning experiences were catalysts for the way Mark Twain depicted characters, differentiated and introduced regional dialects into his literary writings.[32]

Many standup comedians are quick to detect the manifest theme(s) of their culture and the behavior enacted in their society. The penetrating culture critic also uncovers places where covert culture traits may be operating. The researcher of standup comedians' records and live performances can look for a projection of covert culture through the figurative modes of expression —the metaphors and imagery found in spoken words. As psychologists have studied lingual and graphic expressions to detect the unconscious associations of individuals, so systems of imagery and metaphor recurring in imaginative constructions—written, verbal and visual—can be analyzed for the artist's responses, conscious or unconscious, to covert traits of culture.[33] The unreflective artist may merely betray and depict covert traits of culture without analysis. The more sensitive and critical artist will discover, analyze and account for the discrepancies found in their observations of how things *should* operate in the culture but *don't.* The comedian as licensed spokesperson can grasp and articulate contradictions in the culture of which other Americans may be unaware or reluctant to openly acknowledge.

The way the artist's message is heard and incorporated into individual Americans' sense of self and country, past and present, through a few defined images, deserves closer consideration by culture researchers.[34] The standup comedian may implant in his audience what he wants them to believe about the American past, present or future. Also, the context in which a social drama takes place has as much to do with the reception of the message as with how the artist intended the message. The comedian can use his power as a symbol-maker, interpreter and articulator of information to transform past and present experiences into a new cultural focus. As an example, one can imagine the extreme contrast in receptivity to Hal Holbrook's recreation of Mark Twain's views about slavery experienced by participants at a 1981 Ku Klux Klan rally, on the one hand, or if Holbrook had performed the same routine before a college audience at UCLA in 1965. While not all individuals in each audience would share the same pictures of reality, the range from outrage to delight might be somewhat predictable, as the following comedy routine was enacted by Holbrook:

> In my school board days, I had no aversion to slavery. I was not aware that there was anything wrong with it. Local papers said nothing about it. The local pope had taught us that God approved of it, that it was a holy thing, that the doubter need only look in the Bible if he wished to settle his mind. And then the texts were read aloud to us to make the matter sure. If there were passages in the Bible that disapproved of slavery, they were not quoted by our pastors.[35]

Holbrook pauses and reflects. In a lowered voice, as if he is sharing some secret insights with his rapt audience, he continues:

> I wonder how they could lie (emphasis) so—a result of practice, no doubt, and the serene confidence of a Christian with four aces. When I was a boy, I saw a brave gentleman deride and insult a lynching mob and drive it away. For the truth is that no mob has any sand in it in the presence of a man known to be splendidly brave. But where shall such brave men be found? If physically brave will do, well that may be easy. They can be found by the cargo! But morally brave men and women who can face up to church-going gangs of hooded murderers, there don't seem to be very many morally brave people left in stock. . . .[36]

The
Humor
Prism
in 20th-
Century
America

100

He caps a serious revelation with an incongruous solution, ridiculing the enemy. He corrals the community-destroying racism by isolation for the audience to see. What a mocking spectacle is human hatred. Holbrook relates:

> "Why don't we import American missionaries from China and send them into the lynching field? . . . Why those Chinese people are universally conceded to be honest, industrious and honorable. Why don't we give those poor things a rest, huh? Besides, every convert runs the risk of catching our own civilization. We want to think twice before we encourage a risk like that![37]

The social context in which imaginative material occurs in a cultural drama should be examined carefully. Humor has many levels of meanings—some intended by the standup comedian and others discovered by the experiencer in the audience. The seasoned standup comedian will be very aware of his audience's composition and of subtle elements of information operating in the cultural setting. I noticed how standup comedians and their emcee at Garvin's Supper Club in Washington, D.C., mingled with their audiences before a performance to discover audience characteristics. The emcee warmed up the group for the headliners who followed. "Know who these people are," was good advice from veteran comedian Rodney Dangerfield to novice Robert Klein in Klein's early days as a standup comedian. The emcee gathered information about the audience's composition with probing questions, such as "Where are you from? Anyone here from New York? New Jersey? (Snickers emanated from the audience because of the connotation of cultural inferiority associated with New Jersey.) Anyone here Jewish? Does anyone work for the government? Oh, what do you do for a living? What do you think of Reagan—did you vote for him?" The emcee let respondents talk about themselves, revealing their secrets.

The emcee's own comedy routine at Garvin's Supper Club was helped by his quick ethnography of the audience, as he linked association upon association from the informational clues the audience transmitted. He connected appropriate topics in a meaningful chain of associations, imagery and words. This framing and editing ability aided the comedian in aiming referential and social meanings to his audience's general understanding level. Audience and comedian moved in a rhythm of explanation form and met response. Ideas became charged up in this dialogue process.[38] I observed how the emcee and other comedians following the warm-up discarded issues and explanation forms that met little response in the audience and utilized ideas and polarizing strategies that commanded attention and stimulated further meanings. Scatological jokes especially received thunderclap laughs. After the show these comedians said that drug, sex and political jokes met a quick response from the young Washingtonian supper club crowd at Garvin's.

From the comedian's act, the student of culture can note the categorical inventions the artist uses to classify and organize experience. The researcher should be particularly aware of how dissimilar objects and events are treated as if they are related and equivalent, minimizing information overload as the comedian sets the scene for laughs.

Comedians and cultural anthropologists look at the way stylized and formal language modes reflect and affect social roles. The comedian can relate associations and language by matching distinct social class representatives with dialects. For instance,

The
Humor
Prism
in 20th-
Century
America

101

Jonathan Winters noted and demonstrated to his audience how a slowed down Walter Brennan accent becomes John F. Kennedy's. The humor imbedded in that observation relates associations with certain regionalisms which in turn connote social inferiority and superiority. The dynamics of status and deference forms, reflective of the culture's hierarchy, can be illuminated by the comedian. He can portray someone in a lower status position with an exaggerated deferential voice tone, responding to someone more highly ranked. Comic reversals may be enacted to spoof the cultural rule. Specialized professional and occupational vocabularies lampooned by a comedian before an audience who uses such vocabulary can be an identity-bonding communicative act. Links between speech and sexual roles in prescribed verbal behavior can offer glimpses into fundamental beliefs about masculinity and femininity held by segments of American society.

Language is important to both the standup comedian and the cultural anthropologist in its capacity to shape interactive situations, effect bonding and mediate conflict. George Carlin emphasizes the importance of language in one of his routines, when he notes:

The
Humor
Prism
in 20th-
Century
America

102

> Words take care of you. Names are a part of words. Hey, names have real impact. Names have emotional values, especially names that are attached to products or people or really things that are bigger than just stuff. . . . Football team names . . . I would like to root for the Cincinnati Mice. The Hawaii Hamsters. The Georgia Gerbils. . . . Talking about the name George . . . George is a dumb-ass name for it's way down on the list of getting laid just by the sound of your name.[39]

Carlin examines the variations and forms of defensive tactics taken for the protection of the group. He has obviously scanned the newspaper and listened intently to television news reports for different expressions of human aggression described in this routine:

> And to kind of wind up the news tonight, we'll take a look at the news hostility scoreboard. Find out how we're treating each other around the world. According to our scoreboard, we've got 4 civil wars going on right now, 2 brush-fire wars, 4 vest-pocket wars, 4 wars of liberation, 2 police actions, 16 revolutions, 95 commando operations, 52 border clashes,

400 guerrilla operations, 237 cease-fire violations, 44 surprise attacks, 6 outside aggressions, 6 internal upheavals, 3
protective reactionary strikes, 10 counter-insurgencies, 21 violent destructions, 30 warlike acts, 906 hostile incidents, 10
arms races, 18 deliberate provocations, 61 threats to security,
9 dangerous escalations, 6 heightenings of tension, 12 bellig-
erent moves, 2 military confrontations, 14 heated exchanges,
17 reprisals, 3 powder kegs, 2 tinder boxes and an ultima-
tum.[40]

Talking about man's power to destroy his fellow man, he
indicates by voice tone, eye contact, subtle body English and
rapid fire delivery that he is making a social statement which
should be taken with levity, upon first hearing. The standup comedian will aim rhetorical flash words to connect his audience
into the subtleties going on in the situations he describes. He
builds a sense of membership and reinforcement among a group
through his manipulation of language, realizing that not everyone in the audience will share his picture of reality.[41]

The standup comedian and the cultural anthropologist look
for cultural patterns, associations, meanings and values in their
observations of human life. They consider the status of marriage,
new lifestyles, received notions of male and female nature, qualities attributed to adolescents and older Americans, lines of authority existing between parent and child, wealth and status recognition, restrictions imposed on the expression of hostile
impulses within and without the home privacy definitions and
rights, the ordering of physical space, the measurement and con-
firmation of status, as well as self-image, through clothing and
other material goods, property distribution, ownership rules and
the social implications of family.[42]

As the standup comedian describes everyday artifacts and
human behavior, social context can be understood by considering how people feel "about this or that object. What kind of values did they place upon it? What associations, voluntary or invol-
untary, did it call up in them? How might it influence members
of the household?"[43] In one of their routines, Mel Brooks and
Carl Reiner play with the values associated with an artifact familiar to most people in twentieth-century America. Playing an artist, Mel Brooks is interviewed by Carl Reiner in his studio:

The
Humor
Prism
in 20th-
Century
America

103

I notice that you sculpt too. . . . There is a metallic sculpture there that is very interesting. It's just a series of wires in a grid-like effect. Oh, you mean above the door? That's called the air conditioner. The Fedders Company, dey make it and it's very beautiful. Your paintings are very abstract, I notice. Yes, but dey don't blow air out.[44]

Looking at society in a "culture as drama"[45] perspective, so-cial historian John Demos noted that the "most intimate of all the basic theatres of human interaction is the home."[46] This inti-mate theatre is the backdrop against which many standup come-dians play their routines. Bill Cosby, for instance, talks about everyday objects, rules and human behaviors obtaining in Ameri-can homes as he describes child-rearing practices in relation to his daughter, Erin:

We parents ask dumb questions. Therefore, we get dumb answers. For instance, your child is coming across your kitchen floor dragging a tomato on a string. . . . "What are you doing?" [tone of disapproval]. Now it is quite obvious the child is dragging a rotten tomato across the floor on a string. . . . The child answers you very intelligently, now real-izing that they must be doing something wrong. The child says, "Nothing." You have nowhere to go after that. There are no more questions you can ask. They'll "nothing" you to death, man.[47]

The cultural anthropologist and select standup comedians are interested in how humans style their behavior through lan-guage and master their world through symbols. In a live perfor-mance, one notes Bill Cosby's style of utilizing facial expressions, voice tone and other gestures in conveying meanings and in teaching children appropriate and inappropriate rules of behav-ior. He describes in some of his routines the categories and rules that children learn tacitly, describing how children observe adult patterns of behavior, how they hypothesize the rules being used, how they try out imperfect imitations of adult behavior, and how they revise their hypotheses after they are corrected by adults. The result of this teaching is a child talking and behaving in terms of the prescriptions of their behavior. Cosby draws from his own experience with his daughter Erin to get at these points.

Certain standup comedians' routines can be regarded as a kind of behavior pattern moving an audience through a mental fact-finding journey as artists and audience look at the overt and covert cultural forces shaping America. These routines are a body of adult social opinion. They show insights into widely accepted and sometimes rarely acknowledged social and personal values and beliefs. These beliefs may be held by many people in a society or by a maverick group with a competing concept of reality. This portrait of the times in which it was created reflects the subjective intentions of men, social and moral concepts, values, fears, anxieties and doubts operating in segments of American culture at conscious and subconscious levels.

What the artist praises and blames through good and bad characters can also give clues to changes in society. As the comedian listens to Americans thinking and responding in their particular settings, some of these responses catch his or her attention. They may demand a more probing analysis for they might be out of synchronism with America's articulated ideals of freedom and equality for all citizens. Dick Gregory, for example, is especially attuned to the structure of racist institutions that may handicap minority segments of society. The comedian's performance may give voice and resonance to conflicting strains of thought or baffling human behavior occurring in American culture. A graphic portrayal of patterns of psychological response enacted in past or present American society as presented by the comedian may make these patterns visible. These depictions may cause reflection about one's self and society as an unintentional by-product of the performance as connections not seen before are imparted to individuals in an audience.

The setting of audience performance behavior is primarily a time of pure sensory enjoyment where the attention of the individual "may wander away into the stream of consciousness, a curious mixture of language and inner imagery."[48] I suggest that an audience may be engaged in some reflexive stocktaking as the comedian exposes the alienations, injustices, incongruities and immoralities that contaminate human life. As an anonymous cover liner from *The Golden Age of Comedy, Volume I,* suggests, "In night clubs these days you get group therapy, prayer meetings, sociological community. You get thinking . . . you know your mind is doing something, and, you know you're enjoying it, but it isn't until later that you realize that you've been thinking."[49] George Carlin's producer, Tom Berman, noted in a Carlin cover liner that "as his [Carlin's] humor is dissected, one begins to

The
Humor
Prism
in 20th-
Century
America

105

marvel at how deceiving a first listen to his comedy can be. What had seemed funny or outrageous or ridiculous becomes much more than that after repeated listening. For when the laughs are over, there is much to think about, much to be taken seriously."[50]

Reflection about one's self and culture, to be sure, may be an unintentional by-product of being in a certain comedian's audience and not the comedian's primary motivation for coming before an audience. The relaxed scene may especially reserve an opening for indulging in reflection. The individual may imagine himself in the artistic situation enacted by the comedian or in a situation of his own fantasy construction, completely separate from what is happening on stage. When Bill Cosby, for instance, describes the inner feelings of winning, losing, belonging or being excluded, as a professional athlete, his audience may be involved in fragments of remembered sounds, visual images, sensations or emotions,[51] triggered by the comedian. The audience member may recognize himself or herself as a player engaged in a past or present human comedy or tragedy similar to the one described on stage. That person may enjoy the routine because of his own distance from the reality described by the comedian.

Audience members may recall with a sense of superiority a positive social encounter where they felt shamed and inferior. These positive or painful experiences may be re-experienced by the audience, one step removed from immediacy. They may be refelt in a way of amusement or twinges of anger at past unpleasant encounters. The comedian can create an environment in which past and present feelings can be rechanneled into a new cultural focus as he or she mediates these feelings through the vehicle of humor.

Reversing passively experienced events in a revision of reality, adult play may allow the experiencer, in this instance, actively to control circumstances, keep up courage and envision feelings of success and achievement. This allows one to cope with less-than-ideal life conditions. The inversion of reality can result in a healing catharsis. It is an important life-coping strategy. By breaking down the rules and behaviors ingredient in cultural situations, the comedian may increase the participant's awareness of the tacit cultural knowledge with which he operates.

In the way that membership in a special group is many times celebrated in initiation rites to publicly announce an individual's membership in that association of people, so a partici-

pant at a performance may identify with the symbols and concepts accompanying a particular comedian's message. An
individual may share a belief in this message with many others.
The inner states of becoming, changing, belonging and opposing
may be described by the comedian as he proclaims himself in
agreement or opposition to the values of dominant society. The
act of being in an audience can reinforce a special feeling of
membership. Counterculture comedians such as Cheech and
Chong, George Carlin and Dick Gregory speaking to a liberal
college audience about polarizing issues may draw a more uni-
form audience than in a nightclub act. A performance in Las
Vegas may tend to draw a diverse segment of the population who
may or may not share the artist's political and social beliefs. Comedians must aim messages with a broad appeal to a diverse audience rather than an esoteric message to engage their attention.
The nightclub audience may have come purely to be entertained. Thus, different kinds of identity bonding experiences will
happen with different groups and the comedian will vary his or
her message accordingly.

In Las Vegas, an individual may be distracted from the comedian's message by the anticipated allure of the gaming tables
after the performance or by anger felt at sums of money lost
prior to the performance. An accompaniment of leisure activities
for some people is an intake of drugs or liquor and anticipated
sexual encounters which may further distract the participant
from the communicative act on stage. It is also possible that the
performance may have stimulated a good time with no particularly important accompanying thought processes or the participant may have been made uncomfortable by the comic's beliefs
and responded by tuning out part of the message or even by fall-
ing asleep.

The audience may come to understand something about
what it means to be handicapped by society's sexual and cultural
rules pertaining to sex or minority status through examples of
those situations enacted by the standup comedian. What happens
to the individual's "consciousness when he or she attempts to
understand the alien cultural knowledge of an unfamiliar
group"[52] is posed by cultural anthropologist John Caughey. A
fragment of a Dick Gregory routine demonstrates his anger as an
aware Black toward a renowned white sociologist whom he ac-
cuses of misunderstanding Blacks. Gregory is angry because he
feels these statements by white "experts" perpetuate misconcep-

The
Humor
Prism
in 20th-
Century
America

107

tions, misinformation, misinterpretations and overtly prejudicial
reporting about minorities. He makes some particularly stinging
criticisms about Daniel Moynihan:

> We tired of a white racist system thinking for us. Look at
> that Moynihan freak—he really lets hisself think he knows
> more about niggers than we do. . . . Moynihan may be a hell
> of a sociologist when he writes about white folks but he
> doesn't know nothing about us. He proved that on his first
> little outrage—talking about the matriarchal society. Talking
> about the Black woman being stronger than the Black man.
> . . . My Black woman never will be stronger than me. Do you
> understand your insanity?[53]

Constructions of "playlike worlds" visited in a reflexive
mental state outside the confines of objective social life may represent the ideal culture America falls short of achieving or as
John Caughey calls them—"American Dream Images."[54] His
scholarly attention to this body of mental images bears some
similarity to folklorists' work involving an examination of children's folklore. In this body of scholarship, folklorists look for
clues about how children deal with taboo subjects and feelings
they may be unable to individually confront by examining images imbedded in superstition, games, jeers, rhymes, songs,
pranks and stories.[55] Because responsibility rests so heavily on
most adults and actual realities of self and the world often fall
short of the culture's idealized versions of appearance, personal
ability, career and living standards, the act of entering playlike
worlds may help many adults, as Caughey suggests, maintain a
less-than-satisfying reality or catalyze an impetus for social
change. He suggests that "painful imaginings often goad people
into more responsible conduct as well."[56] In our work- and
production-oriented culture, reflexive time has yet to be fully
appreciated for the counterbalance it provides to work experience.

Some anthropologists and standup comedians have carried
their critiques of aspects of their culture into advocate action.
Anthropologist James Spradley effected a more humane understanding of urban nomads along with law enforcement policy
changes by presenting the findings of his ethnography relating
to "hobos" to the Seattle City Council. In a similar spirit, Dick
Gregory has been jailed for his participation in civil rights
marches, demonstrations and hunger fasts. He has used his po-

sition as licensed spokesman to make his audiences aware of the way power structures work in American society against minority groups as he perceives the dynamics of American society. He says of himself: "I've got to make jokes about myself, before I can make jokes about them and their society—that way, they can't hate me. Comedy is friendly relations."[57]

From attention to newspaper articles, television newscasts, listening to and watching people in ordinary and extraordinary life dramas, the comedian gathers material for routines. Jonathan Winters confided that he gets ideas from history, people, art and ordinary situations encountered in the course of a day. Nat Hentoff, reviewing Dick Gregory's career on "The Best of Dick Gregory" album cover, noted about Gregory's manner of obtaining material:

> I never saw anybody read a newspaper the way Gregory did. . . . He dug for truth. He dug hard. . . . He would pounce on some item, often small and obscurely placed, hand it to his researcher and tell him where it could be linked with some other equally fragmentary piece of information. And from that gradually evolving edifice of interpretation would come startingly funny, and revealing, two or three minutes in the next night's performance. . . . In time, of course, more than a two-minute turn would come from relentless piecing together of half-leads, scraps, shadows of facts and other detritus of the news, which most people would have ignored, if they had seen them at all.[58]

In the same way, an anthropologist may spend many days of fieldwork carefully examining what, at first appearance, may seem to be some minor elements of inconsequential human behavior. These instances of inconsequential human behavior, ideas or artifacts, when pieced together with insights from other societies studied, may by their interconnections lead to a profound discovery in the field of anthropology.

The comedian, like the anthropologist, can reveal the structure of institutions that may anger or handicap certain segments of society. By setting up these revelations humorously, the comedian can provide a healthy release of tension, discomfort and anger. The comedian can make feelings present and experienced by an audience humorously visible. For instance, Bill Cosby suggested to his Las Vegas gambling casino audience in one record that the house was fixed. Many individuals in the audience already knew that. He tells them, nonetheless:

> I happen to know from years of working here that it's all on their side and if you don't think it is, then just go out there and see where all the money is. I mean they make their own chips. Let's face it, we don't make our own money and they're just the opposite of us. They got all their money laid right out there so you can see it. . . . And they say you can have it, but. *But*, that's a heavy "but." *But*. That's the heaviest but you'll ever see.[59]

Cosby goes on to describe a trip to Las Vegas as a woman's opportunity to spend time alone with her husband and to display her new wardrobe. She finds herself elegantly attired at the gaming tables only to fall asleep while her husband enjoys the dominant role in gambling, oblivious to the renewal of the courtship role his wife had hoped for in this leisure situation away from the home front. The comedian can tap into the felt annoyance, anger, outrage, disappointment and indignation the customers may be actually feeling in this situation from their different perceptions of what the occasion means in the way of expected behavior. The comedian can release these feelings by airing them with the group.

The standup comedian and the cultural anthropologist look deeper beneath actually feeling in this situation from their different perceptions of what the occasion means in the way of expected behavior. The comedian can release these feelings by airing them with the group.

The standup comedian and the cultural anthropologist look deeper beneath the surface of human behavior at the thought forces at work in a society. They ask what is really at work in human consciousness. They examine the mental molecules that make up social structures. We need with them a kind of understanding which bestows a power to see from many perspectives so we can order our world with wisdom and perception. In this rapidly changing, multilayered society of pluralistic heritages which is America, the individual seems controlled by seemingly implacable and impersonal forces. These forces appear to govern even the most intimate aspect of man's life. The humorous response counters this sense of anomie by keeping one's humanity and sensitivity to self and world intact.

The comedian and the anthropologist share a way of seeing. This involves the capacity to stand outside themselves and to emphasize with people who are different in order to more fully understand their actions and beliefs. Perhaps the standup comedian has taken the place, in our present culture, of the storyteller in primitive cultures—the grandfather or grandmother who could relate an experience through a story or tribal myth to communicate cultural knowledge. In this way children learned the values of the tribe.

The comedian's routines are stories for the adult and like the myths in primitive cultures may answer his need for explanations of good and evil in human experience, help him manage fear and anxiety and by constant admonitions of what happens when there is social chaos, underline the normative outlines of his culture. They come to view their own culture in the way an anthropologist approaches an alien culture. From this perspective and the revelations that result, many standup comedians have all the markings of fine culture critics.

Notes

1. Edward T. Hall, *The Silent Language* (New York: Doubleday, 1973), p. 52.
2. Peter Berger, *Invitation to Sociology: A Humanistic Perspective* (New York: Doubleday Anchor, 1973), p. 125.
3. Hall, p. 30.
4. Bernard Bowron, Leo Marx, and Arnold Rose. "Literature and Covert Culture," *American Quarterly* IX, 4 (Winter 1956), pp. 380–81.
5. John Demos, *A Little Commonwealth: Family Life in Plymouth Colony* (New York: Oxford Univ. Press, 1970), p. 12.
6. Bob Newhart, *The Best of Bob Newhart* (California: Warner Brothers, 1967).
7. Ibid.
8. Ibid.
9. John L. Caughey, "Ethnography, Introspection and Reflexive Culture Studies," *Prospects: A Journal of American Culture Studies* (New York: Burt Franklin and Company, Inc., 1982), pp. 115–39.
10. George Carlin, *An Evening with Wally Lando Featuring Bill Slaszo* (New York: RCA Records, 1972).
11. Bill Cosby's "The Golfer" from Flip Wilson, Redd Foxx, Bill Cosby and Dick Gregory, *Just Four Laughs*, Volume 2 (New York: Sceptor Records, Inc., 1972).
12. Bowron, Marx and Rose, p. 377.
13. Ibid., p. 378.
14. Rusty Warren, *Sexplosion* (Cover Liner). (Los Angeles: Crescendo Record Company, 1977).
15. Carlin.

The
Humor
Prism
in 20th-
Century
America

111

16. Dick Gregory's "Confused" from Wilson, Foxx, Cosby and Dick Gregory, *Just Four Laughs*, Volume 2.

17. Michael Benamon and Charles Carameilo, eds. "Frame, Flow and Reflection: Ritual and Drama as Public Liminality" by Victor Turner. *Performance in Postmodern Cultures* (Madison: Coda Press, 1977).

18. Clifford Geertz, *The Interpretation of Cultures* (New York: Basic Books, 1973), p. 16.

19. Elenore and Smith Bowen (Laura Bohannan), *Return to Laughter* (New York: Doubleday, 1964), p. 82.

20. Ibid., p. 254.

21. Warren.

22. Phil Berger, *The Last Laugh: The World of the Standup Comics* (New York, 1975), p. 19.

23. Ibid., pp. 151–52.

24. Hal Holbrook, *Mark Twain Tonight!* (New York: Columbia Records CBS, Inc., n.d.).

25. Ibid.

26. Ibid.

27. Ibid.

28. Ibid.

29. Ibid.

30. Carlin.

31. Henry Nash Smith, "Can 'American Studies' Develop a Method?" *American Quarterly* IX, 2 (Summer 1957), pp. 200–201.

32. Max J. Herzberg, *The Reader's Encyclopedia of American Literature* (New York: Crowell, 1962), pp. 1159–62.

33. Bowron, Marx and Rose, p. 380.

34. For an in-depth discussion of reconstructing patterns of past behavior and belief using imaginative literature as historical evidence see R. Gordon Kelly, "Literature and the Historian." *American Quarterly* XXVII 2 (May 1972), pp. 141–59.

35. Holbrook.

36. Ibid.

37. Ibid.

38. For an analysis of political communications see Marvin Meyers, *The Jacksonian Persuasion: Politics and Belief* (California: Stanford Univ. Press, 1960).

39. Carlin.

40. Carlin.

41. Meyers.

42. These categories are examined by John Demos in his study, *A Little Commonwealth*.

43. Demos.

44. Gene Wise uses the term "culture as drama" in his article "Paradigm Dramas" in "American Studies: A Cultural and Institutional History of the Movement," *American Quarterly* Bibliography Issue, Vol. 31, No. 3 (1979). He notes that he borrowed the metaphor from the theater as a mode of explanation to describe how ideas operate within the cultural context of historical situations. In this explanation mode, ideas ingredient in historical situations are viewed as a series of dramatic acts which play on wider cultural scenes or historical stages. By choosing this metaphor, Wise em-

The
Humor
Prism
in 20th-
Century
America

112

phasizes the dynamic image and trans-actional quality of ideas through an interplay of scene, actors and audience in continual dialogue.
45. Wise.
46. Demos, p. 46.
47. Bill Cosby, *For Adults Only* (New York: MCA Records,Inc., 1971).
48. Caughey, p. 4.
49. Warren.
50. Tom Berman from *Take-Offs and Put-Ons* cover liner (New York: RCA Corporation, 1972).
51. Caughey pp. 15–18.
52. Caughey, pp. 31–32.
53. Dick Gregory, *The Best of Dick Gregory*, Vol. 1 (New York: Tomato Records, 1977).
54. Caughey.
55. Mary and Herbert Knapp, *One Potato, Two Potato* ___ . *The Secret Education of American Children* (New York: Norton).
56. Caughey, p. 24.
57. Gregory.
58. Gregory.
59. Cosby.

Records

Allen Woody. *The Night Club Years (1964–1968)*. United Artists Records, Inc., 1976.
Berman, Shelly. *Outside Shelly Berman*. Verve, MGV 15007, 1959.
Bruce, Lenny. *Lenny Bruce at Carnegie Hall*. United Artists, UA 9800, n.d.
Carlin, Geroge. *An Evening with Wally Lando Featuring Bill Slaszo*. Little David, LD 1008, 1975.
Carlin, George. *FM & AM*, Little David, LD 7214, 1972.
Carlin, George. *Take-Offs and Put-Ons*. RCA Victor LSP 3372, 1967.
Cheech and Chong. *Big Bambu*. Odyssey. OD 77014, 1972.
Cosby, Bill. *For Adults Only*. United Artists, MCA 533, n.d.
Cosby, Bill. *Inside the Mind of Bill Cosby*. United Artists, UNI 73139, 1972.
Fireside Theatre. *I Think We're All Bozos on This Bus*. Columbia, C 30737, 1971.
Fireside Theatre. *Dear Friends*. Columbia KG 31099, 1972.
Gardner, Brother Dave. *Kick Thy Own Self*. RCA Victor, LPM 2239, 1960.
Gardner, Brother Dave. *The Golden Age of Comedy*. Vol. 1, Evolution 3013, 1972.
Gardner, Brother Dave. *The Great Radio Feuds*. Columbia KC 33241, n.d.
Gregory, Dick. *The Best of Dick Gregory*. Vol. 1. Tomato Records, 1977.
Holbrook, Hal. *Mark Twain Tonight!* Columbia Records, OS-3080, n.d.
Holbrook, Hal. *Just Like Old Times. Genuine Original Recordings of Radio's Most Famous Funny Men*. The Radiola Co., 1970.
Just Four Laughs. Vol. 2 (Flip Wilson, Redd Foxx, Bill Cosby, Dick Gregory). Scepter Records, Inc., SPS 5105, 1972.
Lehrer, Tom. *That Was the Year That Was*. Reprise, 1965.
Martin, Steve. *A Wild and Crazy Guy*. Warner Brothers Records, Inc., 1978.
Minkin, William and Sheridan, William. *The Washington Hillbillies*. Casablanca Records and Filmworks, Inc., 1977.
Newhart, Bob. *The Best of Bob Newhart*. Warner Brothers, W 1672, 1967.
Pryor, Richard. *Is It Something I Said?* Reprise, RS 2227, n.d.
Pryor, Richard. *Are You Serious?* Laff Records, LAFF A196, 1976.
Pryor, Richard. *That Nigger Is Crazy*. Reprise, RS 2241, n.d.

Sherman, Allan. *Allan Sherman's Mother Presents My Son, The Folk Singer.* Warner Brothers, W 1475, 1962.

Sherman, Allan. *Son of Jest Like Old Times: More Genuine Original Recordings of Radio's Most Famous Funny Men.* The Radiola Company, 1970.

Tomlin, Lily. *This Is a Recording.* Polydor, PD 244055, 1971.

Tomlin, Lily. *Twenty-Five Years of Recorded Comedy.* Warner Brothers Records, 3BX 3131.

Wilson, Flip. *Flippin'.* Liberty Records, LP 24012, n.d.

Winters, Jonathan. *Another Day, Another World.* Verve V15032, 1962.

Winters, Jonathan. *Movies Are Better Than Ever.* Verve, V 15037, 1964.

Youngman, Henny. *The Best of Henny Youngman.*

The
Humor
Prism
in 20th-
Century
America

114

III.

Multicultural Spaces

The Urban Landscape

Joseph Boskin

To paraphrase a memorable expression by the late historian, Richard Hofstadter, American humor was born in the country and moved to the city in the twentieth century.[1] The sounds of national laughter that once echoed the language and style of a rural and small town landscape, though not quite silent, are certainly quaintly muted. Although a portion of its original subject matter remains intact, contemporary American humor expresses little of its initial form and flavor. When the humor of pre-industrial America is evoked, it is frequently done in tones either nostalgic or derisive.

Yet there appears, on occasion, a sudden reminder of the type of humor that once embraced the environment and generated native laughter. Garrison Keillor's *A Prairie Home Companion*, on radio and in print for over a decade in the 1970s and '80s, rekindled the satiric embers of a quirky and humane community and was an umbilical connection to the powerful tradition of small town expression. Lake Wobegon is a marvelous, indeed almost mystical, connection to a universe—"that time forgot, that the decades can't improve"—that possessed a different set of rules of engagement of time and space, language and relations.

There are, moreover, other salient exceptions to the contemporary scene. Regional differences clearly produce different comedy, as do differing personalities. Talk show hosts—new breed entertainers who attempt to brew frothiness with seriousness—demonstrate markedly divergent styles. Joan Rivers, Johnny Carson and David Brenner, for example, reach out for broad audiences, yet their approaches reflect not only idiosyncrasies but also geographical backgrounds that range from the seaboard to the Midwest, from the small town to the massive city. Of the various hosts, however, Carson, whose *Tonight* show has been

The
Humor
Prism
in 20th-
Century
America

117

This essay was originally published in *Urban Resources*, vol. 4, no. 3 (Spring 1987). Reprinted with permission.

embraced by fervent audiences from the 1960s to the present, represents a combination of town and metropolis. Raised in a small Nebraska town, Carson has spent the bulk of his adult life in New York and Los Angeles, with his humor a reflection of these polar influences. His enduring appeal is due in large part to the innocence of a rural style contained within an urbane delivery.

Country and city had earlier combined in that remarkable group that converged in the 1920s at the now-legendary Round Table at the Algonquin Hotel in New York. The core group of journalists, playwrights, columnists, critics, novelists, short story writers, poets, and entertainers, who employed humor as a language in their conversations and personal relationships, represented a unique fusion of the small town with the big city. Reflective of the 1920s, that pivotal decade of the century, they were aptly labeled by critic Carl Van Doren as the "town wits" operating in an urban setting.

Exceptions aside, the transformation of the locale and character of humor in this century has been extraordinary both in its scope and its totality. Not surprisingly, the change both mirrors and facilitates the social and demographic alterations felt throughout American culture. Among the most dominating social features of this century has been a pervasive urban quality that has hosted a myriad of ethnic and racial groups, particularly Jewish and Black. This amalgam of place, movement, and subculture has created a special type of humor strophe. Yet, even apart from the influence of these groups, it has been the spirit and exactitude of the city itself that has produced the transformation. It is the city with its definitive character and special demands, its particular rhythm and manner, in short, its dominating presence that has stamped on humor its singular distinction in this century.

In what ways? There is, initially, the form itself. The laughter of pre-industrial society was essentially set within a story. In a culture that was based on a confluence of the oral and literate, a narrative expression was of primary import. Plot and joke were entwined. The essence of Mark Twain's humor was contained within the story, not apart from it. This was, of course, the way of the storyteller, now one of America's endangered species. Twain's woven response to the report of his demise in 1906 is a gentle reminder of this lore:

The
Humor
Prism
in 20th-
Century
America

118

This reminds me—nine years ago when we were living in Tedworth Square, London, a report was cabled to the American journals that I was dying. I was not the one. It was another Clemens, a cousin of mine, who was due to die but presently escaped by some chicanery or other characteristic of the tribe of Clemenses. The London representatives of the American papers began to flock in with American cables in their hands, to inquire into my condition. There was nothing the matter with me and each in his turn was astonished, and not gratified, to find me reading and smoking in my study and worth next to nothing as a text for transatlantic news. One of these men was a gentle and kindly and grave and sympathetic Irishman, who hid his disappointment the best he could and tried to look glad and told me that his paper, the *Evening Sun*, had cabled him that it was reported in New York that I was dead. What should he cable in reply? I said, "Say the report is exaggerated." He never smiled, but went solemnly away and sent the cable in those exact words. The remark hit the world pleasantly and to this day it keeps turning up, now and then, in the newspapers when people have occasion to discount exaggeration.

The next man was also an Irishman. He had his New York cablegram in his hand—from the *New York World*—and he was so evidently trying to get around that cable with invented softnesses and palliations that my curiosity was aroused and I wanted to see what the cable really did say. So when occasion offered I slipped it out of his hand. It said "If Mark Twain dying send five hundred words. If dead send a thousand."[2]

In contemporary society, the Mark Twains have given way to the Henny Youngmans. Subject matter is now largely disconnected, reflecting an often fragmented city style. Standup comics and talk show hosts—jumping from one subject to another in rapid, staccato fashion—mirror the swift and agitated movements of the city. Consider the typical routines of comedians over the past half-century. The number of subjects explored within a twenty-minute presentation reads like the Yellow Pages. To recall the comic's act requires near flawless memory and to grasp its thrust demands the rigors of Talmudic training. What is important is rather a particular tone, a comedic mode that conveys a persona—but the subject around which the act flows is secondary.

At the same time, the narrative style is not entirely a remnant of the past. In the acts of the late Sam Levinson, whose central theme was the family, as well as with Bill Cosby, Woody Allen, and Richard Pryor, there persists the storytelling mode. Cosby's approach is to extrapolate from his life those universal experiences, such as going to the dentist, feeding his children breakfast, or describing a hangover, while Allen concocts an absurdist situation that peers into political or social relationships, and Pryor roams widely into unfamiliar terrains, such as his psychological reaction to a heart attack, the voice of the German shepherd next door, or a cocaine inflammation. Yet, this narrative approach makes these four humorists peculiar to the current scene. Their intensely personal experiences reveal them to the public and provide a perspective that is largely absent in the majority of standup comics.

Form and time connect in humor, and time has been similarly altered by the city. Initially perceived as connecting to the seasons, and as being durational, modern time is inextricably bound to the factory in a mathematical way. The clock now directs work *and* play—and humor can never escape from either, particularly play. As the unceasingly moving conveyor belt and the computer have become the model for the industrial and post-industrial societies, so the outpouring joke and joke-cycle have become the essence of modern humor. Should there have been surprise in the 1970s when AT&T in New York City chose Henny Youngman to lead off its "Dial-A-Joke," a one-minute series to complement offerings which included "Dial-A-Prayer?" Youngman's routine is exemplary of most comics and hosts, as well as of the folk routine of jokes that pass through the grapevine across the country on a daily basis. Indeed, if Twain symbolizes the Era of the Tale, Youngman represents the Era of the One-Liner:

- I'm 66, and it takes me all night to do all what I used to do all night.
- My wife has an even disposition—miserable all the time.
- You go to a nudist wedding. You can always tell who the best man is.
- My friend in Texas was so rich he bought his dog a boy to play with.[3]

An outstanding feature of humor for the past four decades has been a series of unending joke-cycles: sick, elephant, light bulb, catastrophe and others. These cycles appear and disappear with a sudden burst of energy, reflecting a national grappling with bewildering events of a sizeable dimension. Who did not hear any of the hundreds of jokes that emanated in the '80s from a seemingly unending series of disasters—the drowning of actress Natalie Wood, the explosion of the spaceship Challenger, the downfall of presidential aspirants Senators Gary Hart and Joseph Biden, or the Wall Street debacle—almost instantly after they occurred? All are in the Youngman tradition:

- What's the only wood that doesn't float? Natalie Wood.
- Where did the Challenger crew spend its vacation? All over Florida.
- The Hart Affair: Watergate, Irangate, Tailgate.
- Biden called his staff together and told them that the only thing he has to fear is fear itself.
- What do you call a former Yuppie stockbroker? Waiter.[4]

As the city undergoes constant change, to such an extent that Tom Wolfe's title *You Can't Go Home Again* has taken on iconical status, so, too, has humor been carried far from its roots. To the current generation, even the humor of the fifties seems outmoded and unfunny. And the humor landscape assumes a more perplexing shape the farther one travels back in time. Contributing significantly to this change has been a communications system that literally encompasses all individuals and institutions. In the McLuhan sense, urban America has become an intimate village; it is no wonder that humor has become truly national in scope. Jokes traverse the country with such ease, energy, and repetition that they have an immediate effect on public policy. Johnny Carson's exposure on his program of the public's jokes about Gary Hart's fling or Joseph Biden's plagiarisms was the surest sign of the demise of two presidential campaigns. In facilitating the flow of humor, the city not only makes possible its spread and impact but also creates a special type of ambience. An important development of these influences is an urban community with its own insistent brand of laughter, a culture code of mirth.

Precisely what kind of ambience this is, though, is easier to describe than to analyze. To use a sports analogy, the difference between pre-industrial and contemporary humor is not unlike the difference between baseball and basketball. Both are unquestionably national events, but each reflects a different concept of time and space. Baseball is a game that developed unrelated to factory time—as Yogi Berra succinctly put it, "It ain't over till it's over"—or to the limitations of space. Basketball, on the other hand, is an urban sport locked into the industrial system—or, as the sports announcer excitedly declares, "The clock just ran out" —and played within a defined plot. Each game provides a distinctive atmosphere and requires a different mindset.

So it is, too, with the two major traditions of American humor. Pre-industrial focused on weaving a set of stories in which the foibles and fun of the folk combined; industrial concentrates on enumerating as many experiences as possible and sees its people overwhelmingly beset by powerful and whimsical forces. Sanford Pinsker cleverly traced these changes to December 1910, the year in which Twain died, and incisively noted that, "Not only had the locale shifted from the keelboat or Western campfire to the city street, but what a comic persona crowed about was more often ineptitude rather than prowess, weakness rather than strength, crippling inferiority rather than swaggering confidence." It's representative figures have been Charlie Chaplin's "Tramp," Robert Benchley's "Little Man," and Woody Allen's "Neurotic Everyman."[5]

Finally, humor's strategic thrust is unmistakably urban, the consequence of an infusion of Jewish and Black cultures. The transformation of a native humor that was originally English and Irish, rural and small town, began to give way under the heavy influence of entertainers and writers who poured into and wrenchingly adapted themselves to the large cities of the eastern and midwestern regions. Immigrant Jews from Eastern Europe in the early decades, later reinforced and enhanced by migrant Blacks from the South, forged a language and practice of humor to express their experiences as dual citizens. A kind of subversive intrusion reflecting minority status at first, the humor has eventually become mainstream, the culture's most dominant form. It is a humor aggressively wicked and sly, prodding and absurdist, bordering on catastrophe and gallows, and representative of the underdog. At the very least, it is meant not only to retaliate against one's oppressors but also to offset them through humorous strategies. As Mel Brooks wryly queried, "If your enemy is laughing, how can he bludgeon you to death?"[6]

Equally significant is that this humor is a scrupulous observer of American culture. It takes note of its flaws and describes them comedically, in ways that enable perspective on the one hand and call attention to its pejorative images on the other. So it was that comedian Dick Gregory in the early 1960s teasingly threatened to picket the U.S. Weather Bureau unless it named a hurricane after a black woman, "Beulah"; and Amiri Baraka and several friends mocked whites by eating watermelons on a busy Washington, D.C., thoroughfare during rush hour in full view of passing motorists.[7]

Minority humor has insisted in its laughter that American culture recognize its pluralism and diversity as well as its hypocrisies and contradictions. Intriguingly, while the two primary outsider groups have utilized humor as a weapon and means of liberation, they have also bound themselves to American optimism and playfulness. But the basis of their outlook—born, bred and bound within the city—has not ceased to reflect an urban brio and combativeness. "How many New Yorkers does it take to change a light bulb?" goes the joke in the cycle of the 1970s, to which the answer is, "None of your Goddamn business."

In retrospect, Hofstadter's insight into American culture, though slightly exaggerated, got it just right: in this century the humor is in the city.

Notes

1. "The United States Was Born in the Country and Has Moved to the City," *The Age of Reform* (New York: Alfred A. Knopf, 1955), 23.
2. Bernard De Voto, ed., *Mark Twain in Eruption* (New York: Harper & Row, 1940), 252–53.
3. See Phil Berger, *The Last Laugh* (New York: Ballantine Books, 1976).
4. Author's Notes, 1981–87.
5. Sanford Pinsker, "On or About December, 1910: When Human Character —and American Humor—Changed," in William Bradford Clark and W. Craig Turner, eds. *Critical Essays on American Humor* (Boston: G. K. Hall, 1984), 190.
6. Kenneth Tynan, *Show People* (New York: Simon and Schuster, 1979), 213.
7. Joseph Boskin, "Beyond *Kvetching* and *Jiving:* The Thrust of Jewish and Black Folkhumor," in Sarah Blacher Cohen, ed., *Jewish Wry: Essays on Jewish Humor* (Bloomington: Indiana University Press, 1987), 74–5.

Saloons and
Burlesques
Joseph Boskin

Burlesque theatre emerged from the burgeoning American metropolis in the second half of the nineteenth century and presided as the only major entertainment that exalted an urban, working-class *zeitgeist.* Burlesque was the show that flaunted Victorian values and symbols, exposed the epidermis, mocked traditional forms of authority, and refracted city life. Its bawdy and raucous format created a comedy of incongruity that attracted males from across the social spectrum. Other forms of mass entertainment—along with its upstart cousin, vaudeville, nickelodeons, and silent film—catered to the family by offering acceptable fare. Thus burlesque became the entertainment most threatening to social order: its borderline comedy and bodily exposure drew censure if not condemnation and the show was always one step ahead of the reformer's axe.

Along with burlesque's sexual connotations was its symbiotic connection to the city, reflecting the problematic relationship of Americans with elements of an urban environment. Although burlesque theatre came to exemplify an urban ethos, it evolved in part from the cafe garden, a European development of the 1840s. The French called them *café-concerts,* a form of entertainment that was set in the open with tables clustered around a stage and served by waiters dispensing liquor, mainly beer. Patrons from different classes were amused by a variety of acts undergirded by coarse humor. Immigrants to the country carried the theatrical concept with them. The result was the concert saloon that flourished on the western and urban frontiers where customers were served by "waiter girls" in short uniforms. By the end of the century there were saloons of all types in large cities and small towns, from Galveston, to Chicago, to Helena, that served different social needs.

From the beginning, saloon culture catered to ethnic communal celebrations, such as weddings and holidays, and provided a gathering place for fraternal orders and political organizations.

The
Humor
Prism
in 20th-
Century
America

124

So patronized were saloons that in Chicago their numbers surpassed groceries, meat markets, and dry-goods stores. One of the most renowned was Harry Hills, located on the lower East Side in New York. Hills presented a variety show with boxing matches, walking contests, Indian Club swing contests, a punching bag for customers, and offered the usual blue songs and dances.[1]

The saloon was largely an all-male habitat that heavily influenced burlesque. In Kathy Peiss's study of working women's amusements at the turn of the century, we learn that in the 1850s there were saloon owners who converted their back rooms and cellars into small concert halls and hired specialty acts to amuse their patrons and encourage drinking. By the following decade there were more than two hundred concert-saloons that in New York alone had spread along Broadway, the Bowery, and the waterfronts, "catering to a heterogeneous male clientele of laborers, soldiers, sailors, and 'slumming' society gentlemen. The conversations of polite society were put aside in these male sanctuaries, where crude jokes, bawdy comedy sketches, and scantily clad singers entertained the drinkers."[2]

Following the Civil War came the saloon "girlie shows," a spectacle that also caught on in circuses, county fairs, variety halls, and semi-respectable theatres. These places were among the first to display women's bodies, a practice that evolved from musical numbers in which women burlesqued men attired in male clothing. The act of displaying the female form actually began in the mid-1840s, however, when women wearing only tights posed as "living statuary" of classical subjects and contemporary sculpture. Throngs of people viewed shapely young females portraying sculptor Hiram Powers's controversial "The Greek Slave," "Psyche Going to the Bath," and "Venus Rising from the Sea."

Building in stages, burlesque lived up to its intrinsic name by offering mirthful sketches excerpted from familiar plays and pantomimed farces, with the addition of scantily clad female dancers. Parts of the female body that had not been exposed or even suggested by rose-tinted tights made their appearance in Chicago at the 1893 World's Columbian Exposition, a celebration of technology and urban accomplishment. Here for the first time audiences viewed belly dancing in Little Egypt's "Cootch dance." "When she dances," a barker bellowed, "every fiber and every tissue in her entire anatomy shakes like a jar of jelly from your grandmother's Thanksgiving dinner. Now, gentlemen, I don't say that she's that hot. But I do say that she is as hot as a red-hot stove on the fourth of July in the hottest county in the state." The "hootchy-cootchy" dance with its emphasis on exposure and teasing provided, Robert C. Toll observed, "a distinctive feature that helped establish the burlesque show as a separate form of American show business."[3] As an intriguing aside, the music of the "hootchy-cootchy" was improvised by Sol Bloom, who later selected the sites for at least ten 42nd Street legitimate theatres in New York City. In any case, the urban hurly-burly show was born.

By the opening of the twentieth century, the city and burlesque were closely entwined. Chicago journalist Jack Burton wrote in 1912 that "the burlesque house is one of West Madison's most popular institutions, like free lunch and 'the largest glass of beer in the city for five cents.'"[4] Competing with other entertainment forms in the city, burlesque became more daring and racier until it culminated in the famous striptease with which it has become identified almost exclusively. "Wives, women and sex—not necessarily in that order—were dominant themes in burlesque comedy," noted Jill Dolan. "Images of women in burlesque bits always implied sex—either the desire for it, its lack, or society's moral sanctions against it."[5]

Throughout its early existence, burlesque maintained its original variety and incongruous inflection in risqué songs, suggestive dances, and bawdy comedic sketches. But if women served as the "come on / come in," they were not necessarily the only reason for burlesque's popular hold on men's imagination. Burlesque flourished with the rise of the industrial city and the arrival of millions of Eastern and Central Europeans who poured into its environs. The Jews, Italians, Poles, Russians, Slavs, and Greeks, as well as traditional groups from the British Isles and Germany, provided the cheap labor supply for the burgeoning factory system.

For the immigrant, and migrant, the demand was not only for jobs and housing but for diversion as well. Conflict between the newcomers and native-born Americans over modes of entertainment was inevitable. Unlike their predecessors, the new immigrants came from cultures more expressive, comparatively tolerant in their sexual attitudes, open to communal drinking and public dancing, and alienated from their institutional moorings. Drinking was a typical, highly divisive issue. Despite prohibitionist

The
Humor
Prism
in 20th-
Century
America

126

tendencies that had been operative in American culture since the early decades of the nineteenth century, the Germans paraded and drank beer on Sunday; the Irish tavern resonated as a place of male bonding and political activity; the Slav bars were filled after work; the Romanians frequented their wine bars; and the Jews and Italians, while minimizing the use of alcohol, were not prohibitionist in their attitudes or practices.

The immigrants, in short, did not subscribe to many of the manners of Victorian culture and therefore frequently found themselves in serious conflict with native-born American groups. As James L. Collier incisively noted, the new industrial city itself was basically anti-Victorian. "Its character was determined not by the Victorian middle class that still resided in it, but by the rough culture of the working people, with their confused, boiling ethnic mix. . . . In the new city, the tone was set by the working class. And that tone was not a Victorian one."[6]

To a considerable extent, then, it was the industrial city that separated the new immigrants from the middle classes. The city exacted a heavy toll on traditional familial and religious institutions in immigrant culture. Its harsh and demanding conditions forced on its inhabitants the need to create a recreational tableau more suitable both to their psychological needs and financial situation. Decorum and respectability were not primary concerns for the substantially large number of young, single males attempting to make their way as semi- and unskilled laborers in the urban factories. These men were joined by a large number of "floaters"—the unemployed, adolescents, and those whose job depended on good weather—who poured into the saloons in the afternoons or frequented burlesque matinee shows. Inclement weather was always a boost to burlesque: "I hope it rains today" was a popular phrase among the managers. And in addition there were the older, disgruntled married men, who with anonymity and easy access, frequented the bars, theatres, and brothels available in the city.

The sheer size of the city, moreover, hid the movements of men who wanted to escape from the restrictions imposed by their family, religious group, or social class. The theatrical environment of burlesque was a world distinct from their lives. The jokes and routines were too bawdy to recount to family members. It was women in the burlesque houses who provided escape from the rigors of industrial work and the restrictions of family roles.

The Humor Prism in 20th-Century America

127

While men were enticed and titillated by women with beauty marks in the shape of stars and moons on their cheeks, by skimpy outfits and partial nudity, and by bumps and grinds and gyrating rumps, they also saw women in an assortment of roles. They encountered women who were burlesque managers, Agnes Barry of Albany and Ora Dresselhaus of Cincinnati's Standard Theatre, for example; and they were challenged by pugilistic ladies such as Miss Juno, described as "a distaff version of Man Mountain Dean," who offered $500 to any man of her own weight she couldn't trounce.[7]

Word of burlesque's venue spread beyond the city and filtered into the hinterlands. Burlesque was, after all, a kind of sexual "education" for many young males and a voyeuristic release for older men. Where the Victorians were enclosing the human body, burlesque routines were unclothing it. When Victorians made nude statuary anathema in the museums, young males turned to whatever means possible to glimpse the female body. Urban shows became a major source of peeking that eventually included the *National Geographic.* "I wanted to study femininity in the raw and see girls devoid of long skirts and high-necked shirtwaists, and the place to see that, I learned, was at Sam T. Jack's burlesque house in Chicago," wrote Jack Burton in about his tenth and awakening year in matters sexual. Despite the intervening years, he was able to recall a scatological song:

> A fly flew into a grocery store.
> He lit on the ceiling, he lit on the floor,
> He lit in the sugar, he lit in the tea,
> If I hadn't watched out, he'd lit on me.

"In this rendition of this ditty, the comic gave the word 'lit' a phonetic twist and made it sound like a naughty, four-letter verb that excited gales of laughter."[8]

In burlesque's routines were mirrored the variety, vitality, and antagonisms of urban existence, and they clearly served as a means of acculturation. By 1914 there were black burlesque shows and ethnic celebrities from working-class sports were integrated into the venue. Former prizefighters, in particular, wound up on the stage. Gene Tunney, who had beaten Jack Dempsey, offered excerpts from Shakespeare; the highly popular heavyweight champion opened up the John L. Sullivan Players in

1907. "He's with burly," declared *Variety* magazine, "and keeping sober."[9]

It was in the cities, then, that burlesque and its more up-scale relation, vaudeville, existed to inform a polyglot population, a nation of strangers, white and black, European and native-born American. Burlesque provided a comedy that introduced strangers to each other, and in its small way opened a window into other cultures. "Burlesque comedy," Jill Dolan wryly noted, "was peculiarly democratic."[10] What she meant was that it was democratic *and* capitalist: an equal opportunity entertainment that exposed the newcomers and minorities alike to stereotypical comedy. Yet goaded by a Social Darwinist mindset that extolled among its unyielding tenets a rigid pecking order, burlesque offered not a melting pot but a salad bowl. More often than not, the comedy was routinized portraiture. Each ethnic group had "its stock prototype on the stage, usually portrayed at the level of the lowest common dominator":[11] the drunken Irishman, greedy Jewish merchant, chicken-stealing black farmer, numbskull Slav, and greasy Italian. Still, as Robert W. Snyder argued, "such portrayals—whether in song, comedy or sketches—could be mined for more complex and humane meanings than appeared on the surface. And representations of ethnics were bound to be problematic at a time when the stresses of immigration and acculturation left many in a state of upheaval."[12]

Nonetheless, there were elements of burlesque's comedy that transcended urban ethnicity by illuminating the timbre and physical character of urban reality. For the tens of millions of immigrants and migrants—the latter driven from their farms by the massive depressions of the 1870s and 1890s—city life was intensely physical. A stressful precariousness summed up the daily enterprise of the working class. Survival entailed extraordinary physical energy as urban workers grappled with machines of all types, from packed trolleys and subway trains to the factory, which was organized around the time clock that tyrannically ruled production. Everyday existence was compounded by a density of bodies crammed into tiny apartments, bodies that spilled out of massive tenements onto crowded streets. It is not surprising that the industrial city exacted a grievous toll in wrenched and abusive family relationships that on occasion resulted in murder.

Burlesque provided both an escape from and confrontation with modern urban circumstances. Is it any wonder that many of the routines in burlesque were physically explosive, shorn of time constraint, bordering on the vituperative and relying heavily on slapstick? All this suggests that the stage was counterpart to the urban milieu—hilarious, distressing, and seemingly disorganized. The tempo of the comedy, like the movement of city streets, was swift and jolting and possessed highly recognizable parameters. Many standard routines included the pie-in-the-face, the female chase, problems of money, gold-digging wives and harping mothers-in-law, the salacious, unobtainable woman, and the defiance of authority. Within immigrant culture there existed a residual suspicion of government that had been part of their Old World cultural baggage. Thus a comedic climax in the show often took place in a courtroom, with prisoners and lawyers squirting water at each other from seltzer bottles, and the judge demanding order with a wooden potato masher. Consistent with burlesque's reflection of urban existence, a number of skits involved murder. The stage, in short, refracted a curious acceptance of urban helplessness.

A sense of victimization permeated the scene, yet the performers *and* viewers, in one way or another, managed to wrest a degree of control through the show's format. There were forms of power located in the theatre. Indeed, it might be argued that burlesque provided not only a momentary refuge from the city's demands but was one of the few places where those involved could achieve a mastery over their own circumstances. The master of ceremonies was the "top banana," a title surely inspired by pop-freudianism, and despite his oversized costume, his stumbling and bumbling, he always remained center stage with his bawdy sexual humor and allusions to women. Women performers were more than sexual objects since they were in control of their audience with suggestive movements. And for their part, the men escaped from what they regarded as circumstances of entrapment by plunking down scarce cash to hear taboo jokes and ogle semi-nude women.

Once parts of the epidermis came into view, however, burlesque became a lightning rod for criticism. As early as the mid-nineteenth century, charges of "indecency," "societal deterioration," "vulgarity," and "sexual licentiousness" were hurled by middle- and upper-class groups, suggesting a myriad of complex anxieties. "Absolute indecency reigns supreme," wrote Samuel Paynter Wilson in Chicago in 1910. "The performers, mostly women of the underworld, are paid to amuse the audiences by kicking up their heels. The higher they kick, the more they are paid. The hooche-kooche and the Salome dances are here given in all their rottenness. Vulgar sayings and gestures are indulged in to a degree that is amazing even in this enlightened age. These shows are liberally supported by all classes of men. Price of admission is low, and the performance suited to the tastes of the audience."[13]

There was a period in the years preceding World War I when burlesque actually reformed itself, forced by competition from vaudeville and other fast-forming entertainments catering to the family. Prices were lowered, cake-walk contests were added, and the jokes fell short of outright vulgarity. But hard times hit the industry in the 1920s and out went any pretense of "refined" theatre. Eager to bring patrons back into the theatre, ingenious managers in the late twenties renamed and restructured the "cooch" dance. It became the "shake" in which all the principals and chorus shook their bodies in unison, a collective action that produced a "tremendous amount of mammary vibration."[14] Then, the distance between the customer's eyes and hands and the desired object was narrowed with the construction of runways extending halfway into the orchestra. As the modern, urban striptease came alive, performers teased their way along jutting stages to hooting men. With these embellishments, burlesque's days became numbered, and in 1942 it was banned from New York and lost much of its attraction around the country as well.

Outrage over the striptease, however, transcended all other issues. Burlesque epitomized for many their fears regarding the city itself. An anti-urban animus that had long permeated American attitudes reached new heights at the turn of the century as burlesque's salacious and taunting routines confirmed anxieties about alterations in the social fabric. The image of the city as the great tempter and underminer of rational disquisition and social order was reinforced by burlesque's comedic and bodily format. Because women were the most visible aspect of burlesque routines, the "degradation" represented by female performers seemed to legitimize the metropolis as destroyer of innocence. "When a girl leaves her home at eighteen," wrote Theodore

Dreiser in *Sister Carrie* (1900), "she does one of two things. Either she falls into saving hands and becomes better, or she rapidly assumes the cosmopolitan standard of virtue and becomes worse. Of an intermediate balance, under the circumstances, there is no possibility. The city has its cunning wiles, no less than the infinitely smaller and more human tempter. There are large forces which allure with all the soulfulness of expression possible in the most cultured human."[15]

Yet these criticisms had little effect on the new immigrants because for them Victorian ideals still held partial compunction. The accent on punctuality, temperance, higher education, self-control, order, and savings as a means of upward mobility, as pathways to success, were at variance with their background and situation in the industrial city. In desperation, nativists sought to acculturate the "foreigners" by establishing classes and creating night schools in order to achieve a society "100% American." They also sought to remove those subversive obstacles that prevented the attainment of an untainted citizenry, burlesque being chief among them. Consequently, the cry for burlesque's elimination was constantly voiced throughout the first half of the twentieth century.

A persistent criticism of burlesque revolved around the fact that it catered almost exclusively to men, with their prurient desires and ogling eyes. While females were certainly viewed as a sexual commodity, in its parallel way their counterparts were the first-generation city-dwellers from European villages and American farms who were treated as a labor commodity. Both, in effect, *produced* for the culture. Burlesque, ironically, brought together working-class men and women, those who were ensnared in an industrial economy that demanded of them only their bodies. And if the comedy was arguably "vulgar" because it accentuated the physical and sexual, it nevertheless reflected the daily experience of those tens of millions squeezed into massive cities. To the criticism that burlesque was "tasteless," it would be well to bear in mind critic Walter Goodman's observation: "Tastelessness has a firm place in the history of American humor, from the frontier to the big city."[16]

In sum, burlesque was one form of theatre among many spawned by the industrial city, but its routines and language came closer than any other to the new city's cacophonous spirit, ethnic mix, social dissension, and comedic force.

Notes

1. James Lincoln Collier, *The Rise of Selfishness in America* (New York: Oxford University Press, 1991), 78; Laurence Hutton, "The American Burlesque," *Harper's Magazine* LXXXI (June 1890): 73.

2. Kathy Peiss, *Cheap Amusements: Working Women and Leisure in Turn-of-the-Century New York* (Philadelphia: Temple University Press, 1986), 142.

3. Robert C. Toll, *On With the Show: The First Century of Show Business* (New York: Oxford University Press, 1976), 225.

4. Jack Burton, *In Memoriam—Oldtime Show Biz* (New York: Vantage Press, 1965), 54.

5. Jill Dolan, "'What, No Beans?' Images of Women and Sexuality in Burlesque Comedy," *Journal of Popular Culture* 18 (Winter 1984): 37.

6. Collier, *Rise of Selfishness in America*, 67.

7. Abel Green and Joe Laurie, Jr., *Showbiz: From Vaudeville to Video* (New York: Henry Holt, 1951), 75.

8. Burton, *In Memoriam*, 42–44.

9. Green and Laurie, *Showbiz*, 75.

10. Dolan, "'What, No Beans?'," 38.

11. Green and Laurie, *Showbiz*, 76.

12. Robert W. Snyder, *The Voice of the City* (New York: Oxford University Press, 1989), 111.

13. Green and Laurie, *Showbiz*, 76.

14. Ibid., 306.

15. Theodore Dreiser, *Sister Carrie* (New York: Doubleday, Page, 1900), 2.

16. Walter Goodman, "Critics Notebook," *New York Times*, May 15, 1986, C22.

The
Humor
Prism
in 20th-
Century
America

The People of the Joke: On the Conceptualization of a Jewish Humor

Elliott Oring

The
Humor
Prism
in 20th-
Century
America

134

There exists a conceptualization of a special relationship between a particular culture and a particular folklore form. For some reason, commentators have seen fit to establish a bond between the Jewish people and the joke. Those who for millenia were characterized as "The People of the Book" may now be characterized without excessive exaggeration as "The People of the Joke." This characterization is well-known and confronts us repeatedly in articles, essays, and anthologies of Jewish humor. For example, Ernst Simon: "Hardly anyone will contest the assertion that Jewish wit has a character all its own." Harry Golden: "Humor has been so much a part of Jewish culture that any kind of activity at all is impossible without it." Or Leo Rosten: "In nothing is Jewish psychology so vividly revealed as in the Jewish joke." Or George Mikes: "The Jewish joke is probably the best of all jokes."[1] This list of quotations could be, of course, greatly extended.

In truth, the relationship is broader than the title implies, for the Jews are regarded as intimate with humor in its broadest range of manifestations rather than solely with its succinct narrative crystallization in jokes. But as these narrative forms have been frequently identified as particularly apropos to the Jewish character, I feel no particular embarrassment concerning the title of this essay, although I will not restrict myself to a discussion of the form.

What is perhaps more peculiar about this characterization of the Jews as a humorous people is that it seems to be endorsed by Jews and non-Jews alike—a pleasant accommodation of esoteric

Reprinted with permission of the California Folklore Society. Originally published in *Western Folklore*, vol. 42, no. 4 (1983).

and exoteric perceptions. There is likewise some accord between "scientific" and "folk" perceptions on this matter, for the image is not only perpetuated in scholarly and literary publications but in oral sources as well. Hence the first (and oft-repeated) joke that is recorded in Immanuel Olsvanger's *Röyte Pomerantsen:*

> When you tell a peasant a joke he laughs three times; Once when you tell it, once when you explain it, and once when he understands it.
>
> When you tell a land-owner a joke he laughs twice; once when you tell it and once when you explain it—he'll never understand it.
>
> When you tell a military officer a joke he laughs only once—when you tell it. Because he won't let you explain it and of course he doesn't understand it.
>
> But when you tell a Jew a joke, he tells you that he's heard it already—and, besides, you're telling it all wrong.[2]

This is, of course, one of those curious examples of meta-folklore in which the attributes of joking are in themselves the subject matter for the joke.[3]

This paper will explore the image of the Jews as a peculiarly humorous people with a distinctive body of witticisms, jokes, and anecdotes. It will examine the *idea* of Jewish humor and the Jewish joke but will not engage in the analysis of jokes per se. My definition of Jewish humor is greatly simplified by this perspective. Jewish humor is simply that humor which has been conceptualized as uniquely, distinctly, or characteristically reflective of, evocative of, or conditioned by the Jewish people and their circumstances. There is no particular concern that these conceptualizations of uniqueness can be demonstrated as matters of fact —it is the orientation itself that defines the subject matter. This perspective affords an escape from many of the difficulties that have plagued other writers on the subject of Jewish humor, writers who failed to formulate adequate or generally shared definitions of the subject matter they were studying.[4] On the other hand, this approach is beset with its own inherent limitations, most notably that it is always one step removed from the humor and jokes themselves, and that it is in no position to identify either new or old instances of Jewish humorous expression until someone else has identified them as such. For what I claim to study is not a literature or a set of behaviors but a conceptualization of literature and behavior. Thus, if Jewish humor is indeed a "myth" as Dan Ben-Amos has suggested,[5] it is this myth that is the focus of our inquiry. Ultimately, the value of this approach can only be justified if we are led to new awareness and understanding. That is certainly the goal of this essay, although we might be satisfied merely to raise the issue to an appropriate level of consciousness so that the inquiry may be broadened and the debate extended to a wider range of scholars and thinkers.

Theoretically our perspective calls for a number of considerations in the analysis of Jewish humor: (1) Who is doing the conceptualizing of the humor? (2) When and where did the conceptualization take place in both chronological and sociological terms? (3) What is the nature of the materials to which the conceptualization applies? and (4) What are the characteristics of the conceptualization itself? These considerations would apply whether the conceptualization in question was formally and reflectively enacted in a printed publication, or whether it was less formally and unreflectively carried out in the normal flow of ordinary, everyday conversation.

For example, there is a recent popular publication entitled *The Big Book of Jewish Humor*, edited and annotated by William Novak and Moshe Waldoks.[6] Our perspective ideally would be concerned to identify editors Novak and Waldoks, to trace the history of their project, which was first published in 1981, to examine the materials they chose to include in their three-hundred-and-eight-page anthology, and most important, to explore both the implicit and explicit conceptualizations of Jewish humor that they present in their work. Similarly, a joke that a person tells in the course of his everyday conversation and conceptualizes as "Jewish" would be open to the same spectrum of queries.

Ultimately if one were to inquire about a great number of oral and printed enterprises in this fashion, one would be in a position to write a history of Jewish humor, with the awareness that because of our curious definition of Jewish humor as a conceptualization rather than as a phenomenon, such a history would necessarily be an historiography. I am in no position to undertake such a history here. Constraints of space prove our salvation. What I shall attempt instead is to put forward some hypotheses for consideration and debate concerning the development of the conceptualizations of Jewish humor. Although these hypotheses are stated with confidence, I have no overpowering commitment to their defense if evidence to the contrary be

The
Humor
Prism
in 20th-
Century
America

136

forthcoming. What I hope to provide is a focus (I hesitate to say "target") for the discussion of the conceptualization of a Jewish humor and the perception of the Jews as distinctly humorous people.

Our first hypothesis may be stated quite straightforwardly: Jewish humor is a relatively modern invention. The conceptualization of a humor that was in some way characteristic or distinctive of the Jewish people begins only in Europe during the nineteenth century. In support of this hypothesis, I merely wish to point out that as late as 1893, Hermann Adler, the Chief Rabbi of London, still found it necessary to defend the Jews against the charge that they were a humorless people.[7] Today, the great collections of Jewish jokes that are instinctively cited to evidence the existence of a Jewish humor are invariably compilations of the twentieth century.

There is no indication that the composers of the Bible or the Talmud or the later commentaries held any awareness of a distinctive Jewish humor. What was conceptualized was a people, a law, a ritual, a language, and a mission in the world that was distinctive—but apparently not a humor. There is evidence that the rabbis were not particularly well disposed toward humor in general;[8] hence they were unlikely to have recorded their impressions of humor in Jewish society other than to condemn its presence. (Exceptions may be noted here with reference to the celebration of Purim in which merrymaking and ritual reversal were positively sanctioned as well as the rise of humorous narratives in the disquisitions or itinerant preachers and Hassidic leaders.) This is not to deny that humor was present in biblical, talmudic, and medieval Jewish society, but only to suggest that it held no special place and was not bound up with any national, religious, or ethnic identity.

If the idea of a Jewish humor was the invention of the nineteenth century, the conceptualization was applied to earlier materials much as the psychological concept of hysteria might be applied to the conceptualization of witchcraft behaviors reported from earlier centuries. For example, in 1893, Abram S. Isaacs published *Stories from the Rabbis* and *Rabbinical Humor* with the intention of demonstrating that the Jewish sages were not "mere dreamers, always buried in wearisome disputations," but men who were as much impelled by "buoyancy" and "moral cheerfulness" as by intellectual motives.[9] In 1905, J. Chotzner expanded

The
Humor
Prism
in 20th-
Century
America

137

the history of humor in Jewish society by identifying little-known Hebrew humorists of the thirteenth, fourteenth, and eighteenth centuries.[10]

At this point I will tender a hypothesis that is little more than a suspicion: Toward the end of the nineteenth century the faculty of humor was felt to be one of the signs of a civilized humanity, and Jews felt the necessity to demonstrate that they had participated in this humanity since their emergence as a people.[11] Consequently, Jewish scholars perused biblical, talmudic, midrashic, and other literary sources to evidence this claim. At present, I lack any weighty evidence to support this contention, but in the enormously successful book *Sex and Character* published in 1903, Otto Weininger, an anti-Semite of Jewish origins, argued that Jews were not readily disposed to humor. According to Weininger, humor recognized the transcendental and was essentially tolerant while wit and satire were essentially intolerant. Thus, "Jews and women are devoid of humour, but addicted to mockery."[12] Granted that the differences between humor, wit, and satire introduce an unnecessary complication here, nevertheless Weininger's thesis indicates that during this period humor could be and was used as a criterion for bestowing or denying the status of full partnership in civilization.

In their attempts to demonstrate that the prophets and sages were capable of humor, both Isaacs and Adler offered a rudimentary conceptalization of a Jewish humor. Each respectively viewed the humor he had culled from earlier sources as a reflection of the "Hebrew spirit that refused to submit to the yoke of any conqueror,"[13] or as "a resilience which enabled . . . [the Jew] to elude effectually all the attempts made at every age, and in every clime, to lay him low."[14] A similar position had been voiced almost twenty years earlier in the *London Athenaeum* in a comment on Heinrich Heine: "In his wit and humor, Heine was a true child of the Hebrew race. However original he may have been, he exhibited the character and peculiarities of Hebrew humor, of the wittiest and most light-hearted people of the world, which in the midst of unparalleled misfortunes and suffering, has preserved an incredible buoyancy and unconquerable spirit of satire."[15]

It is important to note that in the quests for evidence of humor among the Hebrews, the humor was always viewed against the backdrop of Jewish history and experience—a history that was conceptualized as a history of defeat, exile, segregation, and unending persecution. This points to an important clue in our attempt to understand the special relationship that is perceived to exist between the Jews and humor. Since no empirical comparative assessments of the quantity and quality of Jewish humor have been attempted (nor are they likely to be possible), the privileged relationship that is held to obtain between the Jews and humor must derive from elsewhere. Hence, my next hypothesis: The conception of a Jewish humor derives from a conceptualization of Jewish history as a history of suffering, rejection, and despair. Given this history, the Jews should have nothing to laugh about at all. That they do laugh and jest can only signal the existence of a special relationship between the Jews and humor and suggests that the humor of the Jews must in some way be distinctive from other humors which are not born of despair.

B. Rohaytn provides a particularly poignant example of how this conceptualization of Jewish experience might effect the notion of Jewish humor. Rohatyn had been interested in all forms of Jewish folklore and had collected songs, legends, Märchens, proverbs, folk belief, medical practices, customs, and usages. He knew of the existence of humorous narratives but "did not consider it necessary to document them."[16] Rohatyn, however, was profoundly moved by the blood libel trials that took place at the turn of the century. The trials made Rohatyn keenly aware of how much his people had suffered. He reflected:

> Any means of consolation that otherwise stands open to the Jews seemed to me to fail, and yet how often had our ancestors suffered similar fates and had, as it were, overcome them. Their deep and firm faith had helped them—but also their indestructible and enduring joyfulness, their ability to laugh. Can one better overcome sorrow and gnawing pain than by laughing them away? I began to become aware of the monuments of joy and laughter of our Fathers as they lived in their humorous products, and so I began to collect witticism and anecdotes of the Jews. What began for me as a consolation and as a pleasure gradually took on the character of an objective scholarly interest.[17]

Ultimately, it was only within the context of Jewish despair and suffering that Rohatyn could conceptualize a Jewish humor.

My next hypothesis derives almost directly from the preceding one: If the background of Jewish suffering did condition the expectation of a distinctive Jewish humor, there was only a lim-

The Humor Prism in 20th-Century America

139

ited range of possibilities for articulating this history of suffering with humor. The possibilities were that the humor was *transcendent*, that the humor was *defensive*, or that the humor was *pathological*. In fact, each of these possibilities was explored in the conceptualization of Jewish humor; each possibility suggests a solution to the problem of why the Jew should laugh.

The idea that Jewish humor was in some respects transcendent we have already encountered with Rohatyn and in Isaacs's conceptualization of the humor of the ancient rabbis as a triumph of the Hebrew spirit. The major exponent of this conceptualization of Jewish humor, however, was not a scholar, but the dean of Yiddish authors, Sholem Aleichem. Its primary manifestation is in the character of Tevye the dairyman. There is no need to peruse the literature here because Aleichem's conceptualization of Jewish humor as transcendent has been clearly recognized.[18] For Sholem Aleichem himself, the conceptualization was quite explicit. In 1911 he wrote:

> I tell you it is an ugly and mean world and only to spite it one mustn't weep! If you want to know, that is the real source, the true cause of my constant good spirits, of my, as it is called, "humor." Not to cry out of spite! Only to laugh out of spite, *only to laugh.*[19]

The
Humor
Prism
in 20th-
Century
America

140

Humor is transcendent when it reflects the unwillingness of the individual to surrender to the impossible conditions of existence and attempts to achieve a measure of liberation from the social, political, economic, and even cosmic forces that remain beyond one's control. Jewish humor is thus conceptualized as transcending the conditions of despair and consequently is distinctive in its reflection of an unperturable optimism and zest for living. This conceptualization has found its way into numerous popular anthologies of Jewish humor under the slogan of "laughter through tears" or in the characterization of Jewish humor as fundamentally "philosophical."[20]

The characterization of humor as defensive was expressed by Adler, who portrayed it as a "weapon . . . whereby the Jews . . . have been able to survive in the fierce struggle for existence."[21] This conceptualization was greatly amplified in 1905 in Sigmund Freud's *Jokes and Their Relation to the Unconscious*, which although not ostensibly about Jewish humor utilized numerous examples of what Freud termed "Jewish jokes." Freud's psychodynamic theory of joking regarded jokes as playful facades which often betrayed serious purposes—particularly hostile or critical purposes.[22] Freud's observations provided a ready-made framework for a conceptualization of Jewish humor as a set of defensive, even retaliatory, measures undertaken in the context of an oppressive environment. Thus according to Alter Druyanow, compiler of the three-volume collection of jokes *Sefer ha-Bedihah ve-ha-Hidud*, there were a host of conditions against which the Jewish joke rebelled: most prominently the oppression of the non-Jew, the *Goy*. But there were conditions within Jewish society as well which were felt to be oppressive—occupations, the rich, the rabbis, and even God Himself—at which the Jewish joke directed its sharp criticisms.[23]

The conceptualization of the Jewish joke as pathological, an irrational response to the Jewish condition, derives from an aside by Freud on the matter of Jewish jokes in *Jokes and Their Relation to the Unconscious*:

> A particularly favorable occasion for tendentious jokes is presented when the intended rebellious criticism is directed against the subject himself, or, to put it more cautiously, against someone in whom the subject has a share—a collective person, that is (the subject's own nation for instance). The occurrence of self-criticism as a determinant may explain how it is that a number of the most apt jokes . . . have grown up on the soil of Jewish popular life. They are stories created by Jews and directed against Jewish characteristics. . . . Incidentally, I do not know whether there are many other instances of people making fun to such a degree of its own character.[24]

The
Humor
Prism
in 20th-
Century
America

141

Although Freud was not the first to conceptualize self-criticism as distinctive of Jewish humor,[25] set within the framework of his psychology of the unconscious, his observation resonated with new meaning. The observation conditioned analysts Martin Grotjahn's and Theodor Reik's masochistic conceptualizations of Jewish wit.[26] In truth, both Grotjahn and Reik clearly recognized positive psychological dimensions in Jewish humor, but their fundamental conceptualization of Jewish humor was within the context of psychopathology. Such conceptualizations of the Jewish joke, of course, accorded very well with more general theories of Jewish self-hatred; and the notion that a pathological self-hatred

underlies self-critical Jewish jokes is so strongly implied that it often has to be explicitly denied.[27]

As far as I can determine, conceptualizations of Jewish humor rely primarily upon these three characteristics—transcendence, defense, and pathology—the very characteristics that logi-
cally permit the articulation of Jewish suffering and despair with
humor. Theoretically, these characteristics are distinct. As they
are practically applied to the conceptualization of Jewish humor,
however, these distinctions are blurred. Thus Nathan Ausubel,
one of the most popular purveyors of Jewish folklore and humor,
presents all three possibilities in concert when introducing the
concept of Jewish humor to his readers:

> By laughing at the absurdities and cruelties of life they [the
> Jews] draw much of the sting from them. . . . His [the Jew's]
> satire and irony have one virtue: you never suspect for a
> moment that his barbs are directed at you. . . . Don't be sur-
> prised if you find . . . a large amount of self-criticism dis-
> guised as irony, satire, and caricature.[28]

The concatenation of these three characteristics by Ausubel is
perhaps only to be expected. The three characteristics often
seem to be hopelessly intertwined. Thus the transcendent humor
of Tevye the dairyman invoked by Sholem Aleichem is belied by
Sholem Aleichem's own desperate and spiteful laughter. Indeed,
dark and dangerous undercurrents of pathology have been
noted in his humorous stories.[29] Even Freud acknowledged that
critical and hostile jokes were in some sense liberating and in his
later years came to emphasize the liberating function of humor.[30]
And the masochism conceptualized by Grotjahn and Reik was
not regarded as a perversion, and ultimately could be directed to
purposes of defense and liberation.[31]

It would seem that recent conceptualizations of Jewish humor remain firmly rooted in the constructs and categories I have
described. Certainly, there have been efforts to identify more
precisely the conditions and causes of self-criticism,[32] or the particular character of the dilemmas that the humor was designed
to transcend,[33] or the changes in the intensity and targets of hostility and criticism.[34] But it would not seem that any new conceptualizations have arisen.

It is these same conceptualizations that even determine pre-
dictions concerning the fate of Jewish humor. Some have seen

The
Humor
Prism
in 20th-
Century
America

142

the end of Jewish humor in the rise of a Jewish State, where humor as a weapon has become obsolete.[35] Others foresee a merger between dilemmas of the Jew and "modern man," with the sheer nihilism of the modern age overpowering the transcendental abilities of the Jewish joke.[36] Still others regard the transcendence of Jewish humor as offering an escape from modern forms of despair and imply that Jewish humor and the humor of modernity are merging.[37] Ultimately, as we have seen, it is not really Jewish humor that is at stake. Conceptualizations of the Jewish joke are merely crystallizations of conceptualizations of the Jewish people, their history, and their identity. The notion of Jewish humor will persist as long as there remain conceptualizations that fundamentally distinguish Jewish history and experience from the history and experience of a world of nations.

Notes

1. Ernst Simon, "Notes on Jewish Wit," *Jewish Frontier* 15 (1948): 42; Harry Golden, *The Golden Book of Jewish Humor* (New York, 1972), p. 12; Leo Rosten, *The Joys of Yiddish* (New York, 1968), p. xxiv; George Nikes, *Laughing Matter* (New York, 1971), p. 111.

2. Immanuel Olsvanger, *Röyle Pomerantsen* (New York, 1965), p. 3.

3. Alan Dundes, "Metafolkfore and Oral Literary Criticism" in *Analytic Essays in Folklore*, ed. Alan Dundes (The Hague, 1975), pp. 52–53.

4. See the critique of Heda Jason, "The Jewish Joke: The Problem of Definition," *Southern Folklore Quarterly* 31 (1967): 48–54.

5. Dan Ben-Amos, "The 'Myth' of Jewish Humor," *Western Folklore* 32 (1973): 112–31.

6. William Novak and Moshe Waldoks, eds., *The Big Book of Jewish Humor* (New York, 1981).

7. Hermann Adler, "Jewish Wit and Humor," *The Nineteenth Century* 33 (1893): 457–469.

8. Alter Druyanow, *Sefer ha-Bedihah ve-ha-Hiddad*, 3 vols. (Tel Aviv, 1963), 1:ix.

9. Abram S. Isaacs, *Stories from the Rabbis* (New York, 1911), pp. 7, 114.

10. J. Chotzner, *Hebrew Humor and Other Essays* (London, 1905).

11. Nathan Ausubel seems to agree: "Wit and irony can be regarded as the likely attributes of a civilized mentality." Nathan Ausubel, ed., *A Treasury of Jewish Folklore* (New York, 1948), p. xx.

12. Otto Weininger, *Sex and Character* (London, 1906), pp. 318–319.

13. Isaacs, p. 7.

14. Adler, p. 458.

15. *London Athenaeum*, 15 January 1876; cited in Sig Altman, *The Comic Image of the Jew* (Rutherford, 1971), pp. 144–145.

16. B. Rohatyn, "Die Gestalten des Juedischen Volkshumor," *Ost und West* 11 (1911): 122.

17. Ibid., p. 123.

18. Shmuel Niger, "The Humor of Sholem Aleichem," in *Voices from the Yiddish*, ed. Irving Howe and Eliezer Greenberg (Ann Arbor, 1972), pp. 41–50.

19. In Charles A. Madison, *Yiddish Literature: Its Scope and Major Writers* (New York, 1968), p. 96.

20. For example, Ausubel, *Jewish Folklore*, p. xx; Nathan Ausubel, ed., *A Treasury of Jewish Humor* (Garden City, N.Y., 1951), p. xvi; Rosten, p. xxiv; Novak and Waldoks, p. xiv.

21. Adler, p. 458.

22. Sigmund Freud, *Jokes and Their Relation to the Unconscious* (New York, 1960), pp. 102–116.

23. Druyanow, pp. ix–xix. Also see Donald C. Simmons, "Protest Humor: Folkloristic Reaction to Prejudice," *American Journal of Psychiatry* 120 (1963): 567–569.

24. Freud, pp. 111–112.

25. Adler, p. 468.

26. Martin Grotjahn, *Beyond Laughter* (New York, 1966), pp. 21–25; Theodor Reik, *Jewish Wit* (New York, 1962), pp. 217–242.

27. Kurt Lewin, "Self-Hatred Among the Jew" in *Resolving Social Conflicts* (New York, 1948), pp. 186–200; for a denial see Ausubel, *Jewish Humor*, p. xix: Novak and Waldoks, p. xv.

28. Ausubel, *Jewish Humor*, pp. xvi, xvii.

29. Irving Howe and Ruth Wisse, eds., *The Best of Sholem Aleichem* (New York, 1979), pp. ix–xxi.

30. Freud, p. 105; Sigmund Freud, "On Humour" in Sigmund Freud, *Character and Culture* (New York, 1963), pp. 263–269.

31. Grotjahn, p. 22; Reik, p. 202.

32. Bernard Rosenberg and Gilbert Shapiro, "Marginality and Jewish Humor," *Midstream* 4 (1958): 70–80.

33. Irving Kristol, "Is Jewish Humor Dead?: The Rise and Fall of the Jewish Joke," *Commentary* 12 (1951): 431–436.

34. Ed Gray, "The Rabbi Trickster," *Journal of American Folklore* 77 (1964): 331–345.

35. Salcia Landmann, "On Jewish Humor," *Jewish Journal of Sociology* 4 (1962): 198.

36. Kristol, p. 436.

37. Ruth R. Wisse, *The Schlemiel as Modern Hero* (Chicago, 1971).

African-American Humor: Resistance and Retaliation

Joseph Boskin

"Who steals my history?" intoned Welsh poet Dylan Thomas, in words that symbolically represent the narrative history of blacks in American society. "Who steals my history?" is a question that signifies indictment. History is memory that refracts, refines, and expands consciousness; whoever plunders someone else's history maims not only the person but also the ties that link one to others in the larger community.

To the disgrace of those who defined American culture—who, ironically, themselves created out of the ashes of their backgrounds a new destiny—African Americans were the only ethnic group whose history was grossly distorted and virtually eradicated. The effectiveness of such efforts moved James Baldwin in *Notes of a Native Son* to write: "He is unique among the black men of the world in that his past was taken from him, almost literally, at one blow . . . I am told that there are Haitians able to trace their ancestry back to African kings, but any American Negro wishing to go back so far will find his journey through time abruptly arrested by the signature on the bill of sale which served as the entrance paper for his ancestor."[1]

Baldwin's younger contemporary, sailor-turned-writer Alex Haley, the author of *The Autobiography of Malcolm X*, consumed ten years and his own funds in tracking down his family roots to the Kunte Clan in West Africa. His was an extraordinary odyssey that took him from the warm reminiscences of storytelling aunts in North Carolina, who repeated the anecdotal family connection, to cold archival records in Washington and other places, and finally to the embrace of the Kunte people in The Gambia. Haley listened in awe as the griot retold the genealogical history that included his faraway ancestor, Kunte Kinte, who had been kidnapped and enslaved. No other immigrant, from Asia or Europe, individual or family, faced this predicament: all could *read-*

ily connect back in time and place, and trace in detail their own odyssey to North America.

Deprived of their past, African Americans were further forbidden participation in the present, save as laborers beholden to the interests of another. Their connection to the narrative of the New World was minimal, as slaveowners and others responsible for the national record simply denied their intellectual presence and downplayed their capital significance. Rather, documents were replete with economic data and stereotypes but the African's intrinsic worth to the physical expansion and creative development of the country was disregarded.

But if the written record for and about blacks was disavowed, there was always black memory orally transmitted. "When the country was not looking at Negroes," Ralph Ellison commented in a dialogue with Robert Penn Warren in the mid-1960s, "when we were restrained in certain of our activities by the interpretation of the law of the land, something was present in our lives to sustain us. This is evident when we go back and look at our cultural expression, when we look at the folklore in a truly questioning way, when we scrutinize and listen before passing judgment. Listen to those tales which are told by Negroes themselves."[2]

Before the activities of the Civil Rights and Black Power movements, few whites had ever heard of those tales told by African Americans. Folklorists, writers, musicians, and civil rights activists were privy to the language and lore of the black community but they were few in number and communicating power. Occasionally, a white writer or entertainer—Joel Chandler Harris and Al Jolson, for example—made heavy use of black materials and expressions but they came to black culture with an outsider's presumptuousness.

Segregation in almost all areas of life—particularly in the areas of entertainment and mass communication—compounded the situation by preventing the emergence of black storytellers. The accounts that came forth through the music and black minstrels, in blues and jazz and musical comedies from the 1890s to the 1920s, undercut some aspects of the pejorative images of blacks present in American culture. Largely absent from the stages, radio, and film, however, were dramas and comedies about blacks that grappled with the human condition. Consequently, prior to the 1970s, few outside the black community

The
Humor
Prism
in 20th-
Century
America

146

could have identified such gifted and talented comedians as "Moms" Mabley, "Slapsey" White, Pigmeat Markham, Redd Foxx, George Kirby, Timmy Rogers, and a host of others. A wider audience was familiar with the piquant articles and books of Langston Hughes, yet he was virtually unknown to the majority of people outside of the urban Northeast.

A clue to the obscurity of black folklore, particularly its humor, can be discerned from the astonished thoughts of Ogden Nash, a premier writer of humorous verse, in his review in the mid-1960s of Langston Hughes's work, *The Book of Negro Humor*:

> The range of humor here collected is a surprise. One would not have expected so many kinds, from so many sources. There are the contemporary comics . . . There are jokes having to with jive and the blues! There are anecdotes from the pulpit. There are stories from Orleans and Harlem.[3]

Yet by 1966, when Stokeley Carmichael uttered that prophetic rallying cry "We Want Black Power! We Want Black Power!" before a group of Mississippi sharecroppers, whites were confronted daily by acts of political defiance and comedic assault. *Invisible Man*, Ralph Ellison's incisive work that had symbolically capsulated a historic past, was no longer applicable to the generations after the 1950s, with the rise to national prominence of black comedians such as Dick Gregory, Godfrey Cambridge, Bill Cosby, Richard Pryor, Skip Wilson, Eddie Murphy, and Whoopi Goldberg. For the first time, whites were exposed through comedy to black language and culture, on a national scale.

Whether the majority realized it or not, the dynamics of black humor stemmed in large part from a vigorous folk tradition that fused African and North American motifs. But it was the black experience in the New World, first of slavery and then of segregation, that shaped in a major way the format and tone of black laughter. Three and a half centuries of oppression produced a particular style of resistance humor that entwined defiance, cunning, inventiveness, and retaliation. Stories, anecdotes, jokes, and pranks record black counteraction to oppression and also provide insight into the character of the oppression itself.

Folklorists have identified as a primary form of response the employment of *protest tales*. "These stories," observed Donald C. Simmons, "usually by means of sarcasm, humor or parody of a prejudice's absurdity, primarily function to preserve the ego identity of minority group members compelled to suffer attacks on their group image through repeated contact with the majority group's unflattering stereotypes." Such stories abet "in conserving mental health through sublimating the anger, anxiety, shock and emotional disgust felt when the group image is attacked, by allowing the individual to release the suppressed aggression via *protest humor.*"[4]

The style in which the humor was transmitted among African Americans played a significant part in the repertoire of resistance. How it was expressed was as important as what was actually conveyed. The emphasis on style created, in Daryl C. Dance's phrase, a scenario "full of drama." Tellers of the tales did more than recount anecdotes: they acted them out, rhythmically embellished them, devised a code of double entendres, and established a hierarchal importance. In describing the evolution of African-American humor, Dance noted:

> The vocabulary is made interesting by the use of Negro slang expressions, jive talk, Biblical expressions, stock phrases, a great many obscenities, and an unmatched love of the double entendre. Much of the humor, particularly in the toasts and the dozens, is characterized by a musical, rhythmical quality, a love of verbal play and a delight in rhyme and pure sound. Many of the jokes and tales are highly colored by the influences of the fervent religious services with the chants and shouts of the minister and the impassioned responses of the congregation, as well as by the rhythm and stock phrases of the blues.[5]

The
Humor
Prism
in 20th-
Century
America

148

Resistance formed the contours of slaves' humor as they responded to their situation. Awareness of the need to mask one's feelings and practices occurred very early in response to the knowledge of entrapment: "I fooled Old Master seven years / Fooled the overseer three / Hand me down my banjo / And I'll tickle your bel-lee"[6] began a slave ditty that reflected many occurrences over the decades. This kind of self-concealment is demonstrated in the experience of a white scholar at a Southern university early in the twentieth century. In an attempt to trace the origins of folk songs, he sought to record the chants of black chain gangs. Direct efforts were frustrating as the singers halted their singing when he approached them and the odd rhythms and intonations proved unintelligible. In his office one day, he heard a labor gang breaking up worn pavement with sledgehammers to the accompaniment of melodious chants. Stationing himself unobtrusively on a campus wall, nonchalantly looking in the opposite direction while straining to hear the words he suddenly caught the gist of the song:

> White man settin' on the wall (hanh)
> White man settin' on the wall (hanh)
> White man settin' on the wall all day,
> A-wastin' his time,
> A-wastin' his time.[7]

The scholar, in short, was ensnared in the improvisational technique long honed by slaves anxious to protect their privacy.

Resistance connotes overcoming. Accounts of former slaves recorded in the 1930s and '40s are replete with illustrations of individual defiance and group laughter. "Jack was mean but he was a slick one," commented a fifteen-year-old in describing the escapades of an elderly slave on a North Carolina plantation:

> He was funny, too, and if he ever made up his mind not to do a thing all hell couldn't change him. He would get out of it in one way or another. Once the mistress wanted him to drive her to church on Sunday morning. When the message came to him, he swore he wouldn't drive and she sent for him. We all laughed at him because we thought he surely would have to go. But while he was talking to her he let his knife slip and cut his hand between the first finger and the thumb. "There now I have ruined my hand standing here whittling." Mistress excused him from driving. He went back to his house and such laughing I have never heard as he told us how he outwitted her.[8]

Obstinacy was just one form of resistance. Subtle ridicule was another tactic. Indeed, as Gilbert Osofsky noted in *Puttin' on Ole Massa*, "A private sense of irreverence for their master's plans . . . was the subject of much slave humor." On a Virginia plantation the following conversation was said to have occurred between the servant Pompey and his master, as he prepared for a duel with someone:

> Pompey, how do I look?
> O, massa, mighty.
> What do you mean "mighty," Pompey?

The
Humor
Prism
in 20th-
Century
America

149

> Why, massa, you look noble.
> What do you mean by "noble?"
> Why, sar, you just look like one *lion.*
> Why, Pompey, when have you ever seen a lion?
> I see one down in yonder field the other day, massa.
> Pompey, you foolish fellow, that was a *jackass.*
> Was it, massa? Well, you look just like him.[9]

Slaves contrived nicknames for their masters, mimicked their physical styles, composed ditties mocking their masters' attempts to understand them, wove African-trickster tales of vulnerable animals and stronger prey, and when the occasion demanded, play-acted a comical dumbness to escape retaliation: all these tactics were maintained and embellished throughout the next century of segregation.

A particular psychological facet of resistance was the process of inversion, the reversing of superior/inferior roles. Through this technique, the behavior of whites assumed the very stereotypical traits ascribed to blacks and thereby highlighted the ludicrous. In *Jokes and Their Relation to the Unconscious* (1905), Sigmund Freud explained, "A Joke will allow us to exploit something ridiculous in our enemy which we could not, on account of obstacles in the way, bring forward openly or consciously; once again, then, the joke *will evade restrictions and open courses of pleasure that have become inaccessible.*"[10]

Thus, one of many black responses takes the stereotype of inferior intelligence, a major component of racist ideology, and reverses it:

> A colored maid and her white employer became pregnant at the same time and gave birth on the same day. A few months later the white woman came running into the kitchen and exclaimed to the maid: "My baby said his first word today!" In the crib the colored baby sat up and said, "He did? He did? What did he say?"

On the charge of illiteracy, a lampoon on authority:

> In Alabama in 1942, a Negro drove his car through a red signal and was immediately stopped by a policeman. When asked to sign his name on the traffic ticket, the Negro signed an "X." Upon seeing the "X," the cop began hitting

the man on the head and declaring, "Boy, are you trying to be smart by signing my name on that ticket?"

And the following story, in reponse to the accusation of black thievery:

> A white minister arrived in Africa and was met by an African chief and his party. The chief indicated to the minister that his bags would be picked up by his men and transported to the interior. But first the chief wanted to show him around the village. The minister demurred, pointing to his belongings. The chief allayed his concerns, "You don't have to worry about your bags. There isn't a white man within a hundred miles of here."

An equally if not more pertinent variation on stereotype reversal is to be found in those tales countering the story of Genesis. Pro-slavery advocates had adduced from their interpretation of the tale of Ham the rationale for black servitude. The curse of Ham was God's punishment for moral degradation. Black enslavement was thus a proven fulfillment of the prophecy: God had relegated the African to a status of inferiority from the beginning of time. Blacks, therefore, reversed the position of precedence in the story of Genesis. One such interpretation was delivered by a preacher in the Black Belt:

> Brothers and Sisters, the first man the Lord made was Adam. The first woman was named Eve. They had two children, Cain and Abel. The mother and father and all them children were black; they was colored folks.
>
> Now Cain was a bad Negro, always shootin' an' cuttin' and gamblin'. He was jealous of his brother Abel and killed him one day in a dispute. . . . Then the Lord came up behind Cain and said: "Cain, where is thy brother?" That Cain was a sassy Negro, so he didn't turn around to see who 'tis, but just answered up biggity: "Am I my brother's keeper? I ain't got him in my pockets. I s'pose he's off somewhere."
>
> Then the Lord spoke more angry-like. "Cain, where is thy brother?" Then that Negro turned around and saw it was the Lord, and he got so scared that his hair stood right up straight and his face turned right pale—and sisters and brothers, *that is where the first white man come from.*[11]

The Humor Prism in 20th-Century America

151

The laughter of resistance drew its psychological force from many sources, but it was invariably enlarged by the ongoing challenge to survive. Survival necessitated retelling these particular stories not only as a way to maintain ego strength but also as a means of disarming the adversary. On occasion, a tale was told that was so complex in its arrangement and its shrewd assessment that it extended group resolve. A particular situation that involved hungry slaves and how they managed to scrounge the "meats" from the plantation owner is illustrative. The sense of triumph that resulted both from the escapade and from its retelling was due not only to the master's stupidity and viciousness but also to his ignorance of black mentality:

> . . . . I remember Mammy told me about one master who almost starved his slaves. Mighty stingy, I reckon he was.
>
> Some of them slaves was so poorly thin they ribs would kinda rustle against each other like corn stalks a-dying in hot winds. But they gets even one hog-killing time, and it was funny, too, Mammy said.
>
> They was seven hogs, fat and ready for fall hog-killing time. Just before Old Master told them they was to be killed, something happened to all them porkers. One of the field boys found them and come a-telling the master: "The hogs is all died, now they won't be any meats for the winter."
>
> When the master gets to where the hogs is laying, they's a lot of Negroes standing round looking sorrow-eyed at the wasted meat. The master asks: "What's the illness with 'em?"
>
> "Malitis," they tells him, and they acts like they don't want to touch the hogs. Master says to dress them anyway for they ain't no more meat on the place.
>
> He says to keep all the meat for the slave families, but that's because he's afraid to eat it hisself account of the hog's got malitis.
>
> "Don't you all know what is malitis?" Mammy would ask the children when she was telling of the seven fat hogs and seventy lean slaves. And she would laugh, remembering how they fooled Old Master so's to get all them good meats.
>
> "One of the strongest Negroes got up early in the morning," Mammy would explain, "long 'fore the rising horn called the slaves from their cabins. He skitted to the hog pen with a heavy mallet in his hand. When he tapped Mister Hog 'tween the eyes with that mallet, 'malitis' set in mighty quick,

The
Humor
Prism
in 20th-
Century
America

152

but it was an uncommon 'disease,' even with hungry Negroes around all the time."[12]

The poetry of the tale partly obscures the pain undergirding its roots, a bittersweet tone that flows through much of the resistance humor as blacks constantly and persistently assessed white behavior. A mythical sign at the outskirts of a southern town warned blacks of impending disaster:

> If you can read this sign, run—
> If you can't read this sign, run anyway.[13]

Macabre expressions and jokes circulated through African-American communities during and after the slave period. Sigmund Freud classified this form as "gallows" humor. Its presence, wrote sociologist Antonin J. Obrdlik, was an unmistakable "index of good morale and of the spirit of resistance of oppressed people."[14] Irony is often found at the edge of destruction:

> Negro (just arriving in town): Mr. Policeman, can you tell me where the Negroes hang out in this town?
>
> Policeman: Yes, do you see that tall tree over there?

Not infrequently, gallows jokes singled out specific individuals. Senator Theodore Bilbo of Mississippi, whose racist pronouncements resonated in his home state and on the floor of the U.S. Senate in the 1930s and '40s, was the object of a typical joke:

> A Negro soldier stationed in Europe after World War II met a French woman and married her. The soldier decided to bring the woman of his dreams back to his home town in Mississippi and wrote to his U.S. Senator, Theodore Bilbo, of his plans. A few weeks later he received a reply from the Senator's office: "Have hung your letter in my office. Am waiting on you."

That racist ideology attains a ridiculous sublimity in a tale recounted by historian Solomon Jones:

> One hot day in a small town in Mississippi my uncle drove his mule and wagon to town. Now in that town no Negro could own a white mule. So my uncle had a black mule and a white mule.

He stopped and went into the general store. While inside, someone scared the black mule and it ran away. A white woman was crossing the road at the time of the incident and the mule ran over her. The mob that gathered ran my uncle out of town, burned the wagon, and hung the mule.[15]

Before their decline in the mid-1960s and '70s, an array of gallows jokes mocked different situations, as indicated by the following story:

Two black men walking down the street were visited by a fairy who told them she would grant their fondest wishes. The first man turned to his friend and said, "I'm going to buy me a white suit, white shoes, white Cadillac, and drive to Miami Beach and lay in the white sand."

He then asked his friend what wish he desired. His friend replied, "I'm going to buy me a black suit, black shirt, black shoes, black Cadillac, and drive to Miami Beach and watch them hang your black ass."

Covert resistance came to an end at the height of the Civil Rights movement when, for the first time in American history, black comics found themselves performing in white nightclubs. Suddenly, in the early 1960s, the boundaries that had for so long restricted their comic creativity came crashing down and an outpouring of wit and humor poured into the popular culture.

Extracting from communal memory and embellishing from community banter, black comedians delivered a running commentary on white culture, all the while drawing attention to their own exclusive history. Dick Gregory began the assault, weaving a routine that demonstrated for his audiences the pattern of resistance that sustained African Americans over the centuries. "It's kind of sad, but my little girl doesn't believe in Santa Claus . She sees that white cat with the whiskers and even at two years old, she know damned well that no white man's coming to our neighborhood at midnight." On the scene at the time was Godfrey Cambridge, who tackled the issue of blacks and property values: "Do you realize the amount of havoc a Negro couple can cause just by walking down the street on a Sunday morning with a copy of the *New York Times* Real Estate Section under the man's arm?" Redd Foxx confronted concern about crime by threatening an unenthusiastic, predominantly white audience: "Why should I be

The
Humor
Prism
in 20th-
Century
America

154

wasting my time with you here when I could be knifing you in the alley?"[16]

Jokes that would have been restricted to the inner confines of the black community made their way to white ears. Throughout the commentaries, segregation remained a stark reality, despite the significant changes brought about by *Brown v. The Board of Education* in 1954, the Civil Rights Act of 1965, and the elimination of Jim Crow statutes and practices. De facto segregation still existed, a circumstance that continued to generate jokes in the mode that had for so long characterized resistance laughter. A tale of the mid-1970s revolved around the imagined first African-American commercial airline pilot:

> Good morning, ladies and gentlemen. This is Captain George Washington Jones speaking. Welcome aboard Flight #606 bound from New York to Los Angeles. We will be taking off in a few minutes after we receive the go-ahead from the tower. Our flight plan today calls for an altitude of 35,000 feet and flying time will be five hours and forty-six minutes. The weather across the country looks good and I anticipate a smooth flight. Now, if you will please fasten your seat belt, and observe the no smoking sign, I'll see if I can get this motherfucker off the ground. Hope you enjoy the trip.[17]

As white-imposed boundaries fell, a militant humor assumed a larger place in the response to ongoing racist customs. Black laundry workers refused to clean Ku Klux Klan robes in North Carolina; black students at northern colleges mimicked white students trying to dance in the black style; and among the many jokes that taunted whites, one involved a black freshman student at Harvard University who inquired of a professor, "Excuse me, where's the library at?" and was immediately informed, "Young man, you don't end a sentence with a preposition!"—to which the student responded, "O.K., man, where the library at, asshole?"[18]

Multiplied across the country, these actions echoed a chorus of militancy in humor that reflected and paralleled the nationalist movement of the 1970s and '80s. Blacks openly defied and mocked whites in jokes, skits, and routines. Performers such as Richard Pryor strove to impart the gnarled history of race relations on television programs, specials, and in concerts before mixed huge audiences. In a *Saturday Night Live* sketch, Pryor and

The Humor Prism in 20th-Century America

155

Chevy Chase collaborated in a dialogue that ran the gamut of racial slurs and images. Pryor is being interviewed by Chase for a custodial job, using a word-association test:

> "White," exclaims Chase.
> "Black," replies Pryor.
>
> "Bean."
> "Pod."
>
> "Negro."
> "Whitey."
>
> "Tarbaby."
> "What did you say?"
> "Tarbaby," Chase repeats, monotone.
> "Ofay," Pryor says sharply.
>
> "Colored."
> "Redneck!"
>
> "Junglebunny!"
> "Peckerwood," Pryor yells.
>
> "Burrhead!"
> "Cracker."
>
> "Spearchucker!"
> "White Trash!"
>
> "Junglebunny!"
> "Honky!
>
> "Spade!"
> "Honky, Honky!"
>
> "Nigger," says Chase smugly.
> "Dead Honky," Pryor growls.[19]

The
Humor
Prism
in 20th-
Century
America

156

From the confrontations prying open the acrimonious past came an enlarged sense of liberation. In various parts of the country, public displays of racist artifacts that had perpetuated derogatory stereotypes appeared. "Images of blacks in popular culture have been an important vehicle for the transmission of the myth of black inferiority," read the explanatory placard at the exhibit of *Black Memorabilia* at Dartmouth College in 1981. Within were 150 ephemera, a collection of demeaning comic objects ranging from toys, games, sheet music, postcards, advertising, book illustrations, and food packages produced between the mid-nineteenth and the early twentieth centuries that portrayed blacks as "slow, lazy, ignorant, stupid, amoral, criminal, unclean, bestial and generally subhuman." "Our explanation is clear," explained Dianne Pinderhughes, a political scientist who had assisted in organizing the show. "It may be unpleasant to view these items and to bring out into the open what may be considered shocking examples of black stereotyping. . . . We want to show how comprehensive a set of stereotypes we have in American society, among blacks and whites, and we want to generate discussion about how we create and maintain stereotypes." Marguerite Barnett-King, former director of the Institute for Urban and Minority Affairs at Columbia University, whose private collection had made up the bulk of the items, viewed the exhibit as a cultural mirror: "When one comes to terms with this material, one sees that the image is not me but an oppressor's idea of me."[20]

Gradually, black comics shifted the mirror away from the behavior of the majority to a reflection on their own existence. Godfrey Cambridge stated in the 1960s that among his aims was to acquaint whites with the "normalcy" of black culture, "with letting people see the truth of our lives."[21] A generation later, a group of young African-American comics in Los Angeles focused on the massive riot that engulfed the south-central area of the city in 1992. Performing at the Comedy Act Theater founded six years earlier in a district nearly destroyed by the violence, the comics dissected the community's behavior. Like shamans, they embraced and criticized, forgave and damned the looting and firebombing that followed the Rodney King verdict that exonerated four white policemen of brutality. "The purpose of making jokes about the riots," explained Keith Morris, "is to make people realize what they've done. I feel that the rioting was justified, but, then, it was *not* justified. . . . You just don't burn down things in the community." This sense of ambivalence found its chorus in the routines. "You know," exclaimed a female performer, "I'm glad the riots happened because those prices have just gotten to be so ridiculous! . . . But they didn't have to burn down Fatburger. That just broke my heart. I mean, is there any justice in the world that people can burn down Fatburger?"[22]

In taking over the comic images that had so long stigmatized blacks, and in grappling with events like the Los Angeles riot of 1992, African Americans achieved a turning point in the humor of resistance. They liberated themselves from the past and moved into a space beyond defiance and retaliation, one that held out the possibility of extending black *and* American humor into responsive, creative realms.

Notes

1. James Baldwin, *Notes of a Native Son* (Bantam Press, 1955), 144.
2. Ogden Nash, "Robert Penn Warren and Ralph Ellison: A Dialogue," *The Reporter* (March 25, 1965), 43.
3. *Los Angeles Times Calendar*, March 13, 1966, 33.
4. Donald C. Simmons, "Protest Humor: Folkloristic Reaction to Prejudice," *American Journal of Psychiatry* 120 (July–December, 1963), 567.
5. Darryl C. Dance, "Black American Humor," *American Humor: An Interdisciplinary Newsletter* 4 (Spring 1977), 3–4.
6. B. A. Botkin, *Lay My Burden Down* (University of Chicago Press, 1945), 3.
7. Gerald W. Johnson, *The Man Who Feels Left Behind* (William Morrow, 1961), 90–91.
8. "Times Got Worse after the War," *Slave Narratives*, Social Science Source Document #2 (Social Science Institute, Fisk University, 1945), 178.
9. Gilbert Osofsky, *Puttin' on Ole Master* (Harper and Row, 1969), 22.
10. Sigmund Freud, *Jokes and Their Relation to the Unconscious*, VIII (London: The Hogarth Press and the Institute of Psychoanalysis, 1905), 103. Freud's emphasis.
11. Langston Hughes and Arna Bontemps, eds., *The Book of Negro Folklore* (Dodd, Mead Publishing Co., 1965), 155.
12. Botkin, *Lay My Burden Down*, 4.
13. Author's notes, Interview with Solomon Jones, Los Angeles, June, 1967.
14. Antonin J. Obrdlik, "'Gallows Humor'—A Sociological Phenomenon," *American Journal of Sociology* 47 (March 1942), 712.
15. Author's notes, Interview with Solomon Jones, Los Angeles, June, 1967.
16. Dick Gregory with Robert Lipsyte, *Nigger: An Autobiography* (Pocket Books, 1970), 132; Mel Gussow, "Laugh at This Negro but Darkly," *Esquire* 62 (November 1964), 94–95; Redd Foxx and Norma Miller, *The Redd Foxx Encyclopedia of Black Humor* (Ward Ritchie Press, 1977), 234–5.
17. Author's notes, Interview with a black social worker, Los Angeles, February, 1973.
18. Author's notes, from a variety of sources, Los Angeles and Boston, 1970s and 1990.
19. *The Best of Chevy Chase* (Warner Home Video, 1990).
20. Rita Reif, "Black Stereotypes Featured in Dartmouth Exhibit," *New York Times*, March 3, 1981; Joseph Boskin, "Stereotypes and Images," lecture delivered at Dartmouth College, Hanover, N.H.
21. Joseph Boskin, "Good-bye, Mr. Bones," *New York Times Magazine*, May 1, 1966, 90.
22. Patrick Cole, "Comics Cope with the L.A. Riots," *Los Angeles Times*, May 11, 1992, F1,4; David J. Jefferson, "Amid L.A.'s Sorrows, Black Comedians See Shards of Laughter," *Wall Street Journal*, May 11, 1992, A1,4.

The
Humor
Prism
in 20th-
Century
America

158

Why Are These Women Laughing? The Power and Politics of Women's Humor

Suzanne L. Bunkers

Suicide? Hardly a laughing matter. That is, of course, unless you're twentieth-century American humorist Dorothy Parker, writing about the subject with an acerbic tone and a wry eye toward the little ironies of life—and death:

> Resumé
>
> Razors pain you;
> Rivers are damp;
> Acids stain you;
> And drugs cause cramp.
> Guns aren't lawful;
> Nooses give;
> Gas smells awful;
> You might as well live.
>
> (Parker 99)

The
Humor
Prism
in 20th-
Century
America

159

Parker's matter-of-fact view, so succinctly presented in "Resumé," *is* funny, yet it also makes readers take seriously the woman who once called herself "a little Jewish girl trying to be cute."[1] Parker's variety of humor, considered unusual in a woman writing during the 1920s and 1930s, has actually evolved as part of a long tradition of women's humor which can be traced back to the seventh-century B.C. poet Sappho and which finds voice in poems such as Emily Dickinson's "I'm Nobody! Who are You?":

> I'm Nobody! Who are you?
> Are you—Nobody—Too?
> Then there's a pair of us?
> Don't tell! they'd advertise—you know!

Reprinted with permission of *Studies in American Humor: The Journal of the American Humor Studies Association,* Elmira College.

> How dreary—to be—Somebody!
> How public—like a Frog—
> To tell one's name—the livelong June—
> To an admiring Bog!
>
> (Dickinson 47–48)

Women's humor has existed for a long time (some say, ever since Eve joked with Lilith that Adam was a rough draft), but only recently have we begun to examine the ways in which women use humor and to ask, "Do women have a special sense of humor?" Robin Lakoff, who has studied women's use of language, makes this observation on traditional American assumptions about women and humor: "It is axiomatic in middle-class American society that, first, women can't tell jokes—they are bound to ruin the punchline, they mix up the order of things, and so on. Moreover, they don't 'get' jokes. In short, women have no sense of humor" (Lakoff 56).

Are these assumptions correct or incorrect? Do women have a sense of humor? Is there such a thing as a special type of humor used by women? If so, what typifies it? The purpose of this article is to explore these questions.

If women have been perceived as having any sense of humor at all, it has been self-deprecatory humor, that is, humor characterized by the joke-teller's laughing at herself and putting herself down. This type of humor is evident in the jokes of such comediennes as Phyllis Diller, whose typical stand-up routine begins, "Bob Hope says I was so ugly when I was brought into the world that the doctor slapped my mother" (Scott 1). Self-deprecatory humor, the stock-in-trade of such women comics as Diller and Joan Rivers, is not a recent phenomenon. Seventeenth-century American poet Anne Bradstreet, in "The Prologue," sent her poems out into the world as if they were her children, prefacing their presentation with her recognition that many who read her works would, because their author was a woman, naturally view the poems as weak and inferior:

> I am obnoxious to each carping tongue
> Who says my hand a needle better fits;
> A poet's pen all scorn I should thus wrong,
> For such despite they cast on female wits;
> If what I do prove well, it won't advance,
> They'll say it's stolen, or else it was by chance.

Let Greeks be Greeks. and women what they are,
Men have precedence, and still excel.
It is but vain unjustly to wage war;
Men can do best, and women know it well.
Preeminence in all and each is yours;
Yet grant some small acknowledgement of ours.
(Bradstreet 62)

The poet's self-deprecatory tone is, of course, somewhat tongue-in-cheek: she makes a pretense of acknowledging her inferiority as a woman poet just before she presents her finely wrought poetry for the world to read. Thus, there is a double-edged quality to her humor. Bradstreet is laughing not so much at herself as she is at those who would, without reading her work and judging it on its own merit, discredit her writing because of her gender.

When we read Bradstreet's disclaimer, we may sit back and smile, not because we are laughing *at* the poet but because we are laughing *with* her. Self-deprecatory humor, when used by women, often functions not to demean a particular woman but to establish a common ground among women. When Nora Ephron writes about the female anatomy, we can identify with her struggle to increase her chest measurement:

> Here are some things I did to help: Bought a Mark Eden Bust Developer. Slept on my back for four years. Splashed cold water on them every night because some French actress said in *Life* magazine that that was what she did for her perfect bustline. (Ephron 5–6)

As we read this account, we might laugh, not because we are revelling in our superiority to Ephron, but because we remember all too well those years in gym class when we chanted mindlessly, "We must, we must, we must increase the bust. The bigger the better, the tighter the sweater. . . ."

In a similar vein, when Erma Bombeck describes her never-ceasing efforts to lose weight, millions of women who have tried unsuccessfully to become a perfect size five can laugh at the ridiculousness of the efforts which Bombeck recounts: "I have dieted continuously for the last two decades and lost a total of 758 pounds. By all calculations, I should be hanging from a charm bracelet" (Bombeck 87). Women's use of self-deprecatory humor has arisen from an acculturation to being told, "You're

The
Humor
Prism
in 20th-
Century
America

161

inferior." Sociologist Paul McGhee, in noting the association of power with the successful use of humor, explains that the initiation of humor has in our culture become associated with males rather than with females because males hold the power. McGhee continues, "For a female to develop into a clown or joker, then, she must violate the behavioral pattern normally reserved for women" (McGhee 183–84).[2] Those who hold the power in a culture develop a preference for humor that victimizes the powerless, while the powerless develop a preference for self-victimizing humor (McGhee 186). This tendency, McGhee reasons, provides one explanation for why women have tended to use self-deprecatory humor. Similarly, Elizabeth Janeway, in her analysis of power relationships, explains that the weak, recognizing their powerless position, repress their anger or allow it to seep out only in indirect ways (Janeway 61). Only when the weak learn to disbelieve in the inevitability of the hold of the powerful over them they can develop what Janeway calls the "first power of the weak," namely, the "ordered use of the power to disbelieve," which begins with the "refusal to accept the definition of oneself that is put forward by the powerful" (Janeway 167).

As applied to women's use of self-deprecatory humor, Janeway's analysis of the dynamics of power dovetails with McGhee's findings that the early socialization of women into passive, powerless roles plays a central part in producing self-deprecatory humor, and that a preference for humor disparaging women is not characteristic of all women but only of those with more traditional sex-role values and attitudes (McGhee 199). What both Janeway and McGhee imply is that, as women begin to identify with one another, the sense of powerlessness decreases and the use of self-deprecatory humor takes on the function of uniting women and of laying the groundwork for the creation of other, more positive, forms of humor.

One such type of humor can be called sarcastic humor. It involves pointing out the ridiculous nature of female stereotypes in order to shatter these stereotypes and to move beyond them. When Lily Tomlin speaks as Ernestine or as Mrs. Judith Beasley, for instance, she is using these female caricatures to illustrate the danger in assuming that such stereotypes are reflections of all women. When Edna St. Vincent Millay assumes the persona of the "little woman" in her sonnet, she does so for the purpose of making clear the persona's understanding of the ridiculousness of the role as well as her refusal to assume it any longer:

> Oh, oh, you will be sorry for that word!
> Give back my book and take my kiss instead.
> Was it my enemy or my friend I heard,
> "What a big book for such a little head!"
> Come, I will show you my newest hat,
> And you may watch me purse my mouth and prink!
> Oh, I shall love you still, and all of that.
> I never again shall tell you what I think.
> I shall be sweet and crafty, soft and sly;
> You will not catch me reading any more:
> I shall be called a wife to pattern by;
> And some day when you knock and push the door,
> Some sane day, not too bright and not too stormy,
> I shall be gone, and you may whistle for me.
>
> (Millay 31)

Sarcasm weaves its way throughout this poem. The speaker mocks her spouse, who has mocked her with his "'What a big book for such a little head!'" Her statement, "Oh, I shall love you still, and all of that" pokes fun at the myth of marital bliss as well as at the image of the submissive wife. The final three lines of the poem drive home the message: readers, as well as the speaker's spouse, now realize that the speaker has rejected the role of the "good wife" and that her spouse's whistling will be in vain.

Social criticism is the cornerstone of sarcastic humor, which provides an outlet for anger that has been repressed for too long. The function of sarcastic humor, as used by women, is to turn the laughter outward rather than inward, to expose the sex-role stereotyping in our culture and to reject, either implicitly or explicitly, these rigidly prescribed images of women. The use of such humor enables women to speak out in a non-violent, assertive way about adverse societal norms and to take the first step toward replacing pejorative images of women with more positive images.

Examples of sarcastic humor abound in everything from women's contemporary poetry to women's country-western music to women's cartoons. In her poem, "For the Straight Folks Who Don't Mind Gays But Wish They Weren't So BLATANT," Pat Parker mocks the double standard of heterosexism In American culture:

> Have you met the woman
> who's shocked by 2 women kissing
> and in the same breath tells you that she's pregnant?
> BUT GAYS SHOULDN'T BE BLATANT.
>
> Or the straight couple
> sits next to you in a movie
> and you can't hear the dialogue
> Cause of the sound effects
> BUT GAYS SHOULDN'T BE BLATANT.

The pseudo-conciliatory tone in the final lines of Parker's poem functions in two ways: it makes fun of stereotypical feminine politeness and at the same time reveals the anger underlying the speaker's refusal to return to the closet alone:

> So to you straight folks
> I say—sure, i'll go
> if you go too,
> but i'm polite—
> so—after you.
>   (Parker 23–24)

The
Humor
Prism
in 20th-
Century
America

164

As an example of sarcastic humor, "For the Straight Folks . . ." has yet two more important functions: it serves as a bonding agent for lesbians who have experienced heterosexism, and it calls for heterosexuals to reject the privilege of the double standard which they have enjoyed for so long. Such a poem carves out new ground for women's humor by calling for readers not only to acknowledge the existence of stereotypes but also to reject them and move beyond them to generate new, non-oppressive roles of women.

Feminist critic Naomi Weisstein, in discussing the uses of humor in the women's movement during the early 1970s, explains the significance of the sarcastic humor we see in poems like Pat Parker's in this way: women's supposed charm has depended on our passivity and muteness as well as on our acceptance of the myth that it is our nature to suffer and be still (Weisstein 90). Once women begin to develop a sense of shared oppression—a recognition that "their misery is not due to some innate inferiory, to their own flawed characters, but that there is something going on outside that is keeping them down"—the silence is broken, and the anger surfaces (Weisstein 90). Women, says Weisstein, "must try out forms [of humor] which throw off the shackles of self-ridicule, self-abnegation; we must tap that capacity for outrage, that knowledge of our shared oppression" (Weisstein 90). Sarcastic humor is the result. Women are no longer so likely to smile demurely or to laugh nervously in order to preserve an appearance of feminine propriety. With the surfacing of anger comes the realization that sarcastic humor can serve as one way for women to regain some measure of social control and thus reduce the feeling of personal and group powerlessness.

We can find sarcastic humor not only in women's poetry but also in such popular forms as country-western and feminist music. When Loretta Lynn sings "The Pill," we laugh at her mockery of the "henhouse" stereotype, but we take seriously her implicit message that women must control our reproductive capacity:

> I'm tired of all your crowin' 'bout how you and your hens play
> While holdin' a couple in my arms and another on the way.
> This chicken done tore up her nest and I'm ready to make a deal,
> And you can't afford to turn it down, 'cause you know I've got the Pill.

In a few short verses of "The Pill," the persona chastises her mate for living by the double sexual standard which allows men, but not women, to "play around"; she rebels against being the quiet, submissive "househen"; and she asserts her right to determine whether she will hatch any more "chicks." Loretta Lynn's song thus becomes a way of doing what writer Tillie Olsen refers to as "breaking silences" about women's lives and experiences, for the song, aired on radio stations across the United States (and banned on several of those stations) calls for women to reassess their own domestic situations and to reject the myth that it is a wife's duty to produce one child after another with no choice in the matter.[3]

Similarly, when we listen to Kristine Lems, a feminist songwriter, singing about breasts, we realize that we have traveled quite a distance from the days when ladies hardly dared speak of bosoms:

> Do you want to pay to take a peek at what drives me insane?
> They're in anthro books galore and I'm sure you'll just adore em,
> Cave women have the same . . . two simple
> Mammary glands! Oh-oh! Mother Nature's dairy delight.
> You can make cream or butter cause it's just a human udder,
> A natural mammalian sight.
> (Kaufman 39)

In "Mammary Glands," Lems goes one step further than Nora Ephron did in "A Few Words about Breasts": Lems shatters the mythology surrounding women's breasts as sexual symbols by poking fun at the "pay-for-a-peek" mentality of male-oriented erotica and pornography. At the same time, Lems jokes about the alternative mythology of women's breasts as "Mother Nature's dairy delight." Breasts, says the songwriter, are not to be disembodied and mythologized as representing either madonna or whore; rather, they are simply "a natural mammalian sight." In penning "Mammary Glands," Kristine Lems has asserted women's right to define our bodies in our own terms rather than to remain silent victims of a debasing cultural mythology.

Willie Tyson's song "Debutante Ball" provides yet another excellent example of how women use sarcastic humor to assert independence from a particular aspect of cultural mythology, in this case, the ritual of the debutante's coming-out ball, which in Tyson's song is juxtaposed with the presentation of a prize heifer in the show ring. The persona in "Debutante Ball" is Mr. Sherwood, a stereotypical Southern Gentleman escorting his "fine bred southern daughter girl" to the Debutante Ball while at the same time preparing his prize heifer, Old Red Satin, for auction:

> The Debutante Ball is my favorite function
> It happens every year about this time
> It coincides with our local cattle auction
> The best breeding stock in the county all in a line
> I run back and forth between the auction and the ball
> Thinkin', "Sherwood, ain't you lucky, ain't you fine
> The best cows on four legs and the prettiest gals on two
> Ain't nobody elses but mine."

The
Humor
Prism
in 20th-
Century
America

166

Sherwood's plans go awry, however, when his confusion about whom to take where results in Old Red Satin's appearance in the ballroom and his daughter's in the center of the sawdust-filled auction ring:

> Every seat was filled at the auction hall
> There was laughter and cigar smoke in the air
> The auctioneer was callin' loud, "All right now, you all
> Put your money on the line, slick back your hair
> What am I bid for this well developed kid
> There's not a thought or rotten tooth in her head
> She's a feeder and a breeder, and if you think you need her
> You can lead her like a milk cow to your bed."

The auctioneer's crass sales pitch is, of course, no different from Sherwood's own, and Sherwood stands in shame as the song concludes with his daughter's defiance of the patriarchal "meat-market mentality":

> You think I'm for sale if you're moneyed and you're male
> And it's true I've been trained to heed your call
> But fools are made by men and when we come through
>   again
> There'll be no auctions, no more Debutante Balls.

Women will chuckle with Willie Tyson's clever analogy in "Debutante Ball," perhaps recalling situations in our own lives where we have been paraded through one ballroom or another, all the while feeling like cattle on the auction block; and women will also feel the anger that Sherwood's unnamed daughter feels welling up inside herself, an anger that must be given voice. "Debutante Ball" works particularly well to reveal how women can use sarcastic humor to critique the institutionalization of sexual control over women in our culture and to reject the authority underlying such control.

Women's use of sarcastic, as opposed to self-deprecatory, humor arises from the perception that our culture has systemized the oppression of women and that humor can function as one avenue for the successful rejection of female powerlessness and for the assertion of female power. As Gloria Kaufman observes, we can differentiate between *female* humor, which "may ridicule a person or a system from an accepting point of view," and *feminist* humor, which is characterized by "the nonacceptance of oppression" (Kaufman 13).[4] *Female* humor, then, may well be self-deprecatory, while *feminist* humor is sarcastic and assertive. *Female* humor turns inward, back on the joke-teller, while *feminist* humor turns outward, directing itself toward others, encouraging them to share a common disbelief in women's powerlessness and to claim power by reclaiming the language and redefining its use.

The wide variety of cartoons and comic strips currently being produced by women artists provides further evidence of how pervasive and persuasive women's sarcastic humor has become.[5] Nicole Hollander's character Sylvia, a middle-aged woman who spends most of her time in front of her television munching on corn chips and Twinkies, also makes sharp and insightful comments about the realities of male-female relationships, the dangers of sex-role stereotypes, and the American obsession with the perfect female body. In one cartoon, Sylvia is conversing with a man who asserts, "Admit it, Syl. You need us. Can you imagine a world without men?" Sylvia replies, "No crime, and lots of happy, fat women" (Hollander, *Mercy*, 22–23). In another cartoon, Sylvia is working away at her typewriter, and her copy reads: "Men, boys! Are you bombarded by sexual signals from your female co-workers? Have you been unfairly accused of sexual harassment? Send for 'cutitout,' the revolutionary electronic device that jams those signals and lets you get on with your work" (Hollander, *Mercy*, 80–81). In a third cartoon, a female friend sits across the table from Sylvia, who peers into her crystal ball and asks, "So how come the tall, dark stranger I see in your future is a woman?" Her friend, saying nothing, smiles back knowingly (Hollander, *I'm in Training*).

Whatever the particulars of Nicole Hollander's cartoons, the general principle remains the same: Hollander uses the cartoon format to stake out new territory for women's humor by satirizing passive, submissive female stereotypes and by creating a character who is flashy, assertive, and unabashedly vocal. Many of Hollander's cartoons, which originally appeared in *Spokeswoman*, a feminist journal published monthly in Chicago during the 1970s, find their way into mass-circulation magazines where they enable an increasing number of women to laugh at life's complexities and at the same time to find an outlet for anger and frustration with traditional female roles in our culture.

This examination of self-deprecatory and sarcastic humor brings us back to our original question: "Is there such a thing as a special sense of humor embodied in women's essays, poetry, music, cartoons, and other popular forms of expression?" This is a challenging question, one that cannot be answered with a simple yes or no. If we accept the hypothesis that humor is shaped by the individual's perception of his or her degree of power in our culture, then it is clear that women's sense of powerlessness in the past has accounted for much of the self-deprecatory tone in humor by and about women. It is also clear that, as women's recognition of a common disbelief in powerlessness has grown, a corresponding trend in women's humor has been a movement away from the self-deprecatory and toward the sarcastic, this movement reflecting a rising consciousness of the potential for women's claiming of power. Because women and men have not experienced the same dynamics of power and powerlessness in our culture, the forms of expression which their uses of humor have taken have been decidedly different. It has not been my objective in this article to conduct an in-depth comparative study of forms of women's and men's humor; however, my analysis of women's humor leads me to conclude that, regardless of gender, an individual who feels that he or she is powerful is less likely to engage in self-deprecatory humor and is more likely to engage in assertive forms of sarcastic humor than is an individual who feels powerless. This is not to say that a powerful individual necessarily uses humor to victimize others, although this potential does exist, especially in a setting where a clearly defined imbalance of power has been systematized and institutionalized.

Thus, I do not conclude that, due to a difference in gender, women and men have decidedly different senses of humor. Rather, I suggest that any analysis of women's and men's uses of humor be informed by an understanding of power, past and present, in our culture, and by an awareness of the politics of power on interacting members in a power relationship.

Gloria Kaufman, in her introduction to *Pulling Our Own Strings: Feminist Humor and Satire*, speaks of the diversity of types of humor used by women and points specifically to feminist humor as a humor of survival—one which has the potential to rehumanize and recivilize us (Kaufman 16). To Kaufman's assessment I would add yet a third important function of women's humor: the potential to revitalize us. Because it focuses our attention on

The Humor Prism in 20th-Century America

169

what has been changed as well as on what remains to be changed in our culture, and because it keeps us laughing as it does so, humor plays an indispensible role in our lives. Mary Daly is right: "There is nothing like the sound of women really laughing. The roaring laughter of women is like the roaring of the eternal sea" (Daly 17). Our laughter unites us; it awakens our feelings of self-worth; and it confirms our sense of power.

Notes

1. Today, Dorothy Parker is best remembered for her witticisms. Although Parker was a respected member of the Algonquin Round Table, she had trouble taking herself seriously as a humorist. In the *Paris Review* interview, Parker said, "I don't want to be classed as a humorist. It makes me feel guilty. I've never read a good tough quotable female humorist, and I never was one myself" (Cowley 77). Parker's comment here is important because it reflects her assumption that "toughness" is not within the realm of female humor.

   Phyllis Diller has also spoken about how cultural assumptions about women and humor affected her early reception by audiences: "I was good but my first show was a bomb. The only joints that would accept a female comic in those days were gay places. Non-gay male audiences were hostile. They still are. Men hated me at the beginning. I was a threat because I was invading a man's field. I was the first female stand-up comic which is very different from great comic actresses such as Lucille Ball or Carol Burnett who work ensemble, but never alone on stage. To this day I won't do my act unless there are women in the audience. Women are the first to laugh when I poke fun at high fashion, cooking, kids and driving. Then the men laugh, too. . . ." (Scott 1).

2. Susan Vass, a member of the Comedy All-Stars, an ensemble of comedians performing at Dudley Riggs Etc. in Minneapolis in 1983, responded in this way to an interviewer's question about whether she felt that she faced a sexual disadvantage as a woman stand-up comic: "I have some theories about that. . . . I think women are not used to bantering. Women are taught to be nice, but men have the locker room banter going on all the time. They have to be sharp or they will go under. I'm still not quick. The guys are ragging on me all the time in the waiting room. They're training me in the instant put-down. Women don't do that to one another. That's mostly a male kind of thing" (Strickler 8C). Vass's remarks verify what Paul McGhee asserts: a female comic is viewed as violating the norm of appropriate behavior for women in our culture. Vass's statement that banter and put-downs of others are not characteristic of women's use of humor reinforces McGhee's claim that male humor, derived as it is from a position of power within our culture, is characterized by forms of expression that tend to victimize others.

3. In an interview published in *People Magazine*, Loretta Lynn noted that her songs are written with an audience of women in mind. "The women buy the records and you'd better let 'em know you're just like they are. You can't start singin' over their heads like you're something better" (Windeler 25).

4. Kaufman makes this distinction: "Feminist humor tends to be a humor of hope, female humor of hopelessness. (This is not to contend that bitter-

The
Humor
Prism
in 20th-
Century
America

170

ness is absent from feminist humor, merely that, compared to female humor, it occurs much less regularly.)" (14)

5. Nicole Hollander is one of a growing number of women cartoonists whose works appear in newspapers and magazines across the United States. Other prominent cartoonists include Cathy Guisewite, whose comic strip, "Cathy," pokes gentle fun at growing up female in America; and Claire Bretecher, whose comic strips provide sharp-witted and often bitter satire of traditional sex roles for males as well as for females.

Sources Consulted

Bombeck, Erma. *I Lost Everything in the Postnatal Depression.* New York: Fawcett Crest, 1970.

Bradstreet, Anne. "The Prologue." In *Norton Anthology of Literature by Women.* Ed. Sandra Gilbert and Susan Gubar. New York: W. W. Norton, 1985.

Cowley, Malcolm, ed. *Writers at Work: The Paris Review Interviews.* New York: Viking Compass Press, 1957–58, 69–82.

Daly, Mary. *Gyn/Ecology: The Metaethics of Radical Feminism.* Boston: Beacon Press, 1978.

Dickinson, Emily. *Final Harvest.* Ed. Thomas H. Johnson. Boston: Little, Brown and Co., 1961.

Ephron, Nora. *Crazy Salad: Some Things about Women.* New York: Bantam Books, 1976.

Hollander, Nicole. *I'm in Training to Be Tall and Blonde.* New York: St. Martin's Press, 1979.

———. *Mercy, It's the Revolution and I'm Still in My Bathrobe.* New York: St. Martin's Press, 1982.

Janeway, Elizabeth. *Powers of the Weak.* New York: Alfred A. Knopf, 1980.

Kaufman, Gloria, and Mary Kay Blakeley. *Pulling Our Own Strings: Feminist Humor and Satire.* Bloomington: Indiana University Press, 1980.

Lakoff, Robin. *Language and Women's Place.* New York: Harper and Row, 1975.

Lynn, Loretta. "The Pill." 45 rpm. MCA Records, 4560186, 1975.

McGhee, Paul E. "The Role of Laughter and Humor in Growing Up Female." In *Becoming Female: Perspectives on Development.* Ed. Claire B. Kopp, in collaboration with Martha Kirkpatrick. New York and London: Plenum Press, 1979.

Millay, Edna St. Vincent. *Collected Sonnets.* New York: Harper and Row, 1959.

Parker, Dorothy. *The Portable Dorothy Parker.* New York: The Viking Press, 1973.

Parker, Pat. *Woman/Slaughter.* Oakland, CA: Diana Press, 1978.

Scott, Vernon. "At 62, Phyllis Diller's Still Making Them Laugh." *The Wisconsin State Journal,* July 24, 1979, section 5:1.

Strickler, Jeff. "'Misfit' Fits the Bill Nicely as Member of Riggs Laugh Squad." *The Minneapolis Star and Tribune,* March 18, 1983: 1C, 8C.

Tyson, Willie. "Debutante Ball," *Debutantes.* Album. Urana Records (Wise Woman Enterprises), 1977.

Weisstein, Naomi. "Why We Aren't Laughing . . . Anymore." *Ms.* (November 1973): 49–51, 88–90.

Windeler, Robert. "Loretta Lynn's 'Pill' Is Hard for Some Fans to Swallow." *People Magazine* (March 31, 1975): 23–25.

A Rose by Any Other Name . . . The Occasional Doo-Dah Parade

Denise L. Lawrence

The
Humor
Prism
in 20th-
Century
America

172

To many Americans, viewing Pasadena's annual Rose Parade is synonymous with observing the first day of the New Year. For nearly one hundred years the city has celebrated its internationally known floral festival and followed with the Rose Bowl football game. Highlighting the parade are self-propelled floats, all fabulously decorated with flowers and vegetable materials, which portray exotic fantasy gardens, romantic historical scenes, and cute cartoon characters. For two hours the floats, dignitaries, marching bands, and show horses gracefully glide down the parade route, enchanting millions of viewers who line the street or sit comfortably at home in front of the television.

In 1986 the tenth anniversary of a lesser-known event, Pasadena's Occasional Doo-Dah Parade, was celebrated. Led by its own official band, Snotty Scotty and the Hankies, the parade treated viewers to such memorable entries as the Bed Pan Brigade, the Junk Food Junkies, and the Marlboro Man Rides Again —in an old-fashioned hearse. As ritualized rebellion, Doo-Dah was intentionally created to oppose its conservative counterpart, the Rose Parade. A contentious, licentious, irreverent parade, Doo-Dah lets its participants express themselves in grotesque imagery and the satire of dissent.[1] The Rose Parade glorifies the pristine beauty of roses and orchids; Doo-Dah's "Lovers of the Stinking Rose" celebrate the garlic, and its "Queens in Search of a Float" parody the Rose Parade's Royal Court.

During the past century the Rose Parade and Rose Bowl traditions have grown to form an important core of Pasadena's folklore and constitute essential ingredients in the city's unique

---

This essay was originally published in *Urban Resources*, vol. 4, no. 3 (Spring 1987). Reprinted with permission.

urban identity. By inverting the Rose Parade and other symbols of the city's tradition, however, the Doo-Dah has recently created a dialogue of street performances. Through these public dramas, participants explore the image of the city and themselves.

Parades and Contemporary Life

Modern cities are exceedingly complex products of human life which appear to bring some harmony to multiple social, economic, and political processes. The traditional focus of the American urban order is Main Street. It is geographically centered, the site of commercial and civic institutions, and a primary conduit for vehicular and pedestrian traffic. Main Street is also the traditional center of civic ritual and symbolic activities. In concentrating multiple functions, it is a public place that can stand for the city, a symbol that is special.

Parades are ritual performances that create time out of time. They establish frames to set special time apart from ordinary time, and they provide an arena within which creativity can be legitimately expressed. As communicative events, parades convey messages expressing and inverting the moral order by playfully manipulating symbols. According to Victor Turner, rituals may create a state of "liminality" in which ordinary social roles are transposed; age, gender, occupation, and hierarchical statuses are often reversed.[2] Turner argues that this symbolic playfulness contributes to a feeling of *communitas*, a sense of unity, that transcends everyday social divisions and potentially conflicting sentiments. By colluding in the creation of illusion, participants are able to reaffirm collectively the meaning of the social and moral order.[3]

The ritual reaffirmation of community in contemporary society, however, must not be overstated. Modern post-industrial life is lived in large, heterogeneous, and fragmented social settings. Today's urbanites continue to pursue communitas through collective public rituals[4] but these events are viewed as nonessential, optional activities.[5] Contemporary society lacks the cohesiveness permitting ritual celebrations to directly and completely reinforce moral codes and the social order; these urban parades and festivals are self-consciously produced and passively experienced.[6] As vehicles for the expression and contemplation of only partial beliefs and values by social segments, they cannot

The
Humor
Prism
in 20th-
Century
America

173

accomplish the task of affirming the whole but instead reveal inconsistencies and provide opportunities for opposition to appear.

The Rose and Doo-Dah Parades comprise Pasadena's two most important public ceremonial events, providing a ritual base for the city's continually evolving identity. The form and content of any parade are malleable and can act as powerful vehicles for communicating messages on a variety of levels. While the Rose Parade has responded to a rather conservative constituency, the Doo-Dah speaks to and for a previously silent community. By purposely breaking the rules, this rebellious newcomer has become a legitimate parade alternative in Pasadena.

The Rose Parade

The Rose Parade originated in the celebration of California's temperate winter climate by affluent midwesterners who fled the cold and snow of hometown Chicago and Cleveland around the turn of the century. In 1890 Pasadenans first began decorating horses and buggies with flowers in celebration of the new year; later, horseless carriages became a popular substitute. Within a few years, athletic competitions such as chariot races, and then football games, were added to the parade's festivities. Today, the Rose Parade is a two-hour media event featuring sixty florally decorated, self-propelled floats, and twenty-two bands, equestrian units, and numerous personalities. As the city and parade grew, so did the parade route. Today it covers five and one half miles, beginning near its original site and continuing on Colorado Boulevard through the center of town toward the more recently developed residential areas.[7]

The Rose Parade is organized and staged by the 1,300 volunteer members of the Tournament of Roses Association, who must apply and be accepted for membership and who actually pay for the privilege of working on the event. Traditionally, members have been white male businessmen and professionals, or employees of large corporations or civic agencies.[8] Work is accomplished by dividing the membership into roughly thirty, hierarchically ranked, specialized committees. Expenses incurred in producing the event are met by revenues generated from proceeds and fees paid for television rights to the football game.

The parade organizers choose the Rose Queen and her court, high school bands, and equestrian units through a com-

The
Humor
Prism
in 20th-
Century
America

174

petitive selection process and critically review float designs before acceptance. Although Tournament members are intimately involved in parade production, they never perform or participate in the actual design, manufacture, or sponsorship of any entry. The massive floral floats are built by specialized float building companies which compete for prizes in artistic design and execution. Float themes, kept simple so that complex messages do not interfere with the passive pleasure of viewing the floral beauty, are chosen to offend no one and to capture the essence of American wholesomeness; they include patriotic sentiments, but not political ones; a fundamental belief in God, but no particular religion; and virginal beauty, rather than sexual explicitness. Prize-winning float sponsors are generally large corporations, who can afford to spend large sums of money to gain an advertising advantage. Some municipalities, foreign governments, and large voluntary associations also enter.

In general, the Rose Parade is well liked in Pasadena. Businessmen and politicians claim that it has generated tremendous revenues for the city, especially for establishments along Colorado Boulevard. Residents also seem to like it, although many wealthy inhabitants of the parade's formation area leave town before New Year's Eve to avoid the rowdy, out-of-town, all-night crowds. Traditional forms of celebration, including uninhibited public drinking and sleeping on the streets and front lawns, take their toll in arrests for disorderly conduct and destruction to private property. Nevertheless, many Pasadena residents are proud to have such a splendid event emanate from their city.

The Humor Prism in 20th-Century America

175

The Doo-Dah Parade

Despite its status as an internationally known media spectacle, in recent years the Rose Parade has not held Pasadena's festive spotlight alone. In a very short time, the Doo-Dah Parade has become a viable alternative to the more traditional event. Its spontaneous origins have since become legend, forming part of the Doo-Dah's own mythology and folklore. On a hot summer's eve in a local bar in Pasadena's original center, the Old Town, a group of artists and members of an aging counterculture community gathered to discuss the problems of their community. By chance the conversation drifted to traditional Rose Parade practices as a new arrival in the Old Town pressed locals for information. They told him that, according to ancient custom, when the first of January falls on a Sunday, out of respect for the sabbath the Rose Parade is held on the second day of the new year. The new arrival suggested that, since New Year's Day 1978 was just such an occasion, they seize the opportunity to make their own statement about Pasadena.

What prompted these artists and their friends to stage their own parade was their perception that Old Town and its way of life was threatened. A number of artists had found affordable housing and studio space there, and many elderly pensioners lived in a number of single-room occupancy hotels. Several coffee houses, restaurants, and bars provided a network of lively gathering places for the community. The City of Pasadena, however, had recently initiated an urban redevelopment scheme which sought to revitalize the Old Town. Although "run down" by middle-class standards, the neighborhood was comfortable, economical, full of life, and considered by residents to be in need of no redevelopment. To demonstrate its vitality, they chose that New Year's Day to stage the first Occasional Doo-Dah Parade.

A much deeper motivation for the Doo-Dah Parade, and reason for its ultimate success, lay in what the Rose Parade had come to represent in Pasadena. Its postwar transformation from a hometown parade into a large-scale, staged media event made it more formal, contrived, and oriented to outside audiences than it had been before. Further, the Rose Parade was tightly controlled by the local elite, who also dominated the business community and civic affairs. The parade reflected the values of this powerful urban minority and tended to exclude members of the larger Pasadena community. Rose Parade members were also indirectly linked to Pasadena's politics and to the redevelopment scheme in Old Town. Thus, organizers of the Doo-Dah Parade saw their chance to gain some publicity while symbolically protesting against a parade which represented, by association, a threat to their treasured way of life.

The Doo-Dah was conceived as an event that would retrace the steps of an earlier Rose Parade down the original main street and through the Old Town, thereby symbolically recreating the meaning of a hometown celebration. Unlike its highly organized, competitive counterpart, the Doo-Dah was intended to be spontaneous—no rules, no parade theme, no contests, no prizes, no

The
Humor
Prism
in 20th-
Century
America

176

censorship of parade entries, and not even an order of appearances. Organization was handled by the Pasadena newcomer, later dubbed "The Czar." Working out of his apartment with the aid of an answering machine, the czar was able to coordinate parade entries and arrange for the proper permits and insurance. A nominal charge for entrants, $15.00 for individuals and families, $20.00 for groups of over six individuals, and $29.95 for businesses, provided funds for basic expenses (several thousand dollars the first year). On January 1, 1978, as unwary revellers waited on Colorado Boulevard for the traditonal Rose Parade to begin, the first Occasional Doo-Dah Parade took place. Although the intention was to hold the parade only once, it was so successful that participants immediately began to plan for the following year.

The earliest Doo-Dah Parades clearly protested against the Rose Parade, the segment of the local population associated with it, and the Old Town redevelopment scheme. The "Torment of Roses" was a popular entry which continues to evolve each year. A shopping cart transports the "Rose Queen," actually a garishly painted man sporting a blond wig and outfitted in a tight satin dress with balloon breasts. During the early years, the "Immoral Minority" and a Richard Nixon impersonator carrying a sign declaring "I'm no Crook!" outraged conservative residents. Pasadena City Planners were satirized by one marcher who, dressed in coat, shirt, tie, and boxer shorts, carried a placard demanding "No More Malz"; it referred to the cornerstone of the city's redevelopment scheme, a new shopping mall on Colorado Boulevard.

In addition to the more pointed commentary, participants in a number of entries, many of which have become standard Doo-Dah fare, held a mirror to themselves. The "Synchronized Briefcase Drillteam" marches with actual bank loan officers dressed in gray flannel suits. The bankers hoist briefcases in coordinated drill patterns as they strut in loosely choreographed steps down the main street. One year, the Pasadena Young Lawyers chased a cardboard ambulance down Colorado Boulevard. "Dr. Jim the Dentist," a real dentist, promotes good dental care by demonstrating the use of a gigantic toothbrush and "Crust" toothpaste on an enormous set of choppers while "Dental Flossie" chimes, "Let the floss be with you." The Cancerettes, sporting cigarette package costumes labeled "Old Mold," "Yucky

The
Humor
Prism
in 20th-
Century
America

177

Strike," and "Fool," try to de-glamorize the bad habit by award-ing themselves the "Surgeon General's Trophy."

Some entrants caricature the opposition or create an ab-surd identity in order to convey some important social message. The Ladies Against Women, from a women's center at a local university, parody anti-ERA traditionalists, claiming that "Tupperware Preserves the Family" and urging us to "Make America Strong Again, Invade a Broad!" Bubba Rubba from Planned Parenthood dresses in a rubberized "prophylactic" cos-tume and carries a placard warning males in the audience, "You'd be more careful too if it was you who got pregnant!"

The Doo-Dah Parade has also established itself as a potent vehicle for political protest. One year "Trickle Down" appeared with the blind, all in Ronald Reagan masks, leading the blind. Periodically, issues such as President Reagan's Star Wars military defense proposal or the continuing U.S. involvement in Latin America will provoke a rash of satirical entries. A short time ago an entry claimed, "Reagan is not senile. He can recall everything, including missiles," while another argued, "Get the U.S. out of El Segundo!" (a reference to a local port).

One of the more clever Doo-Dah entries portrayed a Nancy Reagan impersonator wearing a "Reagan" red dress and seated at a banquet table atop a large float. As a crew of rag-tag peasants pulled her along, "Nancy" threw them scraps of food from her table. A sign over her head read, "Let Them Eat Ketchup," a ref-erence to the federal administration's attempt that year to have ketchup approved as a vegetable for school lunch programs.

For the most part, DooDah participants are middle- and upper middle class white males and females—professionals, busi-ness people, and many students. Members of fairly mainstream voluntary organizations, churches, schools, and service agencies also participate. Doo-Dah's reputation has spread in recent years; now as many visitors as residents perform. While many partici-pants identify themselves as "liberals," few would claim to be as left of center in ordinary life as they appear in the parade. Doo-Dah participants often have, however, a passionate interest in their entry's message and volunteer many hours to perfect its expression.

The Doo-Dah's grotesque imagery, satire, and parody are central to its purpose; it offends in order to communicate. While the Rose Parade has a passive appeal, Doo-Dah performers attempt to engage observers in active, critical thinking about complex social issues. Indeed, the contexts of some Doo-Dah entries are so obscure that audience members are forced to interact with one another and share interpretations of the entries just to comprehend the jokes. Although not all entries please all members of the audience, there is an implicit agreement to tolerate that which one does not like in order to maintain the freedom and spontaneity of the event. Unlike the Rose Parade, Doo-Dah entries are unpredictable and experimental, often tasteless and, just as often, marvelous.

Resistance

Not surprisingly, the Doo-Dah parade upset a good many Pasadena residents during its early years; many local businessmen and politicians were offended by the parade's contentious messages. Attempts to squash the parade focused on the city's granting of permits, with controversy centering around the issues of timing and place. During its first five years, the Doo-Dah Parade was held the week before the Rose Parade and confined to a very small area on Colorado Boulevard and other Old Town streets. As it grew in popularity, the parade route was extended. Intense opposition was led by one local businessman who claimed that congestion created by the parade interfered with customer access to his store during after-Christmas sales. Some businesses were concerned because parade-goers might take parking spaces from customers.

Other attempts to rid the city of this offensive event were led by a city director who argued that summer would be a more appropriate time for the Doo-Dah and that it should be relegated to an area in the bottom of the nearby aroyo away from the central business district. The parade's route became a central issue since, by purposely performing on Colorado Boulevard, the Doo-Dah had intended to recapture the symbolic hometown essence of the original Rose Parade. And, by just preceding the New Year's Day event, the Doo-Dah heightened its message by sharing in the holiday ambience.

Although the arguments against the Doo-Dah focused on ostensibly rational issues, underlying these was unease about the parade's flagrant bad taste and a fear that its irreverent humor would somehow contaminate the "sacred" ground of the Rose

The
Humor
Prism
in 20th-
Century
America

179

Parade. Witness the following letter to the local newspaper: "The Doo-Dah (it rhymes with "blah") Parade is not only a blatant slap in the face to our magnificent Rose Parade, but it is a cheap, tawdry, tasteless community affront . . . a pathetically unimaginative hodge-podge of thrift-shop assemblages . . . a mawkish exhibition of public cavorting by welfare beneficiaries who should be seeking employment."[9]

But after numerous meetings of the city's Board of Directors, the Doo-Dah Parade prevailed, in part because the controversy and perceived offense could not be taken seriously. Ultimately the protest was a parade, a form of play, and was intended to entertain, even if its humor was lost on some community members. Further, since the czar was willing to compromise on various logistical points, the controversy began to look frivolous in light of more serious issues plaguing the city. Eventually, the event was moved to the Sunday after Thanksgiving, but the extended parade route stayed intact, except for a minor adjustment away from the vocal shopowner's business.

Acceptance and Accommodation

The
Humor
Prism
in 20th-
Century
America

180

Although the Doo-Dah parade originated as a local, hometown parade to protest against the Rose Parade, in recent years it has not needed the dominant event to justify its own brand of humor. No longer are entries primarily aimed at local issues and personalities. With Old Town redevelopment clearly established, that battle has been lost. The new Old Town is upscale with chic restaurants and specialty boutiques frequented by a young, well-to-do professional crowd. Although this group is strongly attracted to the Doo-Dah Parade, most are unaware of the irony of its original intent. Parade participants and audience (estimated at over 100,000 for 1986) are now drawn from wider geographic circles. The use and meaning of purely local references has weakened; but Doo-Dah is still an important vehicle for expressing protest on political issues beyond Pasadena. More important, the Doo-Dah continues to provide a unique opportunity for ordinary people to participate in a parade.

During the last five years, the Doo-Dah Parade and its supporters have won increasing acceptance in official circles. In 1985, one of the parade's original founders was elected to the city's board of directors. Although his association with the parade was not used in the promotion of his candidacy, his victory lent a certain legitimacy to the beliefs and values which underlie the event. The Rose Parade organizers themselves have also unofficially softened their opposition. In 1986 the Tournament took a subtle cue from the Doo-Dah's lighter spirit and chose "Laughter" as the official theme for the parade. As 1987 draws to a close, the Pasadena Historical Society, one of the city's most conservative institutions, will begin a ten-year retrospective celebration of the Doo-Dah.

City Streets and the Public Arena

The street is central to the performance of contemporary urban celebrations, more than simply a setting for parades and festivals. It is neither created nor used as an inert object; the street is a social fact.[10] Questions regarding who should use the street, and for what purposes, and who should regulate the use of the street and how, are essential for understanding who should have the right to collectively express themselves in public.

In an excellent study of workingmen's charivari in nineteenth-century Philadelphia, Susan Davis advances a theory of the popular use of the street for parades, linking it to the concept of the public domain.[11] She argues that the American notion of the public sphere is associated with the ideals of a liberal democracy, a belief that all people have equal access rights to public places. This conception, however, implies that public spaces ought to be neutral and that their proper use is not only unbiased but may be uninvolved. Davis suggests that the idea of neutrality is useful for avoiding confrontation with a system's inherent contradictions related to social inequalities and class conflicts. While users of public spaces are deceived into thinking they are free to act, they are in actuality constrained by a variety of rules and institutions which are differentially and selectively applied to them. Thus, streets are not "neutral fields or empty frames for social action," but are "structured and contested spaces."[12]

Although Davis focuses primarily on nineteenth-century Philadelphia, contemporary Americans have inherited many beliefs and values from that earlier time. Pasadena's citizens may recognize that complete public freedom is not possible, even in a democracy, and that the city must, in principle, regulate the organized collective use of public spaces. Belief in the neutrality of public spaces, however, is still problematic. The Doo-Dah's rights to equal access to the street were differentially interpreted by those in positions of unequal power. It was a qualified victory for a liberal democracy when the Doo-Dah Parade won its right to utilize the main street, but the fact that a battle was fought indicates that the public sphere is neither neutral nor void but rather is still a very much contested space.

Conclusion

Pasadena's Rose and Doo-Dah Parades are both public ritual events that renew urban life, identity, and a sense of place through celebration, but they differ in their means for achieving those goals. The Rose Parade creates fantastically beautiful floral illusions, an almost flawless facade. By contrast, Doo-Dah feigns disorder, chaos, and the absurd, offending viewers as it probes social and political issues and explores the contradictions of modern life.

Neither of Pasadena's parades can stand as the sole ritual expression or moral standard for the city. While the Rose Parade asserts community harmony and unity, the Doo-Dah cracks its facade to reveal myriad viewpoints hiding beneath. This symbolic dialogue between the two parades asks if the real Pasadena is respectable, tasteful, and conservative, or provocative, questioning, and liberal. There can be, however, no single answer because modern urban life is socially and politically too diverse and fragmented. Doo-Dah's creation has drawn attention to the traditional event by presenting a meaningful alternative, and many residents have found that parades are a lot more important than they originally thought. Urban celebrations can give us a collective sense of unity, even if it is only a momentary illusion. As we renew commitments to a variety of community values and places through public collective performances, we are reminded that parades are a living version of a city's folklore.

The
Humor
Prism
in 20th-
Century
America

182

Notes

1. The research presented here is based on a continuing field study of the Doo-Dah Parade begun in 1980. Data were collected using participant observation and video and photographic documentation and analysis. See Lawrence, "Parades, Politics. and Competing Urban Images: Doo-Dah and Roses," *Urban Anthropology* 11 (1982), 155–76, for a detailed comparison of

imagery and organizational structures of the Rose and Doo-Dah Parades and analysis of their relevance to community values and local politics. Lawrence (1987) discusses the evolution and routinization of the Doo-Dah Parade.

2. Victor Turner, *The Ritual Process* (Chicago: Aldine, 1969).

3. Victor Turner, "Liminality and the Performative Genres," in *Rite, Drama, Festival, Spectacle: Rehearsals toward a Theory of Cultural Performance*, ed. John J. MacAloon (Philadelphia: Institute for the Study of Human Issues, 1984), 19–41.

4. John J. MacAloon, "Olympic Games and the Theory of Spectacle in Modern Societies," in MacAloon, 241–80.

5. Victor Turner, "Frame, Flow and Reflection: Ritual and Drama as Public Liminality," in *Performance in Post-Modern Culture*, ed. Michael Benamou and Charles Caramello (Madison, Wisc.: Coda Press, 1977), 33–55.

6. Samuel Kinser, "Presentation and Representation: Carnival at Nuremburg, 1450–1550," *Representations* 13 (1986), 1–41.

7. Arnold Rubin, "Anthropology and the Study of Art in Contemporary Western Society: The Pasadena Tournament of Roses," in *Plastic and Graphic Arts*, ed. Justine Cordwell (The Hague: Mouton, 1981), 669–715. Rubin has written an excellent description of the Rose Parade's history and organization and gives a superb analysis of symbolic content of parade entries.

8. In the last ten years the Tournament has sought to increase the participation of women and minorities.

9. *Pasadena Star News*, 14 February 1979.

10. Robert Gutman, "The Street Generation," in *On Streets*, ed. Sanford Anderson (Cambridge, Mass: MIT Press, 1978), 249–64.

11. Susan Davis.

12. Susan Davis, 13.

The
Humor
Prism
in 20th-
Century
America

183

IV.

Events and Script

The Giant and the Child: "Cruel" Humor in American Culture

Joseph Boskin

Reality and humor have a complicated, if not conspiratorial, relationship. Though obviously connected, they often appear to move in contrary directions. The reason, as Sigmund Freud acutely observed, is that humor is the open means by which humans grapple with hidden forces, the object of the strophe being to make merry while the emotions rage. In this sly way, humor confronts reality either by distorting and disguising it, by enlarging and exaggerating its dimensions, or by wrapping it in bows and tinsel.

Of all the aspects of humor, the *joke cycle* in American culture is perhaps its most intriguing and imponderable expression. Its appearance in the twentieth century has been spontaneous but at irregular intervals; its form has remained traditional yet always related to current happenings; and its transmission has been initially oral yet usually communicated to succeeding generations via the popular small-sized paperback book. In the latter half of the twentieth century six major joke cycles have surfaced, all national in scope, whose subject matter has been quite diverse. They are specifically the long standing Polish (1950s–80s), Sick or Cruel (1950s–60s), Elephant (1960s), Light Bulb (1970s), JAP (1970s–80), and Disaster (1980s) jokes.

The popular humor of the immediate post–World War II decades—expressed as "black," "sick," and "cruel" and particularly the joke cycle of the pattern that focused on the Child—illustrate the complexities by which humor responds to swift and unsettling changes that have characterized American society throughout its history. The child-oriented cycle that suddenly

The Humor Prism in 20th-Century America

187

This essay was originally published in *The Lion and the Unicorn*, vol. 13, no. 2 (December 1989). Reprinted with permission of Johns Hopkins University Press.

made its appearance in the latter years of the 1950s and early '60s reflected the deep-seated anxieties of the adult world to the socioeconomic changes that were occurring, transformations that were not only affirmed by their actions as upwardly mobile consumers but were perpetuated by their adherence to bourgeois values as well.

Following the triumph of its global victory, the United States embarked on fulfilling the consumer expectations that had been suddenly and brutally cut short by the Great Depression and then by the requirements of the war itself. Freed from the deprivations of both events, there ensued a frenzied rush to achieve the American Dream: an ensured middle-class status buttressed by durable goods and entitled services. Fueled by the needs of a war-torn world and undeterred by competing national economies, the dynamic prosperity did indeed elevate a substantial majority into the middle classes.

The triumph of American technology transcended the continent. No longer isolated, no longer just an important player in the international scene, the United States assumed a global dominance. The result was the rise of the state as a superpower, the nation as a colossus capable of influencing the internal political policies of countries throughout the world.

Expectedly, the nation's language was swiftly altered to redefine its international place. Ideals, institutions and goods were catapulted into higher orbs, the words reflecting a kind of giantism. The prefix *super* quickly became attached to the American universe, suggestive of the world's most powerful financial, military and technological society. Consequently, grocery stores were expanded into supermarkets; six-lane highways were labeled superhighways that criss-crossed the nation; cities and the surrounding environs swelled into megalopolises; the "Sixty-four Dollar" radio show became the "Sixty-four Thousand Dollar" television program; the average-sized movie screen was enlarged into cinemascope; airplanes traveled at supersonic speeds; oil moved around the globe in supertankers; a football championship became the superbowl played in a superdome; and super-weapons and drugs became commonplace announcements. Words synonymous with *super* were sprinkled liberally throughout consumer culture. Products were labeled "extra large," "giant," "jumbo." Advertisements flashed "super sale" signs and beckoned the multitudes with "super savings." Colloquial expressions, too, fixed on the *super*: a positive response to almost anything became "that's super," "super-duper," or a spaced out "su--per." A special word highlighting a happy state was "supercalafragilistic - expialidocious" from the child/adult film, *Mary Poppins* (1964). A highly successful entertainer or athlete was anointed a "superstar." "Simply great" became one of the many hyperbolic phrases that summed up ordinary situations.

At the conscious level, the *super* image came to symbolize national and international might. Toward this type of symbol, as it has existed throughout mythology, a dual attitude emerged. Giants have been alternately viewed with awe and trepidation, adulation and anxiety, suggesting a lurking demon within the strength of a deity.

American folk humor captured this duality in the postwar decades. On the one hand were the Elephant jokes of the early 1960s that extolled in size and reach the enlarged dimension of the American state. Intriguingly, this particular joke cycle was the product of adult imagination but was subsequently incorporated into the repertoire of children's humor. The jokes rest on the premise that despite its size, the elephant has amazing powers contrary to all laws of nature, such as climbing trees, performing acrobatic feats, wiggling in and out of refrigerators and cars, wearing pajamas, walking on ceilings, and hiding under beds.

The humor of the Elephant jokes made quite clear its connection to virtually every fact of a prosperous society:

> How does an elephant get out of an elevator or phone booth? *The same way he got in.* / How do you keep an elephant from charging? *You take away his credit card.* / How can you tell there's an elephant in the refrigerator? *By the footprints in the butter* (or *jello, pizza, cream cheese*) / How do you housebreak an elephant? *Get fourteen copies of the New York Times—Sunday Edition* / How do you make a hamburger for an elephant? *Take 500 jars of mustard, 60 gallons of catsup, 90 pounds of onions, and then you get this big roll . . .* / What's red and white on the outside and grey on the inside? *Campbell's cream of elephant soup.*

The elephant's presence was not without its dangers:

> What looks like an elephant, flies, and is dangerous? *A flying elephant with a machine gun,* or, *A flying elephant with diarrhea* / Why do trees have leaves? *For elephants to hide behind* / Why

is it dangerous to walk in the forest between 1:00 and 2:00? *That's when elephants jump out of trees* / What's that black stuff between an elephant's toes? *Squashed natives* / Why do natives run through the jungle? *To escape from elephants jumping on them.*

The emergence of "black humor" was another expression that appeared unexpectedly, yet one that had its roots in what novelist Bruce Jay Friedman termed the "chord of absurdity" that characterized the events of the period. "What has occurred," Friedman observed, "is that the satirist has had his ground usurped by the newspaper reporter. The journalist, who in the year 1964, must cover the ecumenical debate whether Jews on the one hand, are still to be known as Christ-killers, or, on the other are to let off the hook, is certainly today's satirist. The novelist-satirist, with no real territory of his own to roam, has had to discover new land, invent a new currency, a new set of filters, has had to sail into darker waters somewhere beyond satire and I think this is what is meant by black humor."[1]

The roots of black humor run deep in American cultural soil. Mark Twain was not the only writer to portray American values and political behavior in a whimsically cynical light against the backdrop of a gilded age filled with robber barons in the business and congressional worlds. And certainly the shattering depressions of the 1890s and 1930s produced their bountiful share of grim jokes, quips, and songs.

But the harsh events of these periods warranted such biting humor. By contrast, black humor arose at a time of bursting economic and material expansion buttressed by a surface optimism regarding the fulfillment of the American Century. This humor encompassed both a literary and popular dimension and disclosed a vast disillusionment regarding vaunted ideals and institutions. Labeled variously as "sick," "cruel," "meanie," "Bloody Marys," "hate," or "gruesomes," the subject matter of the jokes exposed a cynicism toward the very changes that were being heralded as realizing the American Dream. The extreme emphasis upon personal striving and sacrifice, in short, the insistence on individual needs over communal requirements, severely dented familial and religious institutions. The joke cycle of the late 1950s and '60s, then, mirrored the wrenching of relationships. "All of these jokes," wrote Brian Sutton-Smith in his analysis of the cruel joke series, "have in common a disregard for sentiments which are usually taken very seriously. The afflictions of others which are normally treated with considerable sensitivity or tenderness, the love for children which is regarded as 'human nature,' the respect for religious institutions and revered persons which is customarily thought to be basic, are in these jokes made the subject matter of amusement."[2]

It was no coincidence that much of the humor focused on certain sanctified institutions, since these were the very ones being buffeted by severe change. The drive to attain a middle-class "place in the sun"—a drive that had as its many practical consequences in those frantic years two working parents, separate rooms for each child, frequent residential moves, acceptance of mobility as a mode of existence, accent on material culture, and an increase in marital separation and divorce—evoked harsh denunciations and anxiety from many quarters throughout the culture.

The response was the "sick" or "cruel" jokes—especially the jibes that centered on the Child—and revolved around family life. It was a humor that touched on matters of intimacy, role models, and stressed parental actions as the harbinger of unlove and, ultimately, of violence as well. Apart from the subject matter, the very opening phrase of the parent's answer to the logical questions posed by the child in the joke, "Shut Up," itself expressed the harsh sentiment of an earlier period, viz., "a child should be seen but not heard."

As overall expression, the jokes revealed a revulsion to a hostile family environment and particularly to parental antagonisms:

> "Hey, Mom, why does Dad always lose his head?" *Shut up, and sharpen the axe.* / "Mommy, where's Daddy?" *Shut up and keep digging.* / "Mommy, why is Daddy still sleeping?" *Shut up and keep digging.* / "Mommy, why are we pushing the car off the cliff?" *Shut up, or you'll wake up your father.* / "Mommy, why is Daddy swimming so fast?" *Shut up and reload.* / "Daddy, why is Mother lying so still?" *Shut up and keep digging.*

In identical fashion, extended family relations came under generational assault:

"Mommy, Grandma is starting to breathe again." *Shut up, and get that pillow back in place.* / "Mommy, why can't I kiss Grandma?" *Shut up, and close the casket.* / "Mommy, can we play with Grandpa?" *No, you've dug him up enough already.*

The actions of adults were repeatedly criticized as being hypocritical. This view of the elder world as two-faced would eventually find its way into the 1960s phrase: "Don't trust anyone over 30." Prior to the political protest, however, was the younger generational outrage:

"Mommy, I want milk." *Shut up, and drink your beer.* / "Daddy, why is it wrong to gamble?" *Shut up, and deal the cards.* / "Mommy, can I go out and play?" *Shut up and deal.* / "Mother, can I put lipstick on?" *No, you look bad enough already.* / "Mommy, what is an Oedipal Complex?" *Shut up, kid. Come here and kiss your mother.*

Parent-child conflicts had their natural effect on sibling relationships. There were swipes between brothers and sisters:

"Johnny, quit pulling your sister's ear; Johnny, quit pulling your sister's ear"; *All right, Johnny, give me the ear.* / "Mommy, I tied Johnny to the railroad track"; *Well, untie him;* "No, I like to see people with their head and body separated." / "Son, will you quit kicking your sister." *Oh, that's all right. She's already dead.*

Not surprisingly, then, undergirding the child-centered cruel jokes was the child's own sense of rejection, the intense fear of being derided as ugly and unwanted:

"Mommy, what is a werewolf?" *Shut up, and comb your face.* / "Mommy, what is a vampire?" *Shut up, and drink your blood.* / "Mother, why do I have warts on me?" *Because you are a toad, honey.* / "Dad, it's dark down here." *Shut up, or I'll flush it again.* / "Mommy, why are we out in our boat at night?" *Shut up, and tie that cement block around your leg.* / "Mommy, I'm cold." *Get back in that refrigerator right now.*[3]

It would be incorrect to assume that the bulk of "sick" or "cruel" jokes centered solely on the child and the child's nuclear and extended family relations. Rather, the jokes also encompassed significant others, those who were the "father" and "mother" figures writ nationally large, thereby suggesting that the *nation as family* was under humorous siege as well. Gallows jokes were directed at political and religious symbols:

- How did your husband like the show, Mrs. Lincoln?
- Did your husband get his polio shots yet, Mrs. Roosevelt?
- Happy Father's Day, Mr. Lindbergh.
- Happy Easter, Jesus.
- I don't care if your name is Santa Claus; get your hand out of my stocking.[4]

Since humor hides, or disguises, what do these joke patterns reveal about the postwar generation that had to grapple with the complicated changes of family life in those decades? What is the connection between the rise of the nation as a superpower and the humor that focused on the youngest generation— the relationship of power to powerlessness?

The thrust of the humor suggests that there existed an undercurrent of deep anxiety about the giant's ability to wreak havoc with the world of the child. That humor was the only way —certainly, the safest path—available to parents for guilt reduction. Aware that their fierce quest for status was undermining family bonds, yet tuning out their responsibility for the breakup of familial relations, adults simply "joked" their way around it. In doing this, parents were essentially mocking themselves and using child-centered humor was a means of assuaging culpability. Thus the connection between the two joke patterns that emerged in the tumultuous decades of the 1950s and early '60s: the elephant acknowledged as a hurtful giant, the child as its potential victim.

Eventually, like the elephant riddles, the jokes became the property of children. But in initiating and sponsoring this humor, the older generation was intuitively groping for a way out of a dilemma: how to accept a lifestyle that centered so heavily on material accoutrement, that continually uprooted itself and disrupted the continuity of childhood, and that focused on "making it" in the workplace to the detriment of the family-place.

Subliminally understood was that the cost of attaining middle-class status was being paid at the expense of the family and that in creating a desired existence they were in effect creating several undesired consequences, namely, the fragmentation and alienation of family relations.

The
Humor
Prism
in 20th-
Century
America

193

It is significant that the next generation, the counterculture, sought to redefine American values and institutions. The
protest movement called for the rearrangement of gender roles,
rejected the sanctity of marriage, experimented with communal
relationship, quested after spiritual values and plunged into the
world of inner consciousness. A variation on an old nursery
rhyme indicated their distaste for the socioeconomic changes
that had so affected their well-being:

> Humpty dumpty sat on a wall,
> Humpty dumpty had a great fall,
> And all the King's horses and all the King's men,
> Ate egg.[5]

Thus, the Giant and the Child reflected each other in the
transformation of American society in those postwar decades,
and the Child, so to speak, "left them tearfully laughing."

Notes

1. Bruce Jay Friedman, *Black Humor* (Bantam Books, 1965), ix.
2. Brian Sutton-Smith, "'Shut Up and Keep Digging': The Cruel Joke Series," *Midwest Folklore* 10 (Spring 1960): 12.
3. See Sutton-Smith, "Shut Up and Keep Digging," 11–22; Roger Abrahams, "Ghastly Commands: The Cruel Joke Revisited," *Midwest Folklore* 11 (Winter 1961–62): 235–46; and Alan Dundes, "The Dead Baby Joke Cycle," *Western Folklore* 38 (July 1979): 145–57.
4. Sutton-Smith, "Shut Up and Keep Digging," 11–12; Abrahams, "Ghastly Commands," 235–46.
5. Sutton-Smith, "Shut Up and Keep Digging," 21.

The
Humor
Prism
in 20th-
Century
America

194

The Helen Keller Joke Cycle

Mac E. Barrick

In the winter of 1979–1980, students (and teachers) in central Pennsylvania were asking each other such questions as "How did Helen Keller burn her fingers?" and "How did Helen Keller burn her face?" expecting such answers as "Reading a waffle iron" and "Bobbing for French fries." The cruelty of these riddle jokes exacted the same sort of moans from listeners that one expects from good (and bad) puns. The Helen Keller joke is the latest in the series of contemporary joking questions that ostensibly jostle the sensibilities of the hearer while subconsciously relating to a pertinent social problem. Like much contemporary adolescent humor, this joke form draws its inspiration from television.

Parodies of commercials and other ephemera of the visual media have been widely collected,[1] such as the parody on the McDonald's song:

> McDonald's is your kind of place,
> Hamburgers in your face,
> French fries up your nose,
> Dill pickles in your toes,
> Catsup running down your back;
> I want my money back,
> Before I have a heart attack.[2]

Television names figure often in the rhymes and jokes of children; "What is brown and sits in a corner? Gomer's pile" (Shippensburg, Pa., October, 1972) is only one of a series of such jokes (cf. "What's brown and sits on the piano? Beethoven's last movement" [Shippensburg, Pa., October, 1972]), but it inspired central Pennsylvania children to create similar puns on local

The Humor Prism in 20th-Century America

195

commercials: "What's brown and lays on the bottom of the ocean? Dolphin Deposit" (referring to Dauphin Deposit Bank, a frequent advertiser).[3] One such joking question, "Did you hear that little Mikey [of Life Cereal commercial fame] is dead? Someone took his Life away," probably abetted the spread of rumors that little Mikey died from eating a fizzling candy named Pop Rocks.[4]

More significant television events have also found their way into the folklore of today's generation. News shows about the burning of school buses resulting from the enactment of the Civil Rights Act of 1964 inspired a wave of "dead bus" jokes:

> What's yellow, has black stripes and is wounded?
> A wounded school bus.
> (Williamsport, Pa., February 1964)
>
> What's yellow and lies on its side (back)?
> (A dead school) bus.
> (Alta Jablow and Carl Withers, "Social Sense and Verbal Nonsense in Urban Children's Folklore," *Southern Folklore Quarterly* 21 [1965], 251; Knapp, p. 111)
>
> What has four wheels and lies on its back?
> A dead bus.
> (Danny Kaye, CBS-TV, April 14, 1965)
>
> What is black and yellow and squeals when you turn it over?
> A school bus.
> (*Time*, May 29, 1964, p. 51)
>
> What's black and yellow and screams?
> A busload of migrant workers going over a cliff.
> (Shippensburg, Pa., October, 1970)
>
> What's yellow on the outside and black on the inside and it makes you laugh?
> A busload of niggers goin' over a cliff.
> (Shippensburg, Pa., October, 1972)
>
> What's black and yellow and full of little Crispy Critters?
> A burnt school bus.
> (Larry Wilde, *The Official Book of Sick Jokes* [Los Angeles: Pinnacle Books, 1979], p. 24).

The
Humor
Prism
in 20th-
Century
America

196

Such jokes might seem to be a sort of wishful thinking on the part of children who would delight in having their own bus destroyed so they couldn't attend school, but the later variants specify exactly why the bus is screaming or squealing.

The thalidomide scare of the late 1960s, when news films showed grotesque fetuses and deformed babies, was the probable inspiration for such jokes as one of a doctor informing a new father that his wife has just given birth to a "seven-pound, three-ounce eye," but that the worst news is that it's blind,[5] or the following shaggy-dog story:

> This kid was born and he wasn't anything but a head. So his mother and father took care of him until he was eighteen years old. And they said, "What do you want for your eighteenth birthday?" And he said. "I want a drink." So the father rolled him down the street to the bar and laid him up on the bar, and the bartender said, "What do you want?" He said, "I'm eighteen years old, so I want a drink." So the bartender poured a drink in his mouth, and an arm popped out. So he ordered another drink, he had an arm now, and another arm popped out. He kept ordering drinks until he was all there, and then he walked out and started home, and as he was crossing the street, a truck load of sweet potatoes ran over him and killed him. Now the moral of the story is, "Be sure to quit while you're a head."[6]

Clearly the real moral to the story in adolescent terms is that you're not a complete person until you're old enough to drink (legal drinking age in Pennsylvania is twenty-one, not eighteen, however). Anxiety over how one will handle that first drink leads to the warning inherent in the joke, "When drinking, use your head, not your hands." It is not too farfetched to suggest that the joke also warns against the possibility of seduction while under the influence of alcohol (the hands on your body may not be your own) and echoes the public-service announcements on television that alcohol may harm or deform your unborn child.

Alan Dundes has shown effectively how the "dead baby" joke reflects a social concern with unwanted babies being destroyed by abortion or contraception.[7] The visual image of the "baby in a baggie" which appears in a number of these jokes was more likely inspired by the actual disposal of unwanted or stillborn babies in plastic bags behind apartment houses or college dorms than by a conceptual association with prophylactics or diaphragms as Dundes suggests (pp. 154–155). Local news media present vivid descriptions and sometimes photographs of such incidents, providing adolescent audiences with a source of anxiety to be alleviated by the tension-releasing process of the joke.

The
Humor
Prism
in 20th-
Century
America

197

Special dramatic shows do not generally provoke much folk humor, perhaps because they are short-lived or have less appeal to a mass audience. The original showing of "Roots" in January, 1977, produced a few jokes ("Did you hear that Alex Haley committed suicide? He found out he was adopted") but considerable violence on the part of blacks outraged by the treatment of slaves shown in the program. It might be argued that the appearance of "Roots" jokes might have prevented the violence, since humor is often a socially acceptable substitute for aggressive behavior.[8] While to an earlier generation of blacks "the anger and aggression that had to be swallowed and hidden normally could surface in jokes" (Levine, p. 317), the younger viewers of the "Roots" series saw the oppression of their ancestors as no laughing matter and reacted in a way those same ancestors could not or would not. Contemporary black jokelore is often bitterly and actively racist, unlike the more passive humor found in the earlier collections of Richard Dorson,[9] where the Irish and other white ethnic groups are simply depicted as numskulls. The change is well illustrated by the following variants of the same joke, the first told by an Italian from eastern Maryland, the other by a black student from Philadelphia:

The
Humor
Prism
in 20th-
Century
America

198

A colored guy walks into a pet store and sees this parrot sitting there on the perch, wearing glasses and reading the *New York Times*. He thinks to himself, "This bird must be some real cool dude," so he walks over and says, "Polly want a cracker?" The parrot doesn't pay any attention. He says, "Hey, man, Polly want a cracker?" The parrot lowers the paper, looks at him, and goes on reading. He starts to get angry. "Polly want a cracker?" The parrot lowers the paper, looks at him and says, "Nigger want a watermelon?"

I know one my brother told me. It's got sort of racial overtones, ya know; it's about a Puerto Rican who goes into a pet store, and he wants to buy a pet. He's dressed to kill, ya know, and he wants a pet. The man says, "How about a dog?" He says, no, he doesn't want a dog, it's gotta be something special, ya know. He's got an accent and everything, "Something special, man." So he's roamin' around there looking at all the animals, and he sees this parrot. And he goes over and says, "Polly want a cracker?" The parrot just looks at him. doesn't say anything. He says, "Polly want a cracker?" a little louder. And the parrot doesn't say anything. So finally he says, real loud, "Polly want a cracker?" Ya know, and the parrot says, "Spic want a razor blade?"

Obviously urban blacks now see themselves in the same light as earlier ethnic groups being overrun by alien cultures, in this case Hispanics.

The television series "The Holocaust" in 1978 might have instigated violence similar to that sparked by "Roots," were it not for the Jewish propensity to laugh at adversity. The program did inspire a small and short-lived series of "Holocaust" jokes:

> What's the difference between a pizza pie and a Jewish person?
> A pizza pie doesn't scream when you shove it in the oven.
>
> The latest neo-socialist invention coming from Germany?
> A microwave oven with accommodations for six.

These, ironically, were told by a Shippensburg high-school student (May, 1979), son of a man who was a German citizen during World War II. The first, which curiously avoids the epithet "Jew," has a parallel in the sick joke: "Mommy, are you sure this is the way to make pizza? Shut up and get back in the oven."[10]

Though an occasional Helen Keller joke surfaced in the late 1960s and early 1970s, the flood of such jokes swelled appreciably after the presentation on October 14, 1979, of a new NBC presentation of William Gibson's "The Miracle Worker," starring Melissa Gilbert as Helen Keller and Patty Duke Astin as Anne Sullivan. There had been several earlier versions of the play, first performed live on the CBS "Playhouse 90" on February 7, 1957 (starring Teresa Wright, Patty McCormack, and Burl Ives), including a Broadway play (with Anne Bancroft and Patty Duke as Helen) which ran two seasons after opening October 19, 1959, and a movie based on the play with the same actresses in the starring roles. Directed by Arthur Penn, the movie opened May 23, 1962, and ran subsequently several times on television, which might explain the sporadic appearance of earlier Helen Keller jokes. The spate of jokes that accompanied the most recent performance was due to a coincidence of circumstances. Following the enactment of Public Law 94–142, the Education for All Handicapped Children Act, the "mainstreaming" of crippled, blind, and deaf children into the public-school system gradually became a social reality. People in wheelchairs held roll-ins, demanding architectural revisions in public buildings (at considerable public expense) so the handicapped could use those facilities. Television's nightly news programs regularly documented governmental decisions to withhold funds from small-town libraries and other institutions that failed to provide ramps or elevators (at a cost of several times their annual budgets), despite the fact that there were no handicapped people in town to use them, and despite the fact that legislative rollbacks and inflation had already curtailed those budgets. Since "folklore provides a socially sanctioned outlet for the discussion of the forbidden and tabooed [enabling the participant to] . . . treat in fantasy what is avoided in reality" (Dundes, p. 146), young people, hearing these news stories or hearing their parents snort with derision, adapted them to the folkloric form most familiar to them, in the manner of the racial problems of the 1960s, the riddle or joking question. "The Miracle Worker" opportunely provided a visual image easily adaptable to the earlier sick-joke style and the Helen Keller joke felt its way to the fore.

Jokes about the handicapped are not a recent phenomenon. Max Rezwin's sick-joke collections of the late 1950s contained many of them, as did Brian Sutton-Smith's article in 1960.[11] A graduate student from Minnesota, in the German Department at the University of Pennsylvania during the same period, told the following:

"Mother, I want to go swimming with the other kids."
"But, dear, you know you can't go swimming."
"I want to go swimming."
"But your iron lung would sink."

"Can Harold come out and play baseball?"
"But Harold can't play baseball. He's a quadruple amputee."
"We know, we want to use him for second base."

"Mother, I want to play the piano."
"But you can't play the piano."
"I want to play the piano."
"You can't! Your hooks scratch the keys."[12]

Of course, in the 1950s no one seriously considered admitting multiple amputees or children in iron lungs (which might sink in the "mainstream") into the public-school system, so the humor of these jokes lies in the grotesqueness of the image suggested. More real was the threat of poliomyelitis, and children deformed by that disease did participate in most school activities. Nonetheless, polio did not become a joking matter until the Salk and Sabin vaccines were developed in 1953 and 1955, and even then the jokes about it seemed a sort of social warning of the consequences of not receiving the vaccine:

> What has 500 legs and can't walk?
> Two hundred fifty polio victims.

> The first day of school, the teacher asked the pupils how many had had all three polio shots. A number raised their hands.
> "How many have had two polio shots?" More raised their hands.
> "And how many have had only one polio shot?" Several more raised their hands.
> "And is there anyone who hasn't had any polio shots?" And one little boy . . . [pantomimed raising of twisted right arm].[13]

With the government-enforced mingling of handicapped students with normal children in the 1970s came a new wave of jokes about deformed or mentally retarded children.[14] Slang epithets like *spaz* and *sped* were popular.[15] The government's earlier attempts to provide jobs for the disable-bodied had met with the same benign resistance as the earlier establishment of minority quotas in the construction industry.[16] To the postal slogan, "Hire the handicapped," was added a key phrase, "they're fun to watch," that established the pattern for antisocial aggression in folk humor in the face of this new threat to established socioeconomic patterns. It was no longer taboo to gawk at people on wheelchairs and crutches, especially when they put themselves on public display in Special Olympics and other sports events. And when Archie Bunker could make jokes about Sammy Davis, Jr.'s glass eye, anything was permissible, at least on the oral level.

Lacking a well-known public figure of an amputee or wheelchair rider (there were jokes about Ironside, but he was fictional), students seized on Helen Keller to provide a universally recognizable focus for their physical-disability humor. She was an ideal subject, suffering the ultimate handicaps, blind, deaf, mute, yet still functioning in a normal social situation in the same way that the contemporary handicapped were expected to function. Two major categories of the joke appeared, those dealing with

The
Humor
Prism
in 20th-
Century
America

201

Helen Keller's sightlessness and her use of braille, and those relating to her being deaf-mute and her use of sign language:

I. Blindness; use of braille.

1. Did you see Helen Keller's new house in Philadelphia?
Neither did she.
(Camp Hill, Pa., March, 1980; usually told about Ray Charles's new car)

2. "Miss Keller, how did you like the movie?"
(Abrahams, p. 246)

3. Helen Keller's new book: *Around the Block in 80 Days.*
(Wilde, *Sick Jokes*, p. 88)

4. Did you see the new Helen Keller dolls?
You wind them up and they walk into walls.
(Maurice Schmaier, "The Doll Joke Pattern in Contemporary American Oral Humor," *Midwest Folklore* 13 [1963–1964]: no. 67; Robin Hirsch, "Wind-Up Dolls," *Western Folklore* 23 (1964), no. 1; Abrahams, p. 246)

5. The Lenny Bruce doll: wind it up and it laughs at the Helen Keller doll.
(Schmaier, no. 68; Hirsch, no. 8)

6. Wind up the Helen Keller doll and it bumps into the furniture.
(Hirsch, no. 4)

7. How did Helen Keller's parents punish her?
They moved the furniture around.
(Shippensburg, Pa., January, 1980; Wilde, p. 87)

8. How did Helen Keller's parents kill her?
They moved the furniture and yelled, "Fire."
(Harrisburg, Pa., March, 1980)

9. How did Helen Keller burn her hand?
Trying to read a waffle iron.
(Shippensburg, Pa., September, 1972, February, 1980; Camp Hill, Pa., March, 1980; George W. Boswell, "Ole Miss Jokes," *Tennessee Folklore Society Bulletin* 42 [1976], no. 71; Wilde, p. 87)

10. How did Helen Keller burn her face?
Answering the iron.

(Shippensburg, Pa., February, 1980; Wilde, p. 87)

11. How did Helen Keller burn her face?
    Bobbing for French fries.
    (Wilde, p. 87; told as an ethnic joke in the movie "Straight
      Time" [1978])

12. Why couldn't Helen Keller read?
    She wore her hand off sliding down the well.
    (Shippensburg, Pa., September, 1972)

13. How did Helen Keller go crazy?
    Trying to read a stucco wall.
    (Camp Hill, Pa., March, 1980; Wilde, p. 87)

14. Why were Helen Keller's hands purple?
    She heard it from the grape vine.
    (Wilde, p. 88)

II. Deafmuteness; use of sign language

15. What is Helen Keller's favorite song?
    "The Sound of Sound."
    (Wilde, p. 88)

16. Helen Keller says—"Uh! Uh! Uh!"
    (Sutton-Smith, no. 132)

17. Helen Keller on "To Tell the Truth":
    "Contestant Number One, what is your name,
      please?"
    "My name is Helen Keller."
    "Number Two, what is your name, please?"
    "My name is Helen Keller."
    "Number Three, what is your name, please?"
    "Bluh waqf btyx krojv narf."
    (Wilde, p. 86)

18. What did Helen Keller's parents do when they
    caught her swearing?
    They washed her hands with soap.
    (Wilde, p. 87; cf. Rezwin, *Best of the Sick Jokes*, p. 150)

19. Why does Helen Keller masturbate with only one
    hand?
    So she can moan with the other.
    (Shippensburg, Pa., February, 1980; Wilde, p. 88)

The
Humor
Prism
in 20th-
Century
America

203

20. Why did they cut off Helen Keller's finger while rap-
    ing her?
    So she couldn't scream for help.
    (Shippensburg, Pa., February, 1980; Wilde. p. 16. Cf. Ger-
    shon Legman, *Rationale of the Dirty Joke* [New York:
    Grove Press, 1968], pp. 160–161)

21. Why did Helen Keller fall out of a tree?
    She was yelling for help.
    (Shippensburg, Pa., February, 1980. Cf., "How do you get a
    Polack out of a tree? Wave to him.")

22. What did Helen Keller do when she fell down a well?
    She yelled and yelled for help 'til her hands turned
    blue.
    (Wilde, p. 88)

23. Did you hear about Helen Keller?
    She jumped off a bridge and screamed her finger
    off.
    (Wilde, p. 88)

The
Humor
Prism
in 20th-
Century
America

204

There can be little doubt about the influence of "The Miracle Worker" on the popularity and propagation of the Helen
Keller joke. The garden-house scene in the play is an obvious
source for the "moved furniture" riddle jokes (nos. 7 and 8); the
well and the tree (nos. 12, 21, and 22) were important visual elements in the television show; and of course the animal sounds of
the young blind girl and the sign language of the deaf-mutes
would have affected impressionable viewers strongly. True, jokes
about the deaf have a long history in folk literature, but most of
them are based on mishearing or misinterpreting what is said
rather than on an outright inability to hear at all. Gesture riddles
have also been popular in recent years,[17] but few of them relate
gestures to being deaf-mute. One longer joke that does this is the
following:

These forty mutes came into a bar, aren't they the people
who can't talk? Anyway, these forty mutes came into a bar,
and the bartender said, "How am I gonna know what they
want?" And the leader said, "Well, I'll tell you. It's easy.
This [holding up thumb] means one drink. This [two fin-
gers] means another drink. And this [waving five fingers]
means one beer. So this went okay for a while [gestures],
and then they started going [opening mouth and making

faces], and he didn't know what this meant so he took them some more beer. And pretty soon their leader came in and he said, "What do they want?" And he said, "Now you've done it. You went and got them drunk and they're singing."[18]

It is perhaps illogical to imagine this joke being adapted to the Helen Keller joke cycle, dealing as it does with a group of deaf-mutes rather than an individual, but some of the extant jokes are already illogically associated with her. Helen Keller's attempt to answer the telephone (no. 10) which she could not hear ringing defies explanation; the image this joke provides has the same grotesque visual impact as her reading a waffle iron or bobbing for French fries. Since the elephant joke and the later grapes and plums jokes relied heavily on incongruity for their humor, one should expect no more from any subsequent joke cycle. Apparently this is the manner in which today's generation of students prepares itself for life in today's world. The moral evidently is "Life is cruel; don't be surprised at anything," and the message of the Helen Keller joke is perhaps best expressed by the Middle Eastern proverb, "If thou seest a blind man beat him; thou art not better than God."[19]

It is impossible to say what effect Larry Wilde's *Official Book of Sick Jokes*, published in July, 1979, has had on the spread of the present joke genre. It contains thirteen Helen Keller jokes, but only one of the students who recited the jokes knew of the book. The United States postage stamp recognizing the hundredth anniversary of Miss Keller's birth appeared too late (June 27, 1980) to influence the joke's development though it may help to preserve its popularity.

The Helen Keller joke has fulfilled an important social function. Like a classical drama, it has had the cathartic effect of erasing the pity normally felt toward the disabled, so that the joke-teller and his listener now accept these people on equal terms. They may resent what some consider to be pushiness on the part of the handicapped or regret the amount of money spent to accommodate them, but as long as physical disability remains a joking matter, the success of the Handicapped Children Act seems certain. How can you hate someone who makes you laugh?

Notes

1. See, for example, Mary and Robert Knapp, *One Potato, Two Potato . . .* (New York: Norton, 1976), pp. 161–179.
2. Collected from a ten-year-old girl, Carlisle, Pa., September, 1971. Also sung as a Girl Scout campfire song, Shippensburg, Pa., 1979. Cf. Knapp, pp. 163–164.
3. The comparison "lower than whale shit" has often been noted: Archer Taylor, *Proverbial Comparisons and Similes from California* (Berkeley and Los Angeles: University of California Press, 1954), p. 55; *The Frank C. Brown Collection of North Carolina Folklore*, I (Durham, N.C.: Duke University Press, 1952), 494; Darryl Ponicsan, *Cinderella Liberty* (New York: Harper & Row, 1973), pp. 3, 34. Cf. "What's white and lies on the bottom of the ocean? Moby's dick" (Knapp, p. 107).
4. A full-page ad denying the rumors ran in the *Washington Post* (and other papers), February 4, 1979, p. A27. Cf. "Pop Rocks Slander," *New York Times*, June 17, 1979, p. 25.
5. Wilde, pp. 45, 83; Alan Dundes, "The Dead Baby Joke Cycle," *Western Folklore* 38 (1979): 150.
6. Told by a fifteen-year-old high school student, Carlisle, Pa., May 1977. Cf. Wilde, p. 197.
7. "The Dead Baby Joke Cycle," pp. 154–157. Cf. Barre Toelken, *The Dynamics of Folklore* (Boston: Houghton Mifflin, 1979), p. 270.
8. See Leonard Feinberg, "The Secret of Humor," *Maledicta* 2 (1978): 88; Daryl Dance, *Shuckin' and Jivin'* (Bloomington: Indiana University Press, 1978), pp. 179–180; cf. Lawrence W. Levine, *Black Culture and Black Consciousness* (New York: Oxford University Press, 1977), pp. 306–320. See also John H. Burma, "Humor as a Technique in Race Conflict," *American Sociological Review* 11 (1946): 710–715, esp. p. 712.
9. Dorson, *Negro Folktales in Michigan* (Cambridge, Mass.: Harvard University Press, 1956); *Negro Tales from Pine Bluff, Arkansas, and Calvin, Michigan* (Bloomington: Indiana University Press, 1958); *American Negro Folktales* (Greenwich, Conn.: Fawcett Premier, 1967). For the contemporary viewpoint, see Dance, *Shuckin' and Jivin'*, esp. pp. 200–223; and Paulette Cross, "Jokes and Black Consciousness," *Folklore Forum* 2 (1969): 140–161.
10. Max Rezwin, *The Best of Sick Jokes* (New York: Permabooks, 1962), p. 112; Wilde, p. 37.
11. Rezwin, *Sick Jokes, Grim Cartoons and Bloody Marys* (New York: Citadel, 1958); *More Sick Jokes and Grimmer Cartoons* (New York: Citadel, 1959); *Still More Sick Jokes and Even Grimmer Cartoons* (New York: Citadel, 1960). Sutton-Smith, "'Shut Up and Keep Digging': The Cruel Joke Series," *Midwest Folklore* 10 (1960): 11–22. See also Roger Abrahams, "Ghastly Commands: The Cruel Joke Revisited," *Midwest Folklore* 11 (1961–62): 235–246.
12. For the first, cf. Sutton-Smith, nos. 88, 90; Abrahams, p. 245; Wilde, p. 24. For the second, Rezwin, *Best*, p. 19; Sutton-Smith, no. 75; Wilde, p. 8; Toelken, p. 270. For the third, Rezwin, *Best*, p. 30; Sutton-Smith, no. 98; Abrahams, p. 245; Wilde, p. 24.
13. Told by the same graduate student as the previous jokes; Philadelphia, 1958–1960.
14. A thirteen-year-old girl in Carlisle, Pa., recited (November 1974): "My name is Leonardo, / I am a retard-o; / I live on four-fortieth street; / I sit on the steeple and piss on the people."
15. "Spaz is directed at a child who has done something awkward or who has accidentally slobbered a little while talking, not a child who is realy spastic"

(Knapp, p. 66); cf. Joseph Wambaugh, *The Black Marble* (New York: Delacorte, 1978), p. 93: "The man's a spaz! A total spaz!"; Saturday Night Live," NBC-TV, April 22, 1978: "Chas the spaz. . . . Hi there, you big spazaropolis." A *sped* is a retarded *special education* student; Carlisle, Pa., 1979.

16. Cf. Barrick, "You Can Tell a Joke with Vigah," *Keystone Folklore Quarterly* 9 (1964): 166–168.

17. See Jan Harold Brunvand, *The Study of American Folklore*, 2nd ed. (New York: Norton, 1978), p. 69; Charles Keller, *Too Funny for Words: Gesture Jokes for Children* (Englewood Cliffs, N.J.: Prentice-Hall, 1973); Abrahams, p. 243.

18. Told by a fifteen-year-old girl, Carlisle, Pa., January, 1976. Cf. Wilde, p. 84.

19. A. P. Singer, *Arabic Proverbs* (Cairo: Diemer, 1913), pp. 42–43.

The
Humor
Prism
in 20th-
Century
America

Racial Riddles and the Polack Joke

Mac E. Barrick

The
Humor
Prism
in 20th-
Century
America

208

It has long been the practice of established civilizations to regard other races as inferior and to ridicule them.[1] This is particularly true when a member of the "inferior" culture resides within the "superior" or majority group. Frequently the inferiority of the alien, immigrant or foreigner stems solely from his lack of knowledge of the local language and customs, for he may be intellectually and culturally above the level of the local residents.[2] He may be highly intelligent and well-educated, but his lack of awareness and understanding of practical matters in a given area makes him appear stupid. Because of his lack of comprehension and his errors in speech, he is naturally funny to the natives and becomes the subject of their humor. His mistakes are told and retold and frequently caricatured or exaggerated in the telling. He becomes the butt of practical jokes and his reaction to them furnishes material for other anecdotes. Numskull tales in circulation for generations come to be told with them specifically as the central figure. Though the tales remain the same, the subject changes, depending on the group currently considered inferior.

The numskull in the Dutch counties of Pennsylvania used to be the "stupid Swabian," about whom many tales were told.[3] In other areas and at different times, Irishmen, Negroes and Jews were the subject of such humor.

Jokes attributing stupidity to the Irish are much older than is generally believed. Rather than gaining prominence in the mid-nineteenth century after the Irish immigration following the potato famine, they were already being circulated widely at the end of the eighteenth century. Several tales about Irishmen appear in *Joe Miller's Jests or the Wits Vade-mecum* published in London in 1739, at least one of which is a traditional numskull tale:

> 47. An *Irish* Lawyer of the *Temple*, having occasion to go to Dinner, left these Directions written, and put in the Key-Hole of his Chamber-Door, *I am gone to the* Elephant *and*

Castle, *where you shall find me;* and if you *can't read this Note, carry it down to the Stationer's, and he will read it for you.* (p. 13)

The identical story with one slight change was published in the Philadelphia *Inquisitor,* January 13, 1819 (I:3, p. 12). The following story appearing in *Kline's Weekly Gazette* (Carlisle, Pa.) for August 3, 1803, had also appeared in *Joe Miller's Jests* (p. 35, no. 120):

> Two Irishmen being one day a gunning, a large flock of pigeon (!) came flying over their heads. One of them elevated his piece, and firing, brought a pigeon to the ground, "Arrah," exclaimed his companion, "what a fool you are to waste your ammunition, when the bare fall would have killed him."

Another early example illustrates how any joke can be adapted to the particular ethnic group being ridiculed. The *Carlisle Gazette* for August 12, 1789, has the following:

> A Sailor, as he was riding, made a pause, the horse, in beating off the flies, caught his hind foot in the stirrup the sailor observing it, said, "how now dobbin, if your (!) are going to get on, I'll get off, for damn me if I'll ride double with you."[4]

In the *Inquisitor* (I:37, September 8, 1819, p. 147), the identical anecdote appears, but the sailor is now an *Irish* sailor and the oath is changed to "by the powers." Unlike twentieth-century ethnic humor, there is nothing distinctively Irish about the characters in these stories. The same stories could be (and often were) related about Negroes, Jews or Poles. Consider, for example, the following:

> A Irishman meeting acquaintance, thus accosted him: "Ah! my dear, who do you think I have just been speaking to! Your old friend Patrick; faith, and he has grown so thin I hardly knew him: to be sure, you are thin, and I am thin, but *he is thinner than both of us put together.*
> (*Inquisitor,* 1:27, June 30, 1819, p. 107)

Vance Randolph collected a similar jest in Missouri; the Irish were not mentioned, though he notes that the joke occurs in many Irish collections.[5]

Negroes were the butt of many jokes told during the late nineteenth and early twentieth centuries, probably because of the popularity of minstrel and vaudeville shows during that era. Some of these are still told, though generally only by older people.[6] During the 1960s because of the Civil Rights movement, a new type of Negro joke developed, reflecting the bitterness which some people felt toward militant Negroes or in some cases, toward segregationists. The following are typical:[7]

This fellow had a plan for bringing gorillas over from Africa and training them to work picking cotton, but a friend of his told him not to bother, because no sooner would he get them trained than them damn Yankees would came down and free them . . . again.[8]

"Knock, knock."
"Who's there?"
"Ise."
"Ise who?"
"Ise your next door neighbor."[9]

Governor Barnett died and went to Heaven, so when he came to the Pearly Gates, Saint Peter said, "Who are you?"
        "I'm Governor Barnett."
        "We's been waitin' fo' you."

The secretary of the NAACP comes into the Philadelphia Free Library and demands the removal of all books containing the word "Nigger." The librarian remonstrates, and tries to placate him by saying, "We have a lot of books with the word 'bastard' in them, and nobody wants *them* removed." The colored fellow says, "It's not my fault we're organized and you're not."[10]

I remember hearing the story years ago. Some colored fella was saying, "The world isn't made right. Things ought to be divided equal." An' somebody said, "If things was divided equal, you'd just spend yours. Then what?" "Divide again."[11]

One joking-question arising from the Negro problem was later applied to other current events:

What's the fastest thing on two wheels?
—Governor Wallace riding a bicycle through Harlem.
(Lancaster, Pa., June 1965)
What's the fastest thing on four wheels?

—Two Jews on bicycles passing through Saudi Arabia.
(Philadelphia, July 1965)

What's the fastest thing in the world?
—Two Jews in a canoe paddling through the Gulf of Aqaba.
(Philadelphia, June 1967)

What's the fastest thing in the world?
—The Egyptian army.
(Carlisle, September 1967)

Jokes about Jews were rife at the start of the twentieth century and collections of them were sold widely.[12] Of the hundreds of jokes published, some must have originated in oral tradition or fed back into it, but few of these survived. One story still being told is based on the Jew's proverbial ability to profit from disaster:

> There were two Jews talking one time and the one says to the other, "How much is your place worth?" "Ten thousand dollars." "How much insurance do you have?" "Twenty thousand dollars." "Well, why don't ya?" "I tell you why I don't. I got a fire house on one side a' me, a police station on the other, and a swimming pool on the roof. Now, why don't I?"[13]

Contemporary joking-questions still refer to the Jew's interest in money:[14]

Why is money green?
—The Jews picked it before it was ripe.
(Lancaster, December 1965)

How do you get thirteen Jews in a Volkswagen?
—Throw a quarter (nickel) in.
(Lancaster, Dec. 1965; Carlisle, Jan. 1966; Shippensburg, Jan. 1970)

Do you know what this is X X ?
—A Jew co-signing for a colored person.
(Carlisle, November 1967)

As might be expected, many of the anti–ethnic group jokes already in oral circulation came to be applied to new groups of outsiders. Jokes about Italians have never become popular in rural central Pennsylvania, probably because few Italians settled there, but among college students and other more sophisticated levels of society, anti-Italian joking questions spread rapidly. Don-

The Humor Prism in 20th-Century America

211

ald C. Simmons traces the appearance of the genre to lower New England about 1961,[15] but the form was practically unknown in central Pennsylvania before 1965, and its appearance was almost concurrent with the development of the Polack joke. The Italian jokes told in Pennsylvania generally dealt with the proverbial ineptness of the Italian military forces demonstrated during the Spanish Civil War at the battle of Guadalajara (March 1937) and during the early campaigns of World War II.[16] A memorable one-liner states: "The Italian planes came roaring over the hill and defeated the Ethiopian, spear and all." And during the summer of 1967, after the Six-Days War, it was said, "When Italy heard of the war between Israel and Egypt, it surrendered to both sides." The following joking-questions express the same idea:

> How many gears does an Italian tank have?
> —One forward and five reverse. The one forward is for use in case they're attacked from the rear.
> (Carlisle, Jan. 1966, Apr. 1966; Shippensburg, Jan. 1970. Cf. Simmons, "Anti-Italian-American Riddles," p. 477, no. 6.)

> What's this (holding hands in surrender position)?
> —The Italians in World War III.
> (Carlisle, Apr. 1966; Shippensburg, Jan. 1970. Cf. Simmons, p. 47, no. 18).

> What do you call an Italian submarine captain?
> —Chicken of the Sea.
> (Shippensburg, Dec. 1969.)

Only one or two local Italian jokes suggest the degree of denigration found in the New England riddles:

> An Italian and a pig were walking down the street and somebody said, "Where'd you get that greasy thing?" And the pig said, "Back at the corner."[17]

The other implies that Italians are inferior even to primitive African tribes:

> What happened to the bridge between Italy and Africa?
> —The Niggers [i.e., Africans] tore it down.
> (Shippensburg, Jan. 1970. Cf. Simmons, p. 475.)

Many anti-Italian joking riddles are easily changed into Polack jokes.

Essentially the Polack joke is a pseudo-riddle or joking question, which, in the manner of conundrums or Elephant Riddles,[18] enables the questioner to respond to his own question with a funny answer. The jokes usually deal with what are considered to be characteristics of Polish-Americans, brute strength, lack of intelligence,[19] uncleanliness, lack of high personal ambitions, etc. Polack jokes collected in Pennsylvania provide few examples of the obscenely insulting type found by collectors in New England and Nebraska.[20]

The following examples were collected from college students and faculty in central Pennsylvania:[21]

I. Joke-riddles Dealing with Personal Hygiene and Dress:

1. What's this [extended index finger]?
   —A Polack handkerchief.
   (Carlisle, Apr. 1966.)

2. How do you break a Polack's finger?
   A.—Punch him in the nose.
   (Carlisle, Jan. 1966; Shippensburg, Jan. 1970. *It's Fun*, p. 7)

   B.—Wait a few seconds before stamping out your cigarette butt.
   (Carlisle, Apr. 1966.)

   C.—Slam the garbage can on his finger.
   (Lancaster, June 1966.)

3. What does a Polack say after he picks his nose?
   —Grace.
   (Carlisle, Jan. 1966.)

4. Who won the Polack beauty contest?
   —Nobody.
   (Lancaster, June 1966; *It's Fun*, p. 23.)

5. What do you call 28 Polack girls in a swimming pool?
   —Bay of Pigs.
   (Carlisle, Jan. 1966, Apr. 1966; Shippensburg, Jan. 1970. *It's Fun*, p. 14.)

6. How do you get them out of the swimming pool?
   —Throw in a bar of soap.
   (Carlisle, Jan. 1966; Shippensburg, Jan. 1970.)

7. Where does a Polack hide his money?
   —Under the soap.

The
Humor
Prism
in 20th-
Century
America

214

(Lancaster, June 1966; Shippensburg, Jan. 1970. *It's Fun*, p. 18. Cf. Simmons, p. 477, no. 7; Bernard Kalb, "I Remember Danang," *Saturday Review*, Nov. 30, 1968, p. 30: You hear jokes like: "Where's a safe place to hide money from a Vietnamese?" Answer: "Under the soap.")

8. Why won't they let Polacks swim in Lake Erie?
   —They leave a ring (on the docks).
   (Carlisle, Feb. 1966; Shippensburg, Jan. 1970. Cf. Simmons, p. 477, no. 8. There is a current joke: Why did the two hippies get married in a bathtub? They wanted a double ring ceremony.)

9. How do you tell the bride at a Polish wedding?
   A.—She has braided hair in her armpits.
   (Carlisle, Jan. 1966; *It's Fun*, p. 26; *Sex-to-Sexty Stag Treasury* [Ft. Worth, 1967], p. 297: How can you tell a bride at an Arab wedding? She's the only girl there with braided armpits.)

10. What's a Polack tuxedo?
    —A starched bowling shirt.
    (Shippensburg, Jan. 1970.)

11. Why do they carry a garbarge can to Polish weddings?
    —To keep the flies off the bride.
    (Carlisle, Dec. 1967.)

12. What happened when the Ajax white knight came to a Polack neighborhood?
    —The dirt was stronger than he was.
    (Carlisle, June 1966; *It's Fun*, p. 59.)

13. What does a Polack say when he takes the garbage out?
    —Grace.
    (Lancaster, June 1966.)

14. What do you call Polish paratroopers?
    —Air pollution.
    (Carlisle, Dec. 1967; Shippensburg, Jan. 1970.)

15. How can you tell a Polish airplane?
    —From the hair under the wings.
    (Shippensburg, Jan. 1970; Welsch, p. 186; *It's Fun*, p. 22.)

16. How did the Polack get a lump on his head?
    —He was washing his face when the lid fell down.
    (Carlisle, Nov. 1969; *Sex-to-Sexty*, no. 21 [1969], p. 10.)

17. What's the difference between a Polack and a bucket of shit (garbage)?
—The bucket.
(Shippensburg, Jan. 1970; Welsch, p. 184. Cf. Simmons, p. 477, no. 16.)

18. What's a Polack luau?
—A bunch of Polacks sitting around a cesspool with straws.
(Shippensburg, Jan. 1970. Cf. Simmons, p. 478, no. 26; *Sex-to-Sexty Stag Treasury*, p. 543: Know what is a Texas Luau? That's a bunch of Texans sitting around a cesspool with straws.)

19. Why do flies have wings?
—So they can beat the Polacks to the garbage cans.
(Shippensburg, Jan. 1970. Cf. Simmons, p. 477, no. 2.)

20. Why don't Polacks kill flies?
—Because the fly is their national bird.
(Carlisle, Jan. 1966; Shippensburg, Jan. 1970.)

II. Joke-riddles Dealing with Physical Strength:

21. How do four Polacks make popcorn?
—One holds the popper (pot) and the other three shake the stove.
(Lancaster, Dec. 1965; Shippensburg, Dec. 1969; *It's Fun*, p. 10; Welsch, p. 185.)

22. How do four Polacks put in a new light bulb?
—One stands on a stool (ladder) and holds the bulb; the other three turn the stool (ladder).
(Lancaster, Dec. 1965; Carlisle, Jan. 1966; *It's Fun*, p. 30. Cf. Simmons, p. 48, no. 22.)

23. How many Polacks does it take to paint a house?
—One hundred. One to hold the brush and the others to move the house back and forth.
(Carlisle, Jan. 1966.)

24. How many Polacks does it take to wash a car?
—Only two. One to hold the sponge and one to drive the car back and forth.
(Carlisle, Jan. 1966.)

25. How long does it take a Polack to paint a basement window sill?

—Three hours. One hour to paint the sill and two hours to dig a hole for the ladder.
(Shippensburg, Jan. 1970.)

26. What is a Polack carpool?
—Five (six) Polacks carrying a car to work.
(Carlisle, Jan. 1966; *It's Fun*, p. 31.)

27. How does a Polack tie his shoe?
—Pantomime: Put one foot on chair, bend over and tie the other shoe on the floor.
(Lancaster, Dec. 1965; Shippensburg, Jan. 1970.)

28. What are two Polack professions?
—Professional football and professional wrestling.
(Carlisle, Feb. 1966. Cf. *It's Fun*, p. 51: Professional football and professional baseball.)

29. How did the beer companies get the idea for pull-top beer cans?
—Watching Polacks pull the tops off regular cans.
(Lancaster, June 1966; *It's Fun*, p. 74.)

III. Joke-riddles Dealing with Lack of Intelligence:

The
Humor
Prism
in 20th-
Century
America

216

30. Why are there no Polack elevator operators?
—They can't learn the route.
(Carlisle, Jan. 1966.)

31. Why do they give Polacks only a half hour for lunch?
—So they won't have to re-train them.
(Carlisle, Jan. 1966; *It's Fun*, p. 75; Gail Gordon, "Dean Martin Show," NBC-TV, Jan. 9, 1970: You're lucky to have a job. Every time you come back from a coffee break we have to retrain you.)

32. What are the two (three) smallest (shortest) books in the world?[22]
A.—*Italian War Hereos* and *Jewish Business Ethics.*
(Carlisle, Jan. 1966.)

B.—*Italian War Heroes*, the *Irish Social Register*, and the *Polack Who's Who.*
(West Chester, Apr. 1966.)

C.—*Italian War Heroes, Puerto Rican Who's Who,* and *Polish Soap Manufacturers.*
(Lancaster, June 1966.)

33. Why wasn't Christ born in Poland?

—They couldn't find three wise men.
(Carlisle, Dec. 1967.)

34. Why wasn't Christ born in Italy (Poland)?
—They couldn't find a virgin.
(Carlisle, Dec. 1967; Shippensburg, Jan. 1970.)

35. Did you hear about the Polish jigsaw puzzle? One piece.
(Shippensburg, Jan. 1969.)

36. 3x5 card reading on both sides: "How to keep a Polack busy all day. (over)."
(Shippensburg, June 1969.)

37. What do you call 144 Polacks?
—Gross ignorance.
(Shippensburg, Jan. 1970. Cf. Simmons, p. 477, no. 12: What is gross ignorance? 144 Wops [Niggers].)

38. What do you call 288 Polacks?
—Too gross to even talk about.
(Shippensburg, Jan. 1970.)

IV. Joke-riddles Dealing with Lack of Ambition:

39. What is the most wanted job in a Polack neighborhood?
—Riding shotgun on the garbage truck.
(Lancaster, June 1966; *It's Fun*, p. 19.)

40. How many pallbearers do you need at a Polack funeral?
—Two. There's two handles on a garbage can.
(Lancaster, June 1966. Cf. Simmons, p. 477, no. 10; *Sex-to-Sexty Stag Treasury*, p. 554: They only need two pallbearers at a communist funeral . . . after all, a garbage can has only two handles.)

41. How do you tell a Polack funeral?
—All the garbage trucks have their lights on.
(West Chester, June 1966. Cf. Simmons, p. 478, no. 24.)

42. How do you tell a Polish funeral from a Polish wedding?
—One less drunk.
(Kutztown, June 1966.)

43. How can you tell a Polack neighborhood?

The
Humor
Prism
in 20th-
Century
America

217

—From the toilet paper hanging out to dry.
(Shippensburg, Jan. 1970.)

44. Why don't many Polacks commit suicide?
    —You can't get hurt jumping out of a basement
    window.
    (Carlisle, Jan. 1966; Kutztown, Apr. 1966; Shippensburg,
    Jan. 1970; *It's Fun*, p. 18; *Time*, March 4, 1966, p. 47;
    Welsch, p. 183.)

45. Do you know how to (How do you) take a Polack
    census?
    A.—Flood the basements.
    (Shippensburg, Jan. 1970; *It's Fun*, p. 23.)

    B.—Count the basement windows and multiply by
    forty.
    (Lancaster, June 1966.)

46. What do you call a Polack who marries a Negro?
    —A social climber.
    (Shippensburg, Jan. 1970. Cf. Simmons, p. 477, no. 14:
    What do you call an Italian who moves into an all-Negro
    neighborhood?)

47. What's a matched set of Polack luggage?
    —Two brown A & P grocery bags.
    (Shippensburg, Jan. 1970; *It's Fun*, p. 75.)

48. What do you call a Polack with a green beret?
    —A thief.
    (Shippensburg, Jan. 1970.)

V. Miscellaneous Puns

49. What's round and Polish (wears a ridiculous outfit)
    and sits on a wall?
    —Humpty Dumbrowski.
    (Carlisle, Jan. 1966; Shippensburg, Jan. 1970.)

50. Who wears white robes and rides a pig?
    —Lawrence of Poland.
    (Carlisle, Jan. 1966; Shippensburg, Jan. 1970; *It's Fun*, p. 7.)

51. What do you call a Polish bank?
    —A Pole vault.
    ("Cartoon Clubhouse," WHP-TV [Harrisburg], Aug. 19,
    1968.)

52. Who was Alexander Graham Kowalski?

The
Humor
Prism
in 20th-
Century
America

218

—The first telephone Pole.
(Shippensburg, Jan. 1970; Welsch, p. 185.)

Some Polack jokes take the form of narratives rather than riddles:

The garbage man stopped at this house and said, "Any garbage today, Mrs. Dumbrowski?" She said, "Yes, I'll take two bags."
(Shippensburg, Jan. 1970.)

A German, an Irishman, and a Polack made a hundred dollar bet as to which could stay in a stinking pig-pen longest. After an hour, the German came out and said, "I can't stand that. It stinks too bad. Here's the hundred dollars." After another hour, the Irishman came out. Then after another hour, the pig came out.[23]

Did you hear about the Polack who ordered a pizza? And the fellow asked him if he wanted it cut in six or twelve pieces. So he said, "You'd better make it six pieces. I don't think I could eat twelve."[24]

The Poles and the Italians decided to stop making jokes about each other's shortcomings, so they decided to play a football game and decide it that way. So they played hard football for three quarters and there was no score. Then in the middle of the fourth quarter, a factory whistle blew, and the Poles and the referee thought it was the end of the game and ran off the field. So the Italians finally scored . . . ten plays later.
(Shippensburg, Jan. 1969.)

A big Polish fellow had played, well, he hadn't played, but he'd been on the football team all four years he was in college, and he never got off the bench. Every game, he sat on the bench, and he never got in the game. So it came time for the last game of the season, and he wasn't even going to get dressed for the game. His wife, she was a big husky Polack girl, said, "Let *me* get dressed and go instead. I can put on pads and sit on the bench and no one will know the difference. It'll be something to talk about when we come back for class reunions." So she got dressed and sat on the bench, and this game, the team ran up a big score, so the coach cleaned the bench, sent everybody in. So the first play, everybody piled up in the center of the line, and she was on the bottom. When she came to, she was lying on a table in the dressing room with no clothes on, and the coach was massaging her up here, and he said, "Don't worry, you'll be all right as soon as we get these lumps down, and the other thing back out."[25]

Many of the Polack jokes and riddles above are simply re-tellings of older jokes, brought up to date and made part of the Polack series. Many are related to traditional motifs of stupidity and physical prowess and can be compared readily with the following Swabian tales told among the Pennsylvania Dutch:

> The Swabians bought a wheelbarrow, but they didn't push it. Instead, one took hold of the wheel and the other the handles, and thus they carried it home.

> The Swabians are so stupid that the soldiers carry hay on one shoulder and straw on the other; and the captain says, "hay" or "straw" when he desires them to turn to the right or to the left.
> (Brendle and Troxell, pp. 112, 114.)

As was the case with Sick Jokes and Elephant Riddles, the Polack Joke has had wide circulation among high school and college students. Like the Elephant Riddle, the Polack Joke seems to have started in the West and moved eastward, though it has been noted that similar jokes were being told about Italians in New England as early as 1961. Despite the predominance of people of Polish provenience in parts of Pennsylvania, it is highly unlikely that the joke had its origins there. When Jan Brunvand first called my attention to it in September, 1965, I had not yet heard a Polack Joke in Pennsylvania, though by December, the fad had spread rapidly.

Television had little effect on the spread of the Polack Joke, possibly because popular media comedians, quick to adopt most forms of folk humor, were reluctant to use controversial or ethnically derogatory materials until Spiro Agnew made them acceptable in 1968. Bob Hope mentioned the Polack Joke (but cautiously avoided the word Polack) on his first show of the 1968–69 season:

> If it wasn't for the Poles, we'd be telling Hungarian jokes . . .

> You know what a Polish politician is? That's a politician that keeps his hands in his own pockets. (NBC-TV, Sept. 25, 1968.)

Other NBC comics followed suit:

The
Humor
Prism
in 20th-
Century
America

220

The latest in a series of hijackings occurred in Ohio where a man jumped into the cab of a garbage truck and said, "Turn this thing around. We're heading for Warsaw."
(Dick Martin, "Laugh In," NBC-TV, Dec. 16, 1968.)

How do you make a Polish wienie?
First you find an ugly chicken.
("Laugh In," Oct. 6, 1969. The chicken reference chides the government's announcement that hot dogs could now contain chicken parts.)

Polish noodle soup. . . . It's just like any other soup except you eat it without a spoon.
(Charles Nelson Reilly, "Dean Martin Show," NBC-TV, Dec. 18, 1969.)

What plays Friday afternoon on Polish television?
Tuesday Night at the Movies.
(Johnny Carson, "Tonight Show," NBC-TV, Jan. 5, 1970.)

Would anybody have gotten out of bed if Paul Revere had ridden through the countryside shouting, "The Polish are coming, the Polish are coming?"
(Jonathan Winters, "Laugh In," Jan. 12, 1970.)

Richard Rodman, whose joke books contain a wealth of authentic but unscientifically reported folklore mailed in by readers, has published a number of Polack Jokes. He uses the term Slobbovians, explaining that "we hate to hurt anyone's feelings, so Slobbovia is a mythical place we use to tell all the really funny stories that might hurt someone's feelings":

Don't take any crap from a Slobbovian. It might be his lunch.
(*Sex-to-Sexty*, no. 21 [1969], p. 56.)

The Slobbovians made medical history last week. They performed the world's first hernia transplant.
(*Sex-to-Sexty*, no. 26 [1969], p. 55. A television joke in Nov. 1969 told of a Jewish doctor's performing a hernia transplant on an Arab.)

Know how to catch a Slobbovian? Hide behind a rock and make a noise like a welfare check.
(*Super Sex-to-Sexty*, no. 8 [1970], p. 33.)

The Slobbovian Royal Symphony stopped right in the middle of a concerto to clean the spit out of their instruments . . . and it's an all-string orchestra!
(*Super Sex-to-Sexty*, no. 8, p. 35.)

> They had to quit selling Preparation H in Slobbovia. It's
> now illegal to practice brain surgery without a license.
> (*Super Sex-to-Sexty*, no. 8, p. 87.)

Time magazine suggested (March 4, 1966, p. 47) that this
joke-riddle genre represents a refusal on the part of its student
devotees to deal with the adult world and its problems. This may
have been true of the Elephant and Grape-Plum jokes of the
mid-1960s. The Polack Joke, however, is more likely simply a re-
currence of the tendency for a majority group to ridicule a minority living within its domain. It provides an insight into our
times to note that even though the Polack Joke usually lacks the
bitterness often found in racial humor, it deals deliberately with
a very small minority group, one not involved in national controversy, and one that has no influential organization for picketing
or protesting. But even the seemingly innocuous Polack joking-
question has caused some uproar. When *Time* commented on
the phenomenon, it drew a letter from George H. Wostkiewicz of
Massachusetts: "Q. What's black and blue and lies on the floor?
A. Guys who tell Polish jokes."[26] And a U.P.I. report from Warsaw
in April, 1968, noted that the Polish Veterans Union was in-
censed at the popularity of the Polack Joke in the United States:
"The veterans group, Zbowid, set up a special display in its small
white, prewar manor house set back among the trees. It splashed
up a bulletin board display of the American ethnic joke book
'It's Fun to be a Polack (sic)' by Marvin Miller." The report
noted that some Polish pedestrians looked at the board, then
glared at the U.S. Embassy. Others read the jokes and laughed,
thereby proving that some Polacks can read.

The
Humor
Prism
in 20th-
Century
America

222

Notes

1. See Ellsworth Huntington, *Mainspring of Civilization* (New York: Mentor,
   1959), p. 47; cf. Donald C. Simmons, "Protest Humor: Folkloristic Reaction to Prejudice," *American Journal of Psychiatry* CXX (1963): 567.

2. Huntington, op. cit., pp. 84, 106–107. Cf. however, Samuel Bayard,
   "Numskull Tales: A Survey," *Folkways* no. 3 (Jan. 1964): pp. 18–19.

3. See Thomas R. Brendle and William S. Troxell, *Pennsylvania German Folk
   Tales* (Norristown, Pa., 1944), pp. 110 ff.; Albert F. Buffington,
   "Schwoweschtories," *Folkways* no. 3 (January 1964): pp. 22–24.

4. This is motif J1874.2. Cf. Leonard W. Roberts, *South from Hell-fer-Sartin*
   (Berea, Ky., 1964), pp. 126–127 (no. 53).

5. Vance Randolph, *Hot Springs and Hell* (Hatboro, Pa., 1965), p. 42, no. 116;
   cf. notes, p. 196.

Racial Riddles and the Polack Joke

6. Vide, e.g., "Numskull Tales in Cumberland County," *Pennsylvania Folklife* XVI:4 (Summer 1967): p. 51.
7. For other examples, see "You Can Tell a Joke with Vigah," *KFQ* IX (1964): 166–168.
8. Told in Philadelphia ca. 1960 by a graduate student from Texas. Bennett Cerf published a slightly different version in *The Pocket Book of Jokes* (New York, 1945), p. 16.
9. This and the following joke were told by Lycoming College students in Williamsport, Nov. 3, 1963.
10. Told in Carlisle by a Dickinson College professor formerly from Philadelphia, May 31, 1967. Cf. *Sex-to-Sexty*, no. 26 (1969): p. 59.
11. Told by a farmer from Middlesex, near Carlisle, June 1, 1968.
12. The following list is far from exhaustive: Hank Blair, *Would You Believe It* (Chicago: Donahue, n.d.); George Milburn, *The Best Jewish Jokes* (Girard, Kansas: Haldeman-Julius, n.d.); *New Hebrew Jokes* (Baltimore: Ottenheimer, n.d.); *Wehman Bros. Hebrew Jokes,* No. 1 and No. 2; *Wehman's Budget of Hebrew Yarns, Jokes and Stories* (New York, 1919). The same publishers also provided an extensive number of books of Irish, Dutch and Negro jokes; see Vance Randolph, *Hot Springs and Hell,* pp. 281–297.
13. Told in Carlisle, June 22, 1963; originally heard at Enola railroad yards about 1918. Cf. *New Hebrew Jokes* (Chicago: Donahue, n.d.), p. 54:

"Vat's de matter, Ikey?"

"Don't mention it, Ezra, I'm a dinkey-dink. Dat's vat I am."

"Vell, vat's you crying about?"

"I insured my brick-yard for five tousand dollars, and not a dam brick burned, and it cost me four dollars and a halluf for kerosene to make it a sure ting."

14. "Whether or not Jews really are materialistic and money-minded is one thing, but that there is a traditional folk stereotype is indisputable. Moreover, what the folk say may be an indicator of what the folk think. Whether it's a slogan ('Jesus Saves; Moses Invests') or a joking question ('Why do Jews have big noses? Air is free') the mercenary slur is the same." (Alan Dundes, *The Study of Folklore* [Englewood Cliffs, N.J., 1965], p. 43.)
15. "Anti-Italian-American Riddles in New England," *Journal of American Folklore* LXXIX (1966): 475–478.
16. The 1962 movie, "The Best of Enemies," starring David Niven and Alberto Sordi, capitalized on this idea.
17. Carlisle, Apr. 1966. This is based on a common "shaggy-dog" story: "A friend of mine walked into a bar holding a duck in his arms. The bartender said to him, 'Hey, buddy, what are you doing with that pig?' My friend answered indignantly, 'You must be an idiot. Can't you see this is a duck, not a pig?' 'I wasn't talking to you,' said the bartender. 'I was talking to the duck.'" (Dean Martin, "My Favorite Jokes," *Parade*, Jan. 23, 1966, p. 14). A similar joke appears in *Sex-to-Sexty Stag Treasury*, ed. Richard Rodman (Fort Worth, 1967), p. 453.
18. See "The Shaggy Elephant Riddle," *Southern Folklore Quarterly* XXVIII (1964): 266–290. Cf. C. G. Loomis, "Traditional American Wordplay," *Western Folklore* VII (1949): 235–247.
19. In the preface to Marvin Miller's collection of Polack jokes, *It's Fun to Be a Polak!* (Glendale, Calif., [Oct.] 1965), the "editors," Ed Zewbskewiecz,

The Humor Prism in 20th-Century America

Jerome Kuligowski and Harvey Krulka, admit that "few of our people will take offense at this book. Few of our people can read."

20. Cf. Simmons, "Protest Humor," and Roger L. Welsch, "American Numskull Tales: The Polack Joke," *Western Folklore* XXVI (1967): 183–186, esp. 184. See also Robert Reisner, "New Fun with Bigotry," *Cavalier*, Feb. 1966, pp. 24–25, 90–91.

21. The informants, their home residence, and college, are: Paul Heishman, Conestoga Valley H.S., Lancaster, later Dickinson College; Darlene Barrick, Carlisle, Kutztown State College; Rosalee Barrick, Carlisle, West Chester State College; the following Dickinson College students: Floyd Smith, Belmar, N.J.; Lawrence DeFuria, Moylan, Pa.; Lonnie Epstein, Pound Ridge, N.J.; Stephen Cole, Pikesville, Md.; the following Shippensburg State College students: George Hocker, Richard Hofman, and Lee Nell; the following faculty members: Enrique Martinez, Dickinson College formerly of Philadelphia; Frank Bianco, Hans Meurer, and Harold Weigel, all of Shippensburg State College.

22. Cf. *It's Fun*, p. 26: thinnest . . . *The History of Polack Culture*; Simmons, p. 477, no. 13: Book of Italian War Heroes (Book of Italian Etiquette, Puerto Rican Who's Who); *Mad*, No. 117 (March 1968): pp. 24–25: "The Mad Library of Extremely THIN Books," by Frank Jacobs, thirty titles, including "Real Funny Jokes from the Humor Collections of Bennett Cerf," "My Deep Concern over the Population Explosion—Pope Paul VI," and "The Israel's Tourist Guide to Egypt."

23. West Chester, Apr. 1966. Cf. the joke told about another ethnic group a generation ago: "There was a government official came up here from Washington during the war and he saw some goats. But he'd never seen any before so he called up Washington and said, 'I ran into some things up here that have hard heads and beards and stink. What shall I do?' And they told him, 'Let them alone! They're Amish!'" (Carlisle, July 1966.)

24. Carlisle, Feb. 1969. This, like several of the Polack Jokes, was formerly told about the Little Moron. For comparative examples of the Little Moron jokes and riddles, see Ernest W. Baughman, "Little Moron Stories," *Hoosier Folklore Bulletin* II (1943): 17–18; Rudolph Umland, "The Demise of the Little Moron," *Esquire* XX:3 (Sept. 1943): pp. 32–33, 154–155. Cf. also Martin Grotjahn, *Beyond Laughter* (New York, 1957): pp. 78–79: "From the Little Moron Joke to the Graf Bobby Anecdote."

25. Shippensburg, October 28, 1969. Cf. Victor Dodson, *The World's Dirtiest Jokes* (Los Angeles, 1969), p. 18, with the punch line: "As soon as we push your testicles back in place, your penis will pop right back out."

26. *Time*, March 18, 1966, p. 22. Cf. Welsch, p. 185: "What is black and blue and red all over? An Irishman who's been telling Polack jokes on Polaski Avenue."

The J.A.P. and the J.A.M. in American Jokelore

Alan Dundes

Jewish folkore is endlessly rich and one large component of the Jewish folklore repertoire consists of jokes. Some have argued that the Jewish sense of humor, especially as revealed in jokes, has helped Jews survive centuries of anti-Semitic prejudice and discrimination which in its extreme forms culminated in pogroms and the Holocaust. If there is a proportional relationship between repression and jokes such that the greater the repression, the greater the number of jokes protesting that repression, one can even better understand why Jews have so long depended upon the defense mechanism of jokes.

Whereas many Jewish jokes are concerned with the Jews' relationships with the outside world—that is, the gentile or goyish world—there have always been jokes that treat the Jewish world itself, from the inside. The themes of these insider jokes include among others the schnorrer, the marriage arranger, the moyl, the rabbi, and the rabbi's wife (see Howe 1961; Landmann 1963, 1977).

Here I propose to examine the stereotype of the Jewish American Princess (J.A.P.) as displayed in a joke cycle popular in the United States in the late 1970s and early 1980s. Since the J.A.P. cannot be understood in isolation from the Jewish American Mother (J.A.M.), this stereotype will be considered as well.

One theme of Jewish jokes in the United States is the Jewish mother. It has been suggested that such jokes are of relatively modern origin. According to one source, "Jokes about the Jewish mother—the biggest cliché in contemporary Jewish humor—are a relatively recent phenomenon. Traditional Jewish humor had no such jokes" (Novak and Waldoks 1981:268). Another source (Ehrlich 1979:396) claims, "By now, the Jewish Mother is part of

The
Humor
Prism
in 20th-
Century
America

225

Reproduced by permission of the American Folklore Society from the *Journal of American Folklore*, vol. 98, no. 390 (October–December 1985). Not for further reproduction.

all American comedy. Overbearing, overprotective, long-suffering, loudly self-sacrificing, and unintentionally funny, she survives the joke not only as a person of warmth, but as one who cares." There is some question as to just when the stereotype began to come into national prominence and to what extent the stereotype derives from Eastern Europe.

Several authorities have argued that the Jewish mother, especially as a negative stereotype, became "an integral part of the American scene" during the 1960s (Bienstock 1979:184; cf. Baum, Hyman, and Michel 1977:237). In her essay "The Jewish Mother and the 'Jewish American Princess': Fact or Fiction?" Sara Reguer (1979:41) begins by stating that "The Jewish Mother is a purely American phenomenon," although she is aware of the possible connection to the *Yiddishe mama* of Eastern Europe. Zena Smith Blau, in her essay "In Defense of the Jewish Mother," maintains "there can be little question that the constellation of maternal traits commonly referred to as the 'Yiddishe Mameh' was the modal maternal pattern among Jewish immigrants from Eastern Europe" (1967:43). Zborowski and Herzog in *Life Is With People* also claim that the stereotype "has firm roots in the shtetl" (1962:293). Whatever the degree of indebtedness might be to Eastern Europe with respect either to the stereotype or to the jokes about that stereotype, there can be no doubt that the Jewish American Mother is a distinctive folk character in American jokelore.

The
Humor
Prism
in 20th-
Century
America

226

The characteristics of the J.A.M. in jokes include such features as being overly solicitous of her children's welfare (especially her son's health), and being anxious for her daughters to marry well (preferably doctors or lawyers) and her sons to become professionals (preferably doctors or lawyers). The stereotype also refers to the J.A.M.'s forcing food down the throats of her children (for reasons of health) and her excessive, unending demand for attention, love, and visits from her children even after they are married successfully.

The J.A.M. is depicted as enjoying the role of martyr. One might even say that the Jewish American Mother suffers from a martyr complex. She is mater as martyr! She is never happier than when she has something to complain about, with the complaint intended to produce feelings of guilt in her children. One of the classic jokes illustrating the impossibility of totally satisfying or pleasing the J.A.M. is the following:

A mother gave her son two neckties as a present for his birthday, a red one and a green one. The son, to show his appreciation for the gift puts on the red one and is wearing it when he picks her up to take her out for dinner. Says the mother. "What's the matter! You didn't like the green one?"
[cf. Grotjahn 1961:186; Bellman 1965:3; Ehrlich 1979:396 (sweaters); Pollack 1979:187]

On the other hand, J.A.M.s worship their sons.

How do we know Jesus was Jewish? He lived at home with his mother until he was 30, he went into his father's business, and he had a mother who thought he was God.
[cf. Knott 1982:21]

Overprotection is a principal element in the J.A.M. stereotype. One theory is that this is a compensation for Jews generally being underprotected in society (Boroff 1957:7). The following text shows the excessively nurturant J.A.M. with the resultant spoiled child:

A Jewish mother and her son arrive in a taxi in front of a large plush hotel on Miami Beach. The mother in a mink coat and much bejeweled goes in to register and she asks several bellboys to bring in the 2 trunks and 12 suitcases. After they do so, they ask if there's anything else they can do for her. She replies, "Would you please lift my 14 year old son out of the car and carry him up to my room?"

"Oh," says one of the bellboys, "I'm sorry, I didn't realize he couldn't walk."

"He can walk all right," says the mother, "but thank God he doesn't have to."
[cf. Pollack 1979:113]

Perhaps the most common sign of the J.A.M.'s nurturant proclivities is her constant concern with feeding her progeny.

Did you know that there are two signs on El Al airlines planes? "Fasten Your Seat Belts" and "Eat."

In another version, the sign reads:

"Eat, eat, take a little nosh"
[Blumenfeld 1969:65–66]

while in yet another, three signs on El Al read:

> "Fasten Seat Belts," "No Smoking," and "Take a Piece of Fruit."
> [Blumenfeld 1969:80]
>
> Did you know they have two stewardesses on El Al airlines? One who serves the food and the other follows saying "Eat, eat."
>
> Did you hear about the new ship in the Israeli Navy? The S.S. Mein Kind (eat, eat my child).
> [cf. Wilde 1980:32]
>
> Did you hear about the bum who walked up to the Jewish mother on the street and said, "Lady, I haven't eaten in three days."
> "Force yourself," she replied.
> [Knott 1982:21]

It has been observed that there was often an apparent altruistic bent to the J.A.M.'s urging children to eat: eat "*for others*, for mama, for poppa, for other members of the family, and inevitably the appeal was made to eat for the 'poor starving children in Europe'" (Blau 1967:45). We shall see that the J.A.P. who is egocentric, not altruistic, in contrast eats for no one, not even herself!

One of the best of the food-forcing J.A.M. jokes is the following reported in 1958:

> A Jewish gangster has been in a gun fight with police. As he staggers into his mother's East Side apartment, nearly *in extremis*, his hands on a big bloody wound, he gasps, "Ma, ma, I-I've been hit. . . ."
> Mama says, "Eat, eat. Later we'll talk."
> [Rosenberg and Shapiro 1958:80; cf. Wilde 1980:42; Novak and Waldoks 1981:71]

The J.A.M. will do anything to make her children eat:

> What's the difference between an Italian mother and a Jewish mother?
> The Italian mother says, "If you don't eat all the food on this plate, I'll kill you."
> The Jewish mother says, "If you don't eat all the food on this plate, I'll kill myself."
> [Knott 1983a:9]

The J.A.M. ploy inevitably involves the murder threat.
Of course, the J.A.M. makes a difficult mother-in-law, as one
might imagine. The antagonism between the J.A.M. and her
(prospective) daughter-in-law is sharply delineated in a tale that
is also popular in Eastern Europe:

> A Jewish young man asks his mother for her heart which his
> fiancée has demanded as a prerequisite for marriage. The
> mother gladly accedes to this unusual request so that her
> son will be happy. Having torn his mother's heart out, the
> boy is rushing back to show it to his bride-to-be. On the way,
> he stumbles and both he and the heart fall to the ground
> whereupon the heart asks, "Did you hurt yourself, my son?"
> [cf. Mintz 1978:346; for a brief discussion of the tale's distribution,
> see Scheiber 1955]

This tale marvelously encapsulates the J.A.M.'s uncanny ability to
use solicitude as a devastating weapon to create feelings of guilt.
No matter how great the pain for the self-sacrificing martyr-
mater, her only concern is for her son's welfare—even if he
treats her shamefully!

Not surprisingly, we find a predictable double standard with
respect to what the J.A.M. wants for her children and what she
wants for their spouses.

> Two women meet on the Grand Concourse in the Bronx,
> and one says to the other. "How are your children?"
> "Well," says the other. "Oy veh, how awful! My son is
> married to such a woman. She has to have breakfast in bed,
> nu, she has to have a mink stole. . . ."
> The other woman says, "And what about your daugh-
> ter? How is she?"
> "She's married to a dear man. . . . He serves her break-
> fast in bed; he bought her a mink stole."

One of the most typical complaints of the J.A.M. concerns
her married children's failure to visit her or to call her often
enough. From my own Jewish mother—by telephone, of course,
when I called her—I collected the following text:

> A Jewish woman discovers a magic lamp. She rubs it, and a
> genie appears and says she can have a wish, anything she
> wants. What does she ask for? Nothing. She didn't want to

The
Humor
Prism
in 20th-
Century
America

229

wish. She had everything she wanted: a daughter who married a doctor and a son who called her once a week.

Another text refers more to the J.A.M.'s daughter.

> An old Jewish woman goes to her lawyer to have her will made out. She arrives at his office and he says, "Hello, what can I do for you?"
>
> She says. "I want to make my will."
>
> "Okay, what do you want it to say?"
>
> "Well, when I die, I want to be cremated and I want my ashes scattered on the first, the second, and the third floors of Neiman-Marcus."
>
> "Okay, but why would you want to do that?"
>
> "Well, at least that way, I know my daughter will come visit me once a week."
>
> [For another text set in Bloomingdales, see Wilde 1979:43; Novak and Waldoks 1981:274]

The J.A.M. is such a stock character that she is virtually interchangeable within her cohort. Any Jewish Mother can serve in a crisis. This is beautifully illustrated in the following "big city" joke:

The
Humor
Prism
in 20th-
Century
America

230

> The telephone rings and the daughter answers.
>
> "Hello!"
>
> "How are you?" says the mother.
>
> "Oh terrible, terrible."
>
> "What's the matter?"
>
> "The baby's sick, and the maid called in today, Ma, and she's not coming, and the place is a mess. There's nothing in the refrigerator and we're having company tonight for dinner. I'm supposed to go to the Hadassah meeting. I don't know what to do!"
>
> "Don't worry. What's a mother for? I got plenty time. I've made gefilte fish; I've got a couple of chickens; I can bring them. I'll be right over. I'll clean your apartment; I'll wait for the doctor to come over. You go to your Hadassah meeting, and I'll get the dinner ready."
>
> "Oh, ma that would be wonderful."
>
> "Listen, what's a mother for? Before you hang up, how's Stephen?"
>
> "Stephen, who's Stephen?"
>
> "What do you mean who's Stephen? He's your husband."

"My husband's name is Marvin."
(Long pause)
"Is this 841-5656?"
"No, it's 841-6565" (Pause). "Does this mean you're not coming??"
[cf. Wilde 1974:37]

Various explanations of the Jewish mother stereotype have been proposed. According to some sources, the Jewish mother had to be strong because the Jewish father was weak. In Europe the husband was concerned with religious devotion to God while the wife ran the household (Bienstock 1979:175–176), while in America Jewish men had to assimilate more to gain employment, leaving the women trapped in the home to serve as bastions of Jewish culture and values (Zanger 1976:41). According to this view the Jewish mother, often married to a weak, unsuccessful Jewish man, had good reason to lavish her attention, love, and hopes for the future of her children instead (Bienstock 1979:186). So involved is the Jewish Mother with the lives of her children that she has difficulty in letting them leave home. She fears the "empty nest syndrome" more than most (Baum, Hyman, and Michel 1977:241).

If this view is accurate, then it seems reasonable to suspect the apparent selflessness of the J.A.M. She has her own personal reasons for serving as relentless nurturer. One sometimes finds an insidious motive attached to the food-providing image. In return for the nurturance, the J.A.M. demands eternal loyalty and love. As one critic has felicitously phrased it, "Too well we know the Jewish mother our male writers have given us, the all-engulfing nurturer who devours the very soul with every spoonful of hot chicken soup she gives" (Duncan 1980:231). Even the "Eat, eat" jokes have been perceived as "hostile vulgarizations" of the Jewish mother's role as all powerful mistress of the home (Zanger 1976:42). There is even a hint that underlying the J.A.M.'s indulgence is hostility toward her demanding, whining children. This underlying hostility is revealed in jokes.

Four Jewish women meet.
"Oy!" says the first.
"Oy veh!" says the second.
"Oy veh iz mir!" [Oh woe is me!] says the third.
"I thought we weren't going to talk about the kids," says the fourth.

In another text:

> Two Jewish mothers meet. One says to the other, "Do you have any children?"
> "No."
> "So what do you do for aggravation?"

It is interesting that the latter joke's premise involves two Jewish *mothers* meeting even though it turns out that one of the women has no children. This suggests that the J.A.M.'s over-solicitous regard for her children might be an instance of reaction formation caused by guilt for harboring such feelings of hostility and resentment. Perhaps the resentment of the seemingly endless nurturance demands of children is a relatively late development of the 1980s.

> A Catholic, a Protestant, and a Jew are debating the question of when exactly does life begin. The Catholic insists that life begins at the moment of conception; the Protestant disagrees claiming that life begins at birth; the Jew says, "You're both wrong. Life begins when the children leave home and the dog dies."
> [cf. Wilde 1985:62]

The image or stereotype of the Jewish American Princess seems to vary considerably from that of the J.A.M. Interestingly, the stereotype of the "Kugel" in South Africa is virtually identical to the J.A.P., demonstrating that the humor is by no means peculiar to the United States (cf. Klevansky 1982; Levine 1983). In any event, the stereotypical traits are consistent ones. The J.A.P. is spoiled, and spoiled rotten. She is excessively concerned with appearance. She diets. She may have had a nose job. (Did you hear about the Jewish girl who cut off her nose to spite her race and was a thing of beauty and a goy forever? [cf. Wilde 1980:18]). She worries about her fingernails. She is interested in money, shopping, and status. Some of these features—wealth and status, for example—she shares with the J.A.M., but her refusal to cook (and eat) contrasts dramatically with the J.A.M. The J.A.P. is indifferent to sex and she is particularly disinclined to perform fellatio.

One might argue that the J.A.M. is ultimately responsible for creating the J.A.P. Mothers who overprotect their daughters produce women who expect to be catered to and looked after.

Julie Baumgold in her essay "The Persistence of the Jewish American Princess" maintains that "A princess is made by only one thing and that is her mother. Her mother telling her that she is beautiful. Unremittingly, over the years, that she is beautiful; that she is precious, the thing that the man has to earn and deserve" (1971:28). While the J.A.M. is bound by "the role of wife and mother, the all-giving selfless nurturer" (Mintz 1978:352), the J.A.P. rejects these values. Perhaps the J.A.P.'s obsession with high style clothing is a reaction to what the J.A.P. perceives as the J.A.M.'s plain, even dowdy hausfrau apparel. The J.A.P.'s refusal to eat (in order to stay slim) may be a direct response to the J.A.M's insistence upon eating. The J.A.M. lavishes food to show love; the J.A.P. declines to cook or eat, or to indulge in lovemaking.

Perhaps the most common J.A.P. jokes treat the refusal to prepare meals.

> What does a J.A.P. make for dinner? Reservations.
> [Lukatsky and Toback 1982:69; Knott 1982:22; Alvin 1983b:15]
>
> How does a J.A.P. call her family to dinner? "Get in the car, kids."
> [Knott 1983b:18; Thickett 1984:68 (without reference to J.A.P.)]
>
> How does a J.A.P. get exercise? "Waitress" (waving one's arm frantically).

An equally common characteristic of the stereotype is the desire for high status items such as trips to fashionable resorts, or standard prestigious material objects:

> What is a J.A.P.'s favorite wine? "I wanna go to Hawaii (Miami)!"
> What is a J.A.P.'s second favorite wine? "And I wanna go right NOW!"

Other favorite whines include "You never take me anywhere," and "I wanna mink coat" (or diamond ring) (Lukatsky and Toback 1982:76; Thickett 1983:44). The "whining and dining" facet of the J.A.P. also characterizes the so-called J.A.P.I.T. joke. The J.A.P.I.T. is a J.A.P. *In Training*. Her cry is "I want a Diet Pepsi but I want my *own*."

> What do you call 12 J.A.P.s locked in the basement? A whine cellar.

The
Humor
Prism
in 20th-
Century
America

233

With respect to this detail of the stereotype, it is of more than passing interest that Blau (1967:44) remarks,

> In America Yiddishe Mamehs appeared far more permissive, indulgent and self-sacrificing than the typical Anglo-Saxon mother, at least in the years prior to the nineteen-forties. For example, they were a good deal more tolerant of whining and crying, and dependency behavior generally.

This would help explain the J.A.M.'s role in producing J.A.P.s.

But the good life includes more than wine. It includes shopping for quality items.

> How do you tickle a J.A.P.? Gucci Gucci goo.
> [Knott 1982:21; cf. Alvin 1983b:14]
>
> Why do J.A.P.s like circumcised men? They like anything with 20% off.
> What three little words does a J.A.P. never hear? Attention K-Mart shoppers.
> [Thickett 1983:46]

K-Mart is, of course, a bargain store, but the merchandise does not carry the required high status labels. In K-Mart, there are frequent loudspeaker announcements calling attention to a particularly cheap item on sale. A contrasting ethnic joke is: "What are the first three words a Mexican baby will hear? Attention K-Mart shoppers."

> How does a J.A.P. commit suicide? Piles her clothes on top of the bed and jumps off.
> What is a J.A.P. with a colostomy's greatest concern? Finding shoes to match the bag.
> [cf. Thickett 1983:47; Knott 1983a:23]

Another reference to the undue anxiety about personal appearance is contained in the following text:

> What's a J.A.P.'s idea of natural childbirth? Going into the delivery room without any makeup on.
> [cf. Knott 1983a:25]

Of course, shopping for expensive name brands requires adequate financial support.

Why do J.A.P.s wear gold diaphragms? Because they like their men to come into money.
[Lukatsky and Toback 1982:57; Knott 1982:21; Alvin 1983b:14]

Despite the existence of this last text, it is her antipathy to sex that constitutes the hallmark of the J.A.P.

How do you keep a Jewish girl from fucking? Marry her.
[Wilde 1974:99; Tonner 1975:70; Lukatsky and Toback 1982:110]

Have you heard the joke about the Jewish nymphomaniac? Once a month.
[Tonner 1975:56; Wilde 1980:48]

What's the definition of a J.A.P. nymphomaniac? One who only has sex on days she gets her hair done.
[Anonymous 1966:8; Lukatsky and Toback 1982:86]

What is Jewish foreplay? Twenty minutes of begging.
[Wilde, 1980:60; Knott 1982:19, 1983a:10]

This is part of a larger ethnic slur tradition criticizing insensitive males who are oblivious to female sexual needs.

What is Irish foreplay? Brace yourself, Bridget.

What is Italian foreplay? Hey, you awake? (Or slamming the front door and announcing "Hey, Honey, I'm home!")

How does a Jewish couple perform "doggie style" sex? He sits up and begs and she lies down and plays dead.
[Thickett 1983:49; Wilde 1985:65]

What's a Jewish 10? A 9 without a headache (or a 5 with money).
[cf. Wilde 1980:22]

What do you call a J.A.P.'s nipple? The tip of the iceberg.
[Knott 1983a:57]

How do you know when a J.A.P. has an orgasm? She drops her emery board (nail file).
[Lukatsky and Toback 1982:68; Knott 1983a:23; Thickett 1983:47]

What's a J.A.P.'s idea of perfect sex? Simultaneous headaches.
[Knott 1983b:20]

Why do Jewish girls kiss with their eyes closed? 'Cause they can't stand seeing anyone enjoying themselves.
[cf. Janus 1980:264]

The
Humor
Prism
in 20th-
Century
America

235

Many of the J.A.P. jokes combine traits of the stereotype such as disinterest in cooking with disinterest in scx, the use of credit cards and sex, and so on.

> Why does a J.A.P. close her eyes during sex? So she can pretend she's shopping.
> [Knott 1983a:27]

> How does a J.A.P. fake an orgasm? She thinks of going shopping.
> [cf. Thickett 1984:90]

> What is a J.A.P.'s ideal house? 6000 square feet with no kitchen and no bedroom.
> [cf. Thickett 1983:45; Knott 1983a:26]

> What's a J.A.P.'s favorite position? Facing Neiman-Marcus (Bloomingdales).
> [Knott 1983a:23; Thickett 1983:44]

> What's a J.A.P.'s favorite position? Bending over credit cards.
> [Knott 1983b:18]

> Why do J.A.P.s use tampons instead of sanitary napkins? Because nothing goes in without a ring attached.
> [Thickett 1984:51]

> Why is a tampon like a J.A.P.? Because they're both stuck up cunts.
> [Alvin 1984:24]

> What do you get when you cross a French whore with a J.A.P.? A girl who sucks credit cards. [Or:] A woman that will suck the numbers off your credit card.
> [cf. Knott 1982:22; Wilde 1985:64]

In this last text, it is the French whore who accounts for the act of fellatio, not the J.A.P. The J.A.P. in the joke cycle absolutely refuses to indulge in such activities.

> What's the difference between J.A.P.s and poverty? Poverty sucks.
> [cf. Wilde 1985:68]

> What's the difference between a J.A.P. and a job? Most jobs suck after 20 years.

> What's the difference between a J.A.P. and the Bermuda Triangle? The Bermuda Triangle swallows seamen!
> [cf. Knott 1983a:23; Alvin 1983a:14]

What do you get when you cross a J.A.P. and an Apple (IBM)? A computer that'll never go down.

Why do J.A.P.s have crow's feet? From squinting and saying, "Suck *what?*"
[Knott 1983a:27; Wilde 1985:64]

In a variant, the question is: why do J.A.P.s have slanted eyes? This is of interest in view of the apparent similarity to Japanese facial features.

What does a J.A.P. think that sucking and fucking are? Two cities in China.

Why won't a J.A.P. eat soybeans? Because it's a meat substitute.
[Alvin 1983b:13]

How does a J.A.P eat a banana? Under duress.
[Alvin 1983b:13]

In a variant, the answer involves miming a banana held in the left hand, with the right hand pretending to peel three strips about halfway down the feigned banana. Then the right hand is placed behind the neck whereupon it roughly forces the head down to eat the peeled banana (cf. Knott 1982:22). The same theme is found in longer jokes, such as the following:

Several months after the death of her husband, Mrs. Goldfarb speaks to the urn containing his ashes. "You know, Morris, that mink coat I always wanted and you promised me, well now thanks to you, I got it. And you know, Morris, that trip to Hawaii I always wanted and you promised me, well, now thanks to you, I just stopped off there on my tour around the world." Mrs. Goldfarb then empties the contents of the urn on the dining room table. "And you know, Morris, that blow job you always wanted and I promised you? Well, here it is!" (blowing the ashes off the table) [For another version, see Thickett 1983:49]

Just as the J.A.P. refuses to engage in fellatio, she is equally disinterested in cunnilingus.

What's the difference between a J.A.P. and jello? One moves (shakes) when you eat it.
[cf. Wilde 1985:5]

The Humor Prism in 20th-Century America

237

What's the difference between a J.A.P. and spaghetti? One
wiggles when you eat it.

The image or stereotype of the J.A.P. is fairly consistent in
these diverse jokes. There is also a male equivalent of the J.A.P.,
namely, the Jewish American Prince (Sequoia 1982:8–9). According to Levine (1983), in South Africa the prince is called a
"Bagel." But the prince figure seems largely derivative from the
Jewish American Princess. In any case, there are not nearly as
many jokes about princes as princesses. One text is:

What word beginning in "A" means prince in Jewish? A doctor.
[Anonymous 1966:8; Wilde 1974:89]

The J.A.M. and the J.A.P. have entered the mainstream of
American culture not just through folklore and jokelore, but also
from popular culture. Dan Greenburg's best-selling book, *How to
be a Jewish Mother* (1964) includes under "The Basic Techniques
of Jewish Motherhood" such lessons as "Making Guilt Work" and
"Seven Basic Sacrifices to Make for Your Child." Moreover, there
is an entire section devoted to "The Jewish Mother's Guide to
Food Distribution." Among other examples of popular culture
devoted to the J.A.P. is a record "The Jewish-American Princess"
(Anonymous 1971), and a cut-out paper doll book complete with
all accessories including a variety of punch-out credit cards (Sequoia and Brown 1983). An article published in the *Journal of
Popular Film* in 1975 includes the J.A.P. as one of the images of
the Jew found in American movies (Erens 1975:213–217). In addition to records and film, there are whole books describing the
J.A.P., such as Leslie Tonner's *Nothing But the Best: The Luck of the
Jewish Princess* (1975). This was followed by *two* entire J.A.P.
Handbooks (Lukatsky and Toback 1982; Sequoia 1982) which
describe in great detail all the presumed personality characteristics and behavioral propensities of J.A.P.s. These handbooks are
no doubt in part a "Jewish" response to the earlier *Preppy Handbook* (Birnbach 1980), which parodied/celebrated old line aristo-
cratic W.A.S.P. culture. The occurrence of J.A.P. jokes in the
bestselling *Gross Jokes* (Alvin 1983a) and *Truly Tasteless Jokes*
(Knott 1982) paperbacks further popularized the cycle. Of
course, both have also been featured in various novels and short
stories such as Philip Roth's *Portnoy's Complaint* (1969) and Her-

The
Humor
Prism
in 20th-
Century
America

238

man Wouk's *Marjorie Morningstar* (1955). For discussions of the J.A.M. and J.A.P. in American literature, see Baumgold (1971), Zanger (1976), Baum, Hyman, and Michel (1977), Mintz (1978), and Bienstock (1979).

The contrast between the J.A.M. and the J.A.P. is clear enough. In the light bulb joke cycle it is significant that there are texts for both the J.A.M. and the J.A.P. This suggests that the folk consider them two separate stereotypes.

> How many J.A.P.s does it take to change a light bulb? One who refuses, saying "What? And ruin my nail polish?" [Or] Two: one to pour the Diet Pepsi and one to call Daddy.
> [Dundes 1981:263–264; Novak and Waldoks 1981:126; Knott 1982:22]

We find the familiar themes of nail polish, dieting, and dependence upon Daddy. This is markedly different from the Jewish mother text.

> How many Jewish mothers does it take to change a light bulb? None, "So I'll sit here in the dark."
> [Wilde 1980:32; Dundes 1981:264; cf. Knott 1982:23]

Here we have the inevitable complaining mother figure who exults in creating guilt feelings in her progeny for their alleged failure to take proper care of her. Generally speaking, the light bulb joke cycle gave fairly specific and accurate delineations of the stereotypes represented in that cycle, such as:

> How many Harvard students does it take to change a light bulb? One, he holds it, and the whole world revolves around him.

Certainly the pictures of the J.A.P. and the J.A.M. ring true in the light of the other texts reported above. One other minimal pair of jokes that helps to illustrate how the folk differentiate the J.A.M. and the J.A.P.:

> What is the difference between a Jewish Mother and a Vulture? A vulture waits until you are dead to eat your heart out.
>
> What is the difference between a J.A.P. and a vulture? Nail polish.

The Humor Prism in 20th-Century America

239

One question that invariably arises in any discussion of stereotypes is the extent, if any, to which the stereotypes are "true." Are the J.A.M. and J.A.P. strictly fictional caricatures? Or do these stereotypes correspond to actual personality traits? As might be expected, there is a difference of opinion. Some have argued "according to the measurements of social scientists, there does seem to be at least some validity to the Jewish Mother stereotype" (Baum, Hyman, and Michel 1977:244; cf. Blau 1967:43). On the other hand, a 1984 doctoral dissertation in clinical psychology entitled "Personality Traits of the 'Jewish Mother': Realities Behind the Myth" (Pelleg-Sani 1984) studied some 200 women from Houston (50 Jewish women under 50 years of age, 50 Protestant women under 50 years of age, 50 Jewish women over 50, and 50 Protestant women over 50). According to this study, the results did not support the traditional stereotype of the Jewish mother as domineering, nurturing, and controlling through guilt. The study did, however, indicate the existence of the J.A.P. configuration, describing the younger Jewish mothers as demanding, materialistic, and self-indulgent. It is possible that the time frame is a factor. In 1984, one might be more likely to find J.A.P.s than J.A.M.s in Houston. Had the study been carried out 40 years earlier, the J.A.P.s might have been outnumbered by the J.A.M.s. In any event, some contend that the J.A.P. stereotype reflects reality (cf. Baumgold 1971; Reguer 1979).

One of the critical differences between the J.A.M. and the J.A.P. has to do with their respective attitudes toward children. This was perhaps first remarked in a brilliant essay by Martha Wolfenstein (1963). Wolfenstein contrasted a 51-year-old Russian-Jewish mother with a 34-year-old second-generation American whose parents were of Eastern European origin. The attitudes of the older woman included the idea that her infant was helpless and that a mother's duty was to feed and care for him and to keep him from harm. Even when her child grew up, the clinical data revealed that she continued to think of her adolescent son "as a helpless infant who cannot be trusted to do anything for himself and who, if left to his own devices, will injure himself, probably irreparably" (Wolfenstein 1963:425). She observes further, "To this mother, her big athletic boy is still as fragile as an infant, just as vulnerable to the hazards of the environment, and just as dependent on the mother's vigilant care in order to survive" (Wolfenstein 1963:426). In contrast, the second woman, a college graduate, has adopted American mainstream values toward children, especially with regard to the need for individualism and independence. Her complaint was "When will Karen [her daughter] grow up? Why is she still so babyish?" (Wolfenstein 1963:427). Wolfenstein ends her fascinating comparison of Eastern European Jewish and American Jewish mother-child relations with the question of how the transition from the Eastern European Jewish to the American Jewish family is achieved.

Wolfenstein's essay was surely inspired by earlier research by Ruth Benedict (1949), who compared child-rearing techniques in selected European countries. Benedict specifically concentrated upon attitudes toward swaddling in Russia and Poland. In Russia, swaddling was deemed necessary to keep an infant from hurting itself; in Poland, the infant was not considered violent, but rather fragile. The infant was swaddled to "harden" it. In contrast to both Russian and Polish views of swaddling, Jewish swaddling in both countries had a different rationale. There was no suggestion that the baby was inherently violent or that it needed "hardening," Benedict argued. Rather it was the baby's first experience of the warmth of life in his own home. It was, in Benedict's terms, an example of a Jewish complementary system she called "nurturance-deference." "The Jewish binder conceives herself as performing a necessary ace of nurturance out of which she expects the child to experience primarily warmth and comfort" (Benedict 1949; cf. Blau 1967:43).

What Benedict and Wolfenstein's speculations suggest is that the Eastern European Jewish tradition of nurturance did not fit in with American ideals of childcare, especially with respect to creating "rugged individualism." Second- or third-generation American Jews felt the need to reject what they considered to be excessive nurturance: hence the J.A.M. stereotype. In the same way, the J.A.P. represents a curious combination of Jewish and American cultural patterns (Tonner 1975:12). Jewish culture overprotects its children and American culture demands and expects upward mobility for all groups. The ideology (though hardly the practice) is expressed in the idealistic egalitarian phrase that "anyone can be president" (except for women, blacks, Jews, etc.). Thus the Jew who had to struggle just to make ends meet in Eastern and Western Europe found that struggling in the United States could yield much greater material reward.

In this light, we can perhaps legitimately argue that J.A.M.s have helped produce J.A.P.s, but the question "Can a J.A.P. become a J.A.M.?" is more difficult to answer. My feeling is that the answer is no. To the extent that the difference between J.A.M.s and J.A.P.s is generational, there is no way that a J.A.P., once created, can ever become a true J.A.M. It is not easy to imagine how the spoiled could become spoiler, how the indulged could become the indulger, how someone who refuses to cook could force her children to eat, and so on.

Since the J.A.P. joke cycle presents such a decidedly negative stereotype of Jewish young women and since the jokes are told by Jews (both men and women), we may well have an instance of what is called in the literature "self-hate" (cf. Lewin 1941; Liptzin 1957; Rosenberg and Shapiro 1958) or self-depreciation (Dorinson 1981:450). Grotjahn (1961) speaks of the Jewish joke in general as expressions "aggression turned inward." It is, he contends, "a combination of sadistic attack with masochistic indulgence" (1961:184). Dan Ben-Amos has criticized what he calls the illusion of self-mockery in Jewish humor, arguing that the examination of Jewish joke-telling events reveals that the raconteur does not identify himself with the butt of the joke (1973:123), although it is not clear just how Ben-Amos knows this. In his words, "The narrator is not the butt of his story and self-degradation could not possibly be a classical form of Jewish humor." Ben-Amos suggests that there is a generational factor. It is Jews who speak *without* "Jewish" accents who especially enjoy telling Jewish jokes using accents. He feels that "the narrators do not laugh at themselves altogether, but rather ridicule a social group within the Jewish community from which they would like to differentiate themselves" (1973:125). In this view, Ben-Amos echoes Naomi and Eli Katz who conclude from their study of American Jewish humor that the second-generation American Jew "wished to separate himself sharply from the unassimilated immigrant" (1971:219).

Stanley Brandes takes issue with this position, arguing that dialect jokes "could be said as much to unite as to divide distinct generations of American Jewry" (1983:239). It seems reasonable that partly or wholly assimilated Jews tell such jokes for precisely the opposite reason offered by Ben-Amos, namely, to prove their connection with the authentic, "real" Jews—their parents and grandparents who did have pronounced accents. Probably both views are correct. The jokes express genuine ambivalence. On the one hand, American Jews are "better"—meaning more assimilated—because they can speak English without an accent whereas their parents or grandparents could not; on the other hand, American Jews maintain their Jewish identity by telling and listening to Jewish jokes, preferably by using Yiddish in the punchlines. In this way, American Jews succeed in distancing themselves from *and* associating themselves with the past vestiges of their ethnicity. So "self-hate" is combined with what might be called "self-love"!

But how does all this bear on the J.A.P. joke cycle? Is it merely what the Katzs suggest, namely that "the contemporary Jewish joke represents . . . a stage of adaptation on the part of young American Jews who reject what they regard as the excessively vulgar, ostentatious and materially oriented conformity of their Americanized parents to the values of well-to-do suburbia" (1971:220)? In this context, we could interpret the J.A.P. jokes told by young Jewish men and women as a rebellion against either the actual values of their materialistic and upwardly mobile parents, or the stereotype of those values, or both. On the other hand, I have encountered young Jewish women who boldly claim that they are J.A.P.s and proud of it. So there is ambivalence. One may identify with some of the values despite the existence of caricatures of those values and the attempt to distance oneself from such values.

This explanation does not really illuminate why the J.A.P. is depicted as being so adamantly opposed to engaging in sexual activity. And why did the J.A.P. joke cycle emerge when it did in the late 1970s and early 1980s? Both J.A.P. handbooks, remember, were published in 1982. Surely there have been overly protective Jewish mothers and whining Jewish princesses before the 1980s. It is possible that the J.A.P. joke cycle serves another function. In this regard, one must keep in mind that the cycle is also popular among non-Jews. This raises the question of whether J.A.P. jokes should be considered Jewish jokes (cf. Jason 1967). One of the handbooks even argues that "Not all JAPs are Jewish," and goes on to discuss what are termed "WASP JAPs" (Sequoia 1982:10, 22). Reguer (1971:42) goes so far as to claim "You don't

The
Humor
Prism
in 20th-
Century
America

243

have to be Jewish to be a 'Jewish mother' or a 'Jewish American Princess.'"

While there may be an anti-Semitic element accounting for the popularity of the joke cycle to the extent that traditional Jewish materialistic values are lampooned, I suspect that the J.A.P. jokes may be a reflection of anti-feminism. The jokes are in the large sense anti-woman, as are some of the J.A.M. jokes. The J.A.P. is the ultimate in bitchy, whining female behavior. It may be more than a coincidence that the joke cycle came into favor at a time when women's liberation and feminist ideology were becoming increasingly well known (and may have been regarded as threatening by old order male chauvinists). Nevertheless, the J.A.P. can hardly be construed as a liberated woman. She is very much an exemplification of "a woman's place is in the home" or out shopping. She is a woman who thrives on being looked after by men—first by daddy, and later by a professional husband. There is no mention of equal rights in the jokes.

Truly egalitarian values in America, even from a historical perspective, denied the legitimacy of royalty as found in Europe. America has celebrities but no bona fide kings, queens, princes, or princesses. The J.A.P. is therefore something of an anomaly, for her actions and her very nickname suggest that she thoroughly enjoys being treated as a princess.

The acronym for Jewish American Princess happens to form an ethnic slur, Jap (for Japanese), which was commonly used in the United States during the days of World War II. It thus carries at least a nuance of battle and wartime, but in this case, the war is not between the United States and Japan, but the continuing and seemingly endless war between the sexes.

In this light, we may see that the particular details of the J.A.P joke cycle encapsulate the view of American women in the early 1980s as perceived by men and by women themselves. Thanks in part to the feminist-inspired women's liberation movement, housewives have become discontent with some facets of the longstanding domestic role customarily assigned to women. That the J.A.P. hates to cook dinner for her husband and her children is an expression of wishful thinking among such discontented housewives. The traditional subservience of such women is also signaled by the sexual demands made upon them by their frequently insensitive husbands. Here another expression of revolt against the status quo takes a sexual form. The J.A.P. is to-

The
Humor
Prism
in 20th-
Century
America

244

tally indifferent to sex. With respect to her reluctance to perform fellatio (another refusal to "eat"), she signifies her disinclination to engage in acts that presumably give primary pleasure to males. Instead of cooking meals and providing sexual accommodation for male chauvinists, the ideal female is free to spend time for and on herself, shopping for fashionable clothes and beautifying herself. For women, the J.A.P. joke cycle pinpoints what's wrong with the traditional roles women were expected to accept cheerfully in American upwardly mobile, middle-class culture.

It is also true that some women in the 1980s are resentful of the feminist dogma insofar as they do not enjoy feeling guilty for not pursuing separate business or professional careers. They would like to continue to be housewives. For such women, there is a real dilemma. They want to remain housewives, but they bitterly resent the image of themselves as slaves or chattels. The J.A.P. in this sense embodies an ideal solution—she is a housewife, but one who has successfully freed herself from some of the daily, onerous chores such as feeding the children. She does not want to be a "stay-at-home," but wants to travel to fashionable resorts and to sample the good life (which includes high style clothing). To the extent that male chauvinists stand in the way, the J.A.P. opposes them, refusing to indulge in sex, oral or otherwise, preferring instead to go off on a shopping spree armed with a large supply of credit cards. The occasional hostile antimale J.A.P. joke reveals this animosity.

> What does a J.A.P. do with her asshole in the morning?
> Dresses him up and sends him to work.
> [Knott 1983a:112, Wilde 1985:64]

There are other Jewish jokes suggesting that strong Jewish women demean weak Jewish men.

> A first-grade teacher is calling on her pupils to identify animal pictures. She holds up a picture of an elephant and calls on Billy Davis. "That's an elephant," he replies. Georgie Croft is called on to identify a picture of a bear, which he does. The teacher then holds up a picture of a deer and calls on Solly Kaplan. Solly stares and stares at it and finally announces. "I don't know." "Oh, surely you do, Solly," the teacher says. "Think about what your mother calls your father." Solly again stares and stares. "Teacher," he yells out,

"that's a shmuck??"
[Erlich 1979:393]

This joke would seem to corroborate the contention that "In popular literature the Jewish man is frequently portrayed as an impotent *schmuck* who has no authority in his own home" (Baum, Hyman, and Michel 1977:239).

The underlying message of the J.A.P. joke cycle is: "Let men/husbands continue to look after us (just as our Jewish mothers and fathers did) but we shall be our own persons, albeit somewhat self-centered and demanding." If this analysis has any validity, then the J.A.P. cycle is by no means limited to Jewish American Princesses. Rather, the stereotype as delineated in the joke cycle may serve as a useful metaphor for *all* upwardly mobile American females who may be dissatisfied with the older traditional norms of a lifestyle demarcated by the duties of mother and wifehood. To hell with being limited by the restrictive demands of being "the good wife and mother" (Baum, Hyman, and Michel 1977:241).

The J.A.P. cycle may appeal to men for quite a different reason. From the male point of view, women want to have it both ways. They want equality, but they also want to be treated as something special. So the J.A.P. represents the modern woman who wants to be taken care of—to be given unlimited credit cards and taken on glamorous trips—but who doesn't want to cook or participate willingly in sexual intercourse. She seems to be all take and no give! One source aptly notes that the J.A.P.'s "most offensive characteristic is her refusal to defer easily to male authority" (Baum, Hyman, and Michel 1977:238). This may be why some of the J.A.P. joke texts project what appears to be unadulterated male misogynistic hostility.

The
Humor
Prism
in 20th-
Century
America

246

What do you call 48 J.A.P.s floating face down in a river? A start.

If there is any validity to this reading of the J.A.P. joke cycle, then it is much more than a Jewish issue. The J.A.M. is thus not just the Jewish American Mother, but any American mother ignorant of the possible ill-effects of over-indulging her children. Any children who are indulged, who are given more freedom than their parents enjoyed, may grow up to be J.A.P.s, that is, women (and men) who are no longer willing to accept the behavioral and role norms of their parents' generation. J.A.P. jokes may represent parody and caricature, but the basic message stands out for all to see. When workers strike for higher pay and increased benefits, they withhold the services they normally perform. So the J.A.P.s who refuse to cook dinner or provide sexual gratification for the male "head" of the household are doing the same thing. The joke cycle may be fantasy, not fact, but wishful thinking can nonetheless have an impact upon individuals and society at large, especially if it is couched in a joking format.

That there seems to be an unending succession of joke cycles underscores the need for serious study of such cycles. This study must cross conventional academic lines. It requires the input of sociologists, psychologists, literary critics, historians, and folklorists among others. Perhaps a science of jokeloristics may one day develop, which could result in a new and improved form of *cycle analysis.*

Notes

This essay is dedicated to my Jewish mother and my two Jewish American Princess daughters. An abbreviated version of the paper was presented at the annual meeting of the American Folklore Society, October 10–14, 1984, in San Diego. For texts, references, and comments, I am greatly indebted to the following: Alison Cohen, Linda Kahn, Pack Carnes, Bluma Goldstein, Barbara Grossberg, Marna Howarth, Marcelle Marcus, Liz Simons, Steve Stern, Ruth Tsoffar, Pat Turner, and Marcy Williams. Unless otherwise indicated, all texts reported were collected by the author through sporadic informal fieldwork during the period 1980–1984 in Berkeley, California.

The Humor Prism in 20th-Century America

247

References Cited

Alvin, Julius
1983a Gross Jokes. New York: Zebra Books.
1983b Totally Gross Jokes. New York: Zebra Books.
1984 Utterly Gross Jokes. New York: Zebra Books.
Anonymous
1966 Race Riots: An Anthology of Ethnic Insults. New York: Kanrom.
1971 The Jewish-American Princess. New York: Bell Records.
Baum, Charlotte, Paula Hyman, Sonya Michel
1977 The Jewish Woman in America. New York: New American Library.
Baumgold, Julie
1971 The Persistence of the Jewish American Princess. New York 4(12):25–31.
Bellman, Samuel Irving
1965 The "Jewish Mother" Syndrome. Congress Bi-Weekly 32(17):3–5.
Ben-Amos, Dan
1973 The "Myth" of Jewish Humor. Western Folklore 32:112–131.
Benedict, Ruth
1949 Child Rearing in Certain European Countries. American Journal of Orthopsychiatry 19:342–348.
Bienstock, Beverly Gray

1979 The Changing Image of the American Jewish Mother. *In* Changing Images of the Family, ed. Virginia Tufte and Barbara Myerhoff, pp. 173–191. New Haven: Yale University Press.

Birnbach, Lisa, ed.
1980 The Official Preppy Handbook. New York: Workman Publishing.

Blau, Zena Smith
1967 In Defense of the Jewish Mother. Midstream 13(2):42–49.

Blumenfeld, Gerry
1969 Some of My Best Jokes Are Jewish. New York: Paperback Library.

Boroff, David
1959 The Over-Protective Jewish Mother. Congress Weekly 24(27):6–8.

Brandes, Stanley
1983 Jewish-American Dialect Jokes and Jewish-American Identity. Jewish Social Studies 45:233–240.

Dorinson, Joseph
1981 Jewish Humor: Mechanism for Defense, Weapon for Cultural Affirmation. Journal of Psychohistory 8:447–464.

Duncan, Erika
1980 The Hungry Jewish Mother. *In* The Lost Tradition: Mothers and Daughters in Literature, ed. Cathy N. Davidson and E. M. Broner, pp. 231–241. New York: Frederick Ungar.

Dundes, Alan
1981 Many Hands Make Light Work or Caught in the Act of Screwing in Light Bulbs. Western Folklore 40:261–266.

Ehrlich, Howard J.
1979 Observations on Ethnic and Intergroup Humor. Ethnicity 6:383–398.

Erens, Patricia
1975 Gangsters, Vampires, and J.A.P.s: The Jew Surfaces in American Movies. Journal of Popular Film 4:208–222.

Greenburg, Dan
1964 How To Be a Jewish Mother. Los Angeles: Price, Stern and Sloan.

Grotjahn, Martin
1961 Jewish Jokes and Their Relation to Masochism. Journal of the Hillside Hospital 10:183–189.

Howe, Irving
1961 The Nature of Jewish Laughter. American Mercury 72:211–219.

Janus, Samuel S.
1980 The Great Jewish-American Comedians' Identity Crisis. The American Journal of Psychoanalysis 40:259–265.

Jason, Heda
1967 The Jewish Joke: The Problem of Definition. Southern Folklore Quarterly 31:48–54.

Katz, Naomi, and Eli Katz
1971 Tradition and Adaptation in American Jewish Humor. Journal of American Folklore 84:215–220.

Klevansky, Illana Hitner
1982 The Kugel Book. Johannesburg: Jonathan Ball.

Knott, Blanche
1982 Truly Tasteless Jokes. New York: Ballantine Books.
1983a Truly Tasteless Jokes Two. New York: Ballantine Books.
1983b Truly Tasteless Jokes Three. New York: Ballantine Books.

Landmann, Salcia
1963 Jüdische Witze. München: Deutscher Taschenbuch Verlag.
1977 Jüdische Witze: Nachlese 1960–1976. München: Deutscher Taschenbuch Verlag.

Levine, Alan
1983 Unreal Humour of the Kugel & Bagel or Are Kugel's Children Born with Designer Genes? Hillbrow: Kugel & Bagel Promotions Ltd.
Lewin, Kurt
1941 Self-Hatred among Jews. Contemporary Jewish Record 4:219–232.
Liptzin, Sol
1957 The Vogue of Jewish Self-Hatred. Congress Weekly 24(11):11–13.
Lukatsky, Debbi, and Sandy Barnett Toback
1982 The Jewish American Princess Handbook. Arlington Heights, IL: Turnbull & Willoughby Books.
Mintz, Jacqueline A.
1978 The Myth of the Jewish Mother in Three Jewish, American, Female Writers. The Centennial Review 22:346–355.
Novak, William, and Moshe Waldoks
1981 The Big Book of Jewish Humor. New York: Harper and Row.
Pelleg-Sani, Tamar
1984 Personality Traits of the "Jewish Mother": Realities Behind the Myth. Ph.D. dissertation, Psychology Department, United States International University.
Pollack, Simon R.
1979 Jewish Wit for All Occasions. New York: A. & W. Visual Library.
Reguer, Sara
1979 The Jewish Mother and the "Jewish American Princess": Fact or Fiction? USA Today 108(2412):40–42.
Rosenberg, Bernard, and Gilbert Shapiro
1958 Marginality and Jewish Humor. Midstream 4:70–80.
Roth, Philip
1969 Portnoy's Complaint. New York: Random House.
Scheiber, Alexander
1955 A Tale of the Mother's Heart. Journal of American Folklore 68:72, 86, 89.
Sequoia, Anna
1982 The Official J.A.P. Handbook. New York: New American Library.
Sequoia, Anna, and Patty Brown
1983 The Official J.A.P. Paper Doll Book. New York: New American Library.
Thickett, Maude
1983 Outrageously Offensive Jokes. New York: Pocket Books.
1984 Outrageously Offensive Jokes, II. New York: Pocket Books.
Tonner, Leslie
1975 Nothing But the Best: The Luck of the Jewish Princess. New York: Ballantine Books.
Wilde, Larry
1974 The Official Jewish/Irish Joke Book. New York: Pinnacle Books.
1979 More The Official Jewish/Irish Joke Book. New York: Pinnacle Books.
1980 The Last Official Jewish Joke Book. New York: Pinnacle Books.
1985 Official Book of John Jokes. New York: Bantam.
Wolfenstein, Martha
1963 Two Types of Jewish Mothers. In Childhood in Contemporary Cultures, ed. Margaret Mead and Martha Wolfenstein, pp. 424–440. Chicago: University of Chicago Press.
Wouk, Herman
1955 Marjorie Morningstar. Garden City, NY: Doubleday.
Zanger, Jules
1976 On Not Making It in America. American Studies 17:39–48.
Zborowski, Mark, and Elizabeth Herzog
1962 Life Is With People: The Culture of the Shtetl. New York: Shocken.

The
Humor
Prism
in 20th-
Century
America

Many Hands Make Light Work or Caught in the Act of Screwing in Light Bulbs

Alan Dundes

The
Humor
Prism
in 20th-
Century
America

250

Folklorists never lack data, for there is not only the accumulation of folklore from centuries past but new folklore constantly being created in response to each succeeding generation's social and psychological needs. The distressing feature of folkloristics, the scientific study of folklore, is that new folklore does not appear to be any better understood than was the old. Even though modern folklorists have the advantage of virtually being able to observe an element of folklore at its moment of inception, they seem able to do little more than report its existence. Folklorists somehow cannot bring themselves to depart from the longstanding tradition of merely describing. What is needed, of course, is description *and analysis.* Granted that it is much easier to describe than to interpret, but that is no excuse really for the dearth of analytic commentary on folklore old and new.

Among the dozens and dozens of Polack jokes so popular in the late 1960s and 1970s, one particular text asked: "How many Polacks does it take to screw in a light bulb?" The answer(s): "Five—one to hold the bulb and four to turn the ceiling (chair, ladder, house)." William M. Clements in his useful "The Types of the Polack Joke," first published in 1969, indicates that the Indiana University Folklore Archives contained more than twenty versions of this joke.[1] The joke was simply one of many purportedly commenting on the physical ineptitude and stupidity of Polacks.[2]

What is of special interest is that apparently this single joke provided a model or impetus for a whole new cycle of jokes, all based on the initial formulaic question of how many ____s does

This essay originally appeared in *Western Folklore*, vol. 40, no. 3 (July 1981). Reprinted with permission of the California Folklore Society.

it take to screw in a light bulb? This leads one to speculate on the possible genetic interrelationships of joke cycles. As the light bulb cycle may have spun off from the Polack joke cycle, so the Polack cycle may in turn have derived from some earlier cycle.[3] One cannot help wondering what new joke cycle, if any, may be inspired by one or more of the light bulb jokes.

By 1978 and 1979, the light bulb cycle had swept the country, and by 1980, a short note on the subject had appeared in the *Journal of American Folklore* and a popular anthology of some forty texts entitled *How Many Zen Buddhists Does It Take to Screw in a Light Bulb?* had been published.[4] The anthology contains texts only (accompanied by cartoon drawings as illustrations) and ends with an invitation for readers to "join the newest and fastest-growing joke craze since the Knock, Knock!" by sending in additional examples of the genre. The note in the *Journal of American Folklore* presents some of the better known light bulb jokes and asks in conclusion why the cycle came into being. The author claims the answer is complicated and suggests that complex social movements and decision-making in the 1980s "call for comment." Presumably the joke cycle is a response to that call. The author also argues that the underlying impulse for the formation of such jokes may "be more a matter of esthetics." These vague notions do not explain at all why the particular metaphor of screwing in light bulbs was selected as a paradigm for social commentary. Why wasn't one of the many other available Polack (and other) riddling jokes used as the datum for a new cycle? In short, what is the significance, if any, of the choice of the act of screwing in light bulbs as the basis of a series of jokes?

The original (?) Polack joke reflected a stereotype, namely, that Poles or Polish-Americans are stupid, that is, they are not too *bright.* Inasmuch as an illuminated light bulb is a standard popular iconographic symbol for "idea"—as found, for example, in comic strips—it makes a certain amount of sense for a Polack to be unable to screw in a lightbulb, that is, to be unable to come up with a bright idea. But the same attribute of stupidity is *not* necessarily part of the stereotypic features normally associated with the various groups named in the light bulb jokes.

> How many WASPs (White Anglo-Saxon Protestants) does it take to change a light bulb?
>
> Two. One to mix martinis and the other to call an electrician.

The WASP is not stupid but rather is above carrying out such menial tasks as changing a light bulb. Instead he pours himself a drink and pays for a high-priced specialist to come to perform a simple household chore which he could easily do himself.

In ethnic slurs based upon a common action, the stereotype is supposedly revealed in the manner in which the action is carried out. So the only variable in the first line of each joke is the name of the group being pasquinaded. The principal variation occurs in the "answer" to the joking question. In this way, we are told that Californians are "laid back," New Yorkers are rude, etc. Here are a number of groups and their stereotypic activity:

Californians. Ten. One to screw it in and nine others to share the experience.[5]

New Yorkers. Three. One to do it and two to criticize.
or
None of your fucking business!

Pennsylvanians. None. You just hold it up and it glows by itself (referring to the Three Mile Island nuclear facility and its radiation crisis).

Democrats. Thirty. One representative from every social/economic group.

Republicans. Three. One to change the bulb, and two to see how good the old one was.

Graduate students. Only one but it takes nine years.
or
Depends on the size of the grant.
or
Two and a professor to take the credit.
or
Could you repeat the question, please.

Football players. One, but eleven get credit for it.

Law students. Six. One to change it and five to file an environmental impact report.

Pre-Med students. Three. One to stand on a stool to screw it in and two to kick the stool out from under him.

Gay men. Five. One to screw in the Art Deco light bulb and four to stand back and yell "Fabulous!" (or "Marvelous!")

Feminists. That's not funny.
or
Five. One to do it and four to write about it.

The
Humor
Prism
in 20th-
Century
America

252

or

Five. One to change the bulb, two to discuss the violation of the socket, and two to secretly wish that they were that socket.

Psychiatrists. Only one, but the light bulb has to really want to change.

Zen Buddhists. Two. One to screw it in and one to not screw it in.

or

Two. One to screw it in and one to unscrew it.

Jews. So how many Jews does it take to change a light bulb?
JAPs [Jewish American Princesses]. One who refuses saying, "What and ruin my nail polish?"

or

Two. One to call her father and the other to open a can of Diet Pepsi.
Jewish mothers. None. So I'll sit here in the dark.

Blacks. Hey man, whussa lightbulb?

Mexicans. Ask me *mañana, señor,* if you still want to know.

These are representative although the list is not exhaustive. For example, several texts have been aimed at the Iranians as a means of venting anger over the unwarranted seizure of more than fifty American citizens housed in the U.S. Embassy in Iran:

Ayatollahs. None, they didn't have light bulbs in the thirteenth century.

Beverly Hills real estate agents. Fourteen. One to screw it in and thirteen to learn Farsi.

Iranians. One hundred. One to screw it in and ninety-nine to hold the house hostage.

In a joke about the joke cycle, the Iranians are also featured. "The *Village Voice* in New York City ran a light bulb joke contest. First prize was $200. The winning joke was sent in by the Iranians: 'How many Iranians does it take to screw in a light bulb? You send us the prize money and we'll tell you the answer.'"

Having sampled the tradition, we remain in the dark about why the act of screwing in light bulbs should have been selected as a base metaphor for a joke cycle. I believe the efficacy of the metaphor turns on the word "screw." To screw is a common slang term for the conduct of sexual intercourse. And this very usage is found in the light bulb cycle itself. In one version of "How many Californians does it take to screw in a lightbulb?" the answer is: "None. They screw in hot tubs (or Jacuzzis)." (In northern California, this same joke is told about Marin County residents, rather than Californians.) In another light bulb joke "How many Lilliputians does it take to screw in a light bulb?" the answer is "Two. You just put them in a light bulb and let them do it." In the published anthology, we find "What's the difference beween a pregnant woman and a lightbulb? You can unscrew the light bulb!" and "How many mice does it take to screw in a light bulb? Two (with a drawing of two mice engaged in intercourse—in a human face-to-face position)."

The underlying sexual nature of the light bulb joke cycle suggests that the jokes are essentially about impotence. Sexual impotence is a common enough theme of oral (and written) humor. To be sure, some of the light bulb jokes have more to do with delineating alleged stereotypic features of various groups than with anything else. My point is rather that the basic premise of an individual's having trouble screwing in a light bulb has a definite sexual connotation. In addition to the nuances of the verb "screw," one might also mention the phrase "turn on." To "turn on" means to become emotionally aroused either through drugs or through sexual attraction. Thus someone who needs help in "turning on" a light by "screwing" a bulb into a light socket is someone who is sexually inept. Please keep in mind that this double sense of "screwing in light bulbs" is explicitly signalled in the "They screw in hot tubs" text cited above as well as in the feminist text treating the violation of the socket.

Most of the stereotypes delineated in the light bulb cycle are not new. The cutthroat competition surrounding admission into medical schools which causes students to actually go so far as to sabotage fellow students' experiments in chemistry labs so that the saboteurs will finish higher on the class grade curve is unfortunately a sad fact of undergraduate academic life. The spoiled daughter of indulgent Jewish parents who is unduly concerned with her appearance (nail polish, slimness) and the aggressive rudeness of New Yorkers are much older than the light bulb cycle. The light bulb cycle simply utilized already existing stereotype traditions in American culture. And inasmuch as the light bulb joke itself already existed in the Polack joke cycle, we find that the "new" cycle consists of "recycled" older form and

The
Humor
Prism
in 20th-
Century
America

254

content. Still, the Iranian texts are new, having been sparked by the American shame and fury over the Iranian government's holding American citizens hostage for billions of dollars. And the articulation of older stereotypes in the light bulb joke format also represent something new. Folklorists are accustomed to seeing endless combinations of new and old elements in a given item of folklore.

One question we have not yet answered is why the light bulb cycle came to be so popular at the end of the 1970s. The sexual significance of screwing, assuming that it is valid, would not in and of itself explain why the cycle arose when it did. It could theoretically have arisen at any time as far as fears of sexual impotence are concerned. That is hardly a new anxiety peculiar to the late 1970s. My hunch is that the cycle is about power or the lack thereof. Specifically, power in modern times depends upon having sufficient energy resources. Americans have begun to fear that rising oil prices and/or diminishing oil supplies will severely decrease energy supplies ranging from gasoline for automobiles to heating oil for homes or electricity for household appliances. The question is "Will there be enough 'power' to go around?" The burgeoning pressures of increasing population growth around the world suggest that there may well be energy shortages in years to come, just as there are shortages of food and housing now in many parts of the globe. Modern society with its inevitable bureaucracy has made it increasingly difficult to carry out even the simplest tasks. A maze of rules and requirements must be fulfilled before a need can be met. As we become more and more specialized in our work, there are more and more intermediaries in the chain of events intervening between a need and filling that need. Whether one calls an electrician to change a light bulb or one has to wait until an environmental impact report has been filed before changing a bulb, the upshot is the same. The "deferred reward" philosophy remains in effect. One must wait for the light. The Iranians seizure of American citizens confirms Americans sense of a lack of power. And the fact that the Iranian government (as opposed to terrorists) demanded exorbitant sums (e.g., twenty-four billions dollars) before releasing the hostages could have been easily construed as an attempt by Iran to "screw" the United States!

American society has historically had a positive attitude toward change—change is a good thing in a worldview system

The Humor Prism in 20th-Century America

255

which places a high premium on progress. And Americans are impatient with the slowness of other societies with respect to change. Yet as the United States becomes enmeshed in more and more webs of conflicting legislation, it becomes harder and harder to implement change. And so it seems to the average American that it has become increasingly difficult for an individual to effect change—social change, political change, technological change, etc. More and more, it is groups, not individuals, which have become the agents of change. And so it is that we can understand the inflation of numbers with respect to how many people (of a particular group) it takes to change a light bulb. In theory, one person can change a light bulb; in practice, it may take more than one to carry out the task.

If the above analysis is at all valid, we can perhaps better understand the popularity of the light bulb jokes. On the one hand, they reflect the age-old theme of sexual impotence, a metaphor which lends itself easily to minority groups seeking power. But on the other hand, they may reflect a widespread malaise Americans share about energy supplies and the power that comes from energy. The simple necessities such as cheap gasoline and electricity, once taken for granted, are now in some jeopardy. Without electricity, we will all be unable to screw in lightbulbs to any useful purpose. We shall all join the Jewish mother who complainingly sits in the dark. Add to this the American concern about losing political power in the world and about the individual's losing power to control his own destiny and we can see other reasons why the cycle might have mass appeal. We should not be misled by the presence of particular groups named in the cycle for when we joke about the impotence of others, we are joking about our own potential lack of sexual and political power.

The
Humor
Prism
in 20th-
Century
America

256

Notes

1. William M. Clements, *The Types of the Polack Joke, Folklore Forum* Bibliographic and Special Series No. 3 (Bloomington, 1973), 27, E7.6.6, 'The Number of Polacks Needed to Screw in a Light Bulb.'

2. For a discussion of this trait and others in the Polack joke cycle, see Alan Dundes, "A Study of Ethnic Slurs: The Jew and the Polack in the United States," *Journal of American Folklore* 84 (1971): 186–203.

3. I have previously suggested that the American jokes about Polacks had antecedents in a German ethnic slur tradition about Poles. See Dundes, 200–201.

4. Judith B. Kerman, "The Light-Bulb Jokes: Americans Look at Social Action Processes," *Journal of American Folklore* 93 (1980): 454–458; Matt Freedman and Paul Hoffman, *How Many Zen Buddhists Does It Take to Screw in a Light Bulb?* (New York, 1980). Kerman's original manuscript had "Many Hands Make Light Work" as a subtitle, but presumably editorial intervention eliminated it. I have gratefully borrowed if for my own note's title.

5. Most of the texts were collected in Berkeley, California, in 1979 and 1980. I hereby acknowledge valuable assistance in supplying additional texts from Swedish folklorist Bengt af Klintberg (who forwarded to me a set of light bulb jokes he had received from a friend in New York City), Berkeley linguist Nancy Levidow, and my daughter Alison who collected texts from classmates at Harvard. It should be noted that each of the groups named in the light bulb jokes could be the subject of a separate study. For example, Californians, as a group, are featured in analogous jokes—"How many Californians does it take to water a plant? Two. One to pour the Perrier [mineral water] and one to massage the leaves."

The
Humor
Prism
in 20th-
Century
America

Those Sick
Challenger Jokes

Patrick D. Morrow

January 28, 1986. Challenger, after several delays, was ready to take off. This was the tenth flight by Challenger, but this one was special because for the first time, a teacher, Christa McAuliffe, was selected to be a member of the Challenger crew, and give students a lesson about science while orbiting in space. This Challenger voyage seemed to be merely the latest in a series of successful and daring space ventures, using a recently developed design of two booster rockets, an enormous fuel tank filled with powerful liquid propellant, and an attached shuttlecraft, capable of a ground landing. Earlier, a prince from Saudi Arabia flew on an educational mission in a similar vehicle called Discovery. The Arabian prince successfully went skyward and orbited.[1] Challenger had performed quite successfully before, including launching several satellites into orbit; and the U.S. space program seemed to have settled into a series of comfortably routine successes. After all, there had been no serious accident with American space missions since the tragic deaths of three astronauts during an aborted launching in 1967.

The time seemed safely appropriate to turn space success into corporate profits. A page from Spiegel's 1986 Spring catalogue clearly demonstrates that Challenger was now deemed a suitable vehicle for a new, money-making commodity. Spiegel decided to offer a Challenger indoor/outdoor tent for younger children, so that they, too, could feel a part of the space program.[2] Popularity for the tent appeared to be guaranteed, although now the issue is what will the sale price be for this tent. Even a relevant film, *Space Camp* (1986), while delayed a bit in its release, has received considerable popular approval. *Space Camp* is an adolescent fantasy saga about the ultimate technocracy summer camp, where teens (for a hefty fee) get to practice being as-

This essay originally appeared in the *Journal of Popular Culture*, vol. 17, no. 2 (1961). Reprinted with permission.

tronauts. In the story, the teens get into orbit by mistake, but manage to successfully orbit, get through re-entry, and even land the shuttlecraft, while saving the injured adult astronaut on board. Near Huntsville, Alabama, there is an actual Space Camp, run by NASA, which has a waiting list of at least a year for prospective clients. The unscheduled orbiting spacecraft has the inauspicious name of Atlantis, which happens to be the actual name of Challenger's successor.

But let us return to January 28, 1986. All over the United States, schoolchildren prepared to receive Christa McAuliffe's lecture, the first school lesson ever taught from space. Thousands of children were watching the launching on television when, just seventy-three seconds into the ill-fated mission, Challenger and all its rockets and fuel tanks exploded, killing the entire crew of seven. "An apparent major malfunction," stated Mission Control in Houston. Here is the reaction of Paul Hotchkiss, an eleven-year-old student at Drake Middle School in Auburn, Alabama. I asked Paul what he knew about Challenger before the catastrophe happened. "Well," he said, "I knew that there was a teacher going up in space, and everybody was looking forward to her lecture. Everybody was real excited. Nobody ever expected a catastrophe because nothing like this ever happened before in the shuttle program." I then asked Paul what his reactions were immediately after the catastrophe happened. He said, "I don't know. I guess I felt pretty sad. And I felt it was unfair that seven innocent people got killed. After a while, I really got tired of all those sick Challenger jokes that everybody was telling."[3]

Hurt, but very much wanting the now-threatened U.S. space program to continue and progress, schoolchildren from all over the country raised money for the U.S. Space Foundation in Colorado Springs, which by early May had collected over $100,000 to support future space missions.[4] Most of this money the children scrounged out of their own pockets, rather than demanding donations from their parents. The Young Astronaut Council of Washington, D.C., also made renewed efforts to support youth and their interest in "the conquest of space." This is the organization that had provided the funding to bring Christa McAuliffe's son, Scott, age nine, and his third-grade classmates from Concord, New Hampshire, to Florida, so that they all could watch the launch in person. The Council quotes an Eskimo boy from Alaska as saying, "If our ancestors had been

The Humor Prism in 20th-Century America

259

afraid to cross over the ice, we wouldn't be here today."[5] The young are not easily discouraged about the future, since that so clearly belongs to them.

The aftermath of Challenger as catastrophe has unfolded in several phases. The first phase was one of immediate shock, which quickly brought about a series of sick jokes. Most of these jokes assume that listeners know what Challenger was and what happened to it, and that the joke audience has seen at least some of the grim television accounts that immediately followed the disaster, in addition to having read newspaper accounts of what happened and why the catastrophe happened. The following is only a sampling of jokes, and most of them have at least one or two variants. Here are the jokes.

1. *Question:* Do you know what NASA stands for?
   Answer: Needs Another Seven Astronauts.

2. *Question:* Do you know what Christa McAuliffe's last words were to her husband?
   Answer: You feed the dog and I'll feed the fish.

3. *Question:* Where did Christa McAuliffe spend her vacation?
   Answer: All over south Florida.

4. *Question:* Did you hear that Christa McAuliffe has been nominated for the 1986 Mother of the Year Award?
   Answer: Of course—she blew up only *once* in front of her kids this year.

5. *Question:* What were the last words of the Challenger crew?
   Answer: OK. OK! *Bud* Light.

6. *Question:* Did you hear that Tang is no longer the official drink of the space program?
   Answer: Yes, now it is Ocean Spray.

7. *Question:* Do you know what color Christa McAuliffe's eyes were?
   Answer: They were blue. One blew over this way and one blew over that way.

8. *Question:* Why didn't the spaceshuttle astronauts take a shower before they lifted off?
   Answer: They'd rather wash up on shore.

9. *Question:* When is the next spaceshuttle launch?
   Answer: The Fourth of July.

10. *Question:* What were the last words of Christa McAuliffe?
    Answer: What's this little red button for?

11. *Question:* What does Christa McAuliffe teach?
    Answer: English, but she's history now. [Actually, McAuliffe taught science and social studies.]

12. *Question:* Where did the Challenger crew take their vacation?
    Answer: All over Florida.

13. *Question:* How many astronauts can fit in a Volkswagen?
    Answer: Eleven—two in the front seats, two in the back seat, and seven in the ashtray.

14. *Question:* How do we know that Christa McAuliffe didn't have dandruff?
    Answer: They found her head and shoulders on the beach.[6]

Assuming these examples are representative of all sick Challenger jokes, certain features may be observed about these jokes as a class. We note that most jokes feature Christa McAuliffe, rather than any other astronaut. There are no Ellison Onizuka (an Oriental Hawaiian) or Judith Resnick (Jewish) jokes, although these individuals certainly present the possibility of ethnic or racist jokes. The astronauts who were killed are perceived as a group—except Christa McAuliffe. Yet, while the jokes seethe with bad taste, anger, and hostility, there seems to be little personal antagonism against McAuliffe, except for her million dollar life insurance policy from Lloyds of London.[7] Many people, I believe, know the names of one or two of the other dead astronauts, but few know *all* their names, or anything about them as individuals. Of course, launching a million dollar lawsuit against NASA may make the names of Mrs. Michael Smith and late Captain Michael Smith pretty familiar to those who pay attention to national news, in the last third of 1986.

These truly tasteless jokes seem to be a collection of unfair attacks, centering around Christa McAuliffe. But what appears to be unfair treatment of a dead person actually is, as I hope to show later in this article, a cloaking device for attacking what caused her death and those responsible for this perhaps needless tragedy. Looking over these jokes, one can see a bond of kinship between the joke teller and McAuliffe. We can relate to her as a domestic person (jokes 2, 4, and perhaps 3 and 5) and as an incompetent person who found herself, so to speak, in water too deep (jokes 7, 9, 10, and perhaps 11 and the violent 14). There is an additional bond between the joke teller and McAuliffe on the basis of her being perceived as a sort of Everyperson. So while there may be a feeling of relief on the part of the joke teller that he/she did not try to become an astronaut, there is also respect and sadness for McAuliffe—who did. The sentiment of "what happened to her is exactly what would have happened to similarly incompetent me" comes screaming through these jokes. The astronauts, treated as a group of professionals, receive much less sympathy (jokes 5, 6, 8, 12, and most certainly 13).

A number of reasons account for the bitterness of Challenger jokes. First, our astronauts have been embraced as our heroes of today. We naturally expect our heroes to overcome challenge and adversity and not fall, Icarus-like, from the sky. There is even a "true-to-life" film about heroic American astronauts called *The Right Stuff,* based on Tom Wolfe's best-seller and focusing on Senator and former presidential candidate John Glenn.[8] But Challenger astronauts so clearly were fatally overcome by technology and bureaucracy, that anger, betrayal, and intense disillusionment inform these jokes. Advanced technology, the very force that created the arena for these new heroes to emerge, has betrayed us all, so these jokes indicate, with considerable antagonism against one more recent American failure. Worse, this failure was perpetrated by an American agency (NASA) that had largely been accepted as sacred and invulnerable. Clearly one of our most-needed archetypes, the hero, has been violated. However, systems are too huge, complex, intimidating, and ill-defined to attack directly. Thus attaching blame to a victim is a holding pattern, a joke, until the "real" culprits can be identified.

Challenger jokes may be classified as examples of what Freud called "tendency-wit." According to Freud, "Tendency-wit usually requires three persons. Besides the one who makes the wit there is a second person, who is taken as the object of the hostile or sexual aggression, and a third person in whom the purpose of the wit to produce pleasure is fulfilled."[9] In Challenger jokes, a question-and-answer format is typically used. Questioner and respondent take the roles of persons #1 and #3, while the victim, Christa McAuliffe, takes the role of person #2. Freud notes that "tendency-wit" is an ideal vehicle for articulating, usually in some disguised form, intense and subversive hostility. To quote Freud again: "Wit permits us to make our enemy ridiculous through that which we could not utter loudly or consciously on account of existing hindrances."[10] Thus Challenger jokes, using McAuliffe as hostility object, the one astronaut on the mission who was a civilian, thus prone to error like the rest of us mortals, serves as a punching bag, absorbing our deflected vituperation against the technological powers-that-be.

"By belittling and humbling our enemy," as Freud notes, "by scorning and ridiculing him, we directly obtain the pleasure of his defeat in the laughter of the third person."[11] Christa McAuliffe was a victim, and she was killed. Who would want to attack her? The covert objects of attack are the forces, depersonalized and inhuman, that killed her, as, indeed, they could kill any of us unheroic, civilian souls. Or, to quote Jacques Lacan, "[Hitting the mark] takes its place from the necessity, so clearly marked by Freud, of the third listener, always presupposed, and from the fact that the witticism does not lose its power in its translation into indirect speech."[12] The indirect speech of Challenger jokes is the displacement of anger and critical mockery toward the victims, thus creating a covert attack on the system and individuals who caused this catastrophe.

Challenger jokes have also been seen as a healthy way of assuring ourselves that the world is not out of our control. These sick jokes can be seen as a psychological defense mechanism against failure and tragedy. University of Tennessee psychology professor Dr. Howard Pollio has said (in an A.P. news release) that: "Challenger jokes are a negative way of reasserting that there is some order. The joke goes beyond the boundary of good taste, but only to demonstrate that it's still there. . . . When something goes afoul, something that we expected not to lose control, we get scared. Joking about it brings us back to the world where there is control, where there are limits."[13] We should note that these reassuring words address a mass consumption newspaper audience. Challenger jokes show a lot of complexity, despite fre-

The Humor Prism in 20th-Century America

263

quently and conveniently being dismissed as ill-tempered exhibitions of needless cruelty, or even grief.

Grief is certainly a common enough feeling about what happened to Challenger and its crew, but grief alone does not explain very well the rash of these jokes. After all, most Americans did not even have a media image, much less a personal relationship, with this particular group of astronauts. A great deal of horror has been expressed about the Challenger catastrophe, but grief is a complex and very personal emotion that consists of deep sorrow about the injury, illness, or death of someone close to us, or perhaps even intense feelings about our own death, especially if diagnosed as imminently impending. Sending cards of sympathy to astronaut families would, for most of us, clearly be inappropriate.

In fact, while these jokes do have an uncomfortable intimacy about them, the jokes are less about the ones who died than the ones who live on, scarred with the knowledge and consequences of this tragedy. For the first and third figures in Challenger jokes, anger rather than death, is of immediate concern. Rather than the well-known Kubler-Ross paradigm about the unfolding stages we all pass through in accepting grief and death,[14] a more accurate analogy to what we have passed through with Challenger jokes would be the processes a person with a long-term, debilitating, and *not* fatal illness passes through in successive stages. One such disease is multiple sclerosis ("the tragic crippler of young adults"), and indeed, the patient with this disease passes through stages of anger, acceptance, and adaptation, the same stages that many of us who have been hurt by the Challenger catastrophe must pass through.[15] We find it difficult to live in a state of faith and innocence, having been through what happened to Challenger. Adaptation, even more than grief, is what Challenger jokes help us live with, as we move from the anger of disillusionment to the resigned adaptation of living with our very fallible systems.

One of the features of Challenger jokes has been that, as the focus moved away from awareness of the tragedy to questions about what caused it, from citing the faulty booster rocket seals and the freezing January Florida weather to the darkening Rogers Report, which features an ever-unfolding tale of bureaucratic complicities and incompetencies, Challenger jokes entirely ceased as suddenly as they had begun. Why? True, they were immediately replaced by Chernobyl nuclear disaster jokes, but nonetheless, Challenger jokes were a phenomenon of the past. Chernobyl jokes do reveal parallels to Challenger jokes, but jokes about Russian tragedy hardly have the clout of jokes about an American Tragedy. (*Question:* What's the five-day weather forecast for Kiev? *Answer:* Three days.) Perhaps Challenger jokes ceased because our nation had passed through a battling with acceptance phase, and, with all of the rapidly escalating information about so many new factors that apparently contributed to the spaceshuttle catastrophe, had moved to a new stage of learning to adapt. Consequently there were no new Challenger jokes about faulty rocket seals, the Rogers Report, Morton Thiokol Co., engineers as managers, or NASA trying to regain lost credibility and a new launching schedule.

As Elisabeth Kubler-Ross and others tell us, when our feelings of deep unhappiness change, however expressed, from an intense immediacy to any kind of public demonstration, one's "grief" has entered an entirely new stage.[16] Or, to look at Challenger jokes in a somewhat different light, the public memorializing of Christa McAuliffe points to a significant and new mass media adaptation toward feelings about the Challenger catastrophe. This memorializing was accomplished at that lavish 1986 Fourth of July weekend, designed primarily for Americans to celebrate the long-awaited restoration of the Statue of Liberty. In one portion of this internationally televised program from New York City, on the 3rd of July, Henry ("the Fonz") Winkler held court with a student from every state, winners of the "Poem to the Statue of Liberty" Middle School contest which had been conducted throughout the entire country. Winkler's voice was quiet and subdued, his solemn mood emphasized by the indirect, soft lighting. With the reading of a short, patriotic essay by a Vietnamese girl, an immigrant now living in Honolulu, and a considerable amount of praise for "noble ladies who gave their all," the program was dedicated to the memory of Christa McAuliffe. At that point she passed from being our recent tragic nightmare into acceptance in the hallowed halls of history.

The Humor Prism in 20th-Century America

265

Notes

1. See *Arabs and the Stars* (Houston: Aramco World Magazine, January–February, 1986).
2. *Spiegel's Spring Catalogue* (Chicago, 1986), 23.

3. From conversations with Paul Hotchkiss, particularly our tape-recorded conversation of Saturday evening, June 28, 1986.
4. *The Opelika-Auburn News* (May 5, 1986), 3.
5. "Young Astronauts: The Word Is Still 'Go'," Jack Anderson, *Parade Magazine* (May 4, 1986): 20.
6. For help with gathering, selecting, verifying, and editing Challenger jokes, I am indebted to Jill Buchanan, Wyatt H. Daniel, Alex Dunlop, Clay Heron, Blair Hobbs, Paul Hotchkiss, LaClare LaBorde, William E. Morrow, Kari Moroney, and Daniel Zalik. For help with typing I am indebted to Katie Varner and Jea Joiner; and for help with editing I am very much indebted to Dr. Joyce Rothschild.
7. A few people have told me that "she asked for it; she knew the risks." Curiously, these were the same people who expressed jealousy over her life insurance policy.
8. For an excellent study of this film, Glenn, and the astronauts as heroes see Gregory S. Sojka, "The Astronaut: An American Hero with 'The Right Stuff'," *Journal of American Culture* VII (Spring/Summer, 1984): 118–121.
9. *The Basic Writings of Sigmund Freud*, trans. Dr. A. A. Brill (New York: Random House, 1938), 695.
10. Ibid., 698.
11. Ibid.
12. Jacques Lacan, *Ecrits: A Selection*, trans. Alan Sheridan (New York: Norton, 1977), 60. Jokes and wit are Lacanian thematics, if considered a "reflexivity" of his style. I am indebted to Professor Kenneth Watson for much-needed help in dealing with Lacan.
13. Quoted in Steve Baker, "Laughing at Disaster Not as Bad as It Seems," *Sunday Ledger-Enquirer* (Columbus, Georgia), May 18, 1986.
14. Elisabeth Kubler-Ross, *Death: The Final Stage of Growth* (Englewood Cliffs, N.J.: Prentice-Hall, 1975).
15. See *Multiple Sclerosis: A Guide for Patients and Their Families*, ed. Labe C. Scheinberg, M.D. (New York: Raven Press, 1984), esp. 1–44.
16. For an excellent article on the popular American perception of grief, see Charles H. Lippy, "Sympathy Cards and the Grief Process," *Journal of Popular Culture* 17 (Winter, 1983): 98–108.

Bibliography

Barrick, Mac E. "Racial Riddles and the Polack Joke," *Keystone Folklore Quarterly* 15, 1 (Spring 1970): 3–15.

———. "The Helen Keller Joke Cycle," *Journal of American Folklore* 93, 370 (October–December 1980): 441–49.

Berger Arthur Asa. "What Makes People Laugh? Cracking the Cultural Code," *Etc.: A Review of General Semantics* 32, 4 (December 1975): 427–28.

Boskin, Joseph. "Humor in American Culture: The Urban Landscape," *Urban Resources* 4, 3 (Spring 1987): B1–B4.

———. "The Giant and the Child: 'Cruel' Humor in American Culture," *The Lion and the Unicorn* 13, 2 (December 1989): 141–47.

———. "American Political Humor: Touchables and Taboos," *International Political Science Review* 11, 4 (October 1990): 473–82.

———. "People's Entertainment: Saloons and Burlesques in American Culture." Paper delivered at the Conference, "Burlesque: Tradition and Transgression," University of California, Los Angeles, March 13, 1993.

———. "African-American Humor: Resistance and Retaliation." Paper delivered at Central Connecticut State University, African American Lecture Series, November 19, 1992.

Bradley, Sculley. "Our Native Humor," *North American Review* 242, 2 (Winter 1936–37): 351–62.

Bunkers, Suzanne L. "Why Are These Women Laughing? The Power and Politics of Women's Humor," *Studies in American Humor* 4, nos. 1, 2 (Spring/Summer 1985): 82–91.

Dundes, Alan. "Many Hands Make Light Work or Caught in the Act of Screwing in Light Bulbs," *Western Folklore* 40, 3 (July 1981): 261–66.

———. "The J.A.P. and the J.A.M. in American Jokelore," *Journal of American Folklore* 98, 390 (October–December 1985), 456–75.

Hansen, Arlen J. "Entropy and Transformation: Two Types of American Humor," *The American Scholar* 43, 3 (Summer 1974): 405–21.

The
Humor
Prism
in 20th-
Century
America

267

Koziski, Stephanie. "The Standup Comedian as Anthropologist: Intentional Culture Critic," *Journal of Popular Culture* 18, 2 (Fall 1984): 57–76.

Lawrence, Denise L. "A Rose by Any Other Name . . . The Occasional Doo-Dah Parade," *Urban Resources* 4, 3 (Spring 1987): 37–42.

Morrow, Patrick D. "Those Sick Challenger Jokes," *Journal of Popular Culture* 20, 4 (Spring 1987): 175–84.

Oring, Elliott. "The People of the Joke: On the Conceptualization of a Jewish Humor," *Western Folklore* 42, 4 (1983): 261–71.

The
Humor
Prism
in 20th-
Century
America

268

Books in the
Humor in Life and Letters Series

The Contemporary American Comic Epic: The Novels of Barth, Pynchon, Gaddis, and Kesey, by Elaine B. Safer, 1988

The Mocking of the President: A History of Campaign Humor from Ike to Ronnie, by Gerald Gardner, 1988

Circus of the Mind in Motion: Postmodernism and the Comic Vision, by Lance Olsen, 1990

Jewish Wry: Essays on Jewish Humor, edited by Sarah Blacher Cohen, 1991 (reprint)

Horsing Around: Contemporary Cowboy Humor, edited by Lawrence Clayton and Kenneth Davis, 1991

Women's Comic Visions, edited by June Sochen, 1991

Never Try to Teach a Pig to Sing: Still More Urban Folklore from the Paperwork Empire, by Alan Dundes and Carl R. Pagter, 1991

Comic Relief: Humor in Contemporary American Literature, edited by Sarah Blacher Cohen, 1992 (reprint)

Untamed and Unabashed: Essays on Women and Humor in British Literature, by Regina Barreca, 1993

Campaign Comedy: Political Humor from Clinton to Kennedy, by Gerald Gardner, 1994

The Ironic Temper and the Comic Imagination, by Morton Gurewitch, 1994

The Comedian as Confidence Man: Studies in Irony Fatigue, by Will Kaufman, 1997

Tilting at Mortality: Narrative Strategies in Joseph Heller's Fiction, by David M. Craig, 1997

The Humor Prism in 20th-Century America, edited by Joseph Boskin, 1997